NEWGRANGE SPEAKS FOR ITSELF:

FORTY CARVED MOTIFS

&

RELATED SITE FEATURES

JACQUELINE INGALLS GARNETT

Book design, typesetting: Roy Diment VRG
www.members.shaw.ca/vrg

Note for Librarians: a cataloguing record for this book that includes Dewey Decimal Classification and US Library of Congress numbers is available from the National Library of Canada. The complete cataloguing record can be obtained from the National Library's online database at:
www.nlc-bnc.ca/amicus/index-e.html

ISBN 1-4120-5717-5

TRAFFORD

Offices in Canada, USA, Ireland, UK and Spain

This book was published *on-demand* in cooperation with Trafford Publishing. On-demand publishing is a unique process and service of making a book available for retail sale to the public taking advantage of on-demand manufacturing and Internet marketing. On-demand publishing includes promotions, retail sales, manufacturing, order fulfilment, accounting and collecting royalties on behalf of the author.

Book sales in Europe:

Trafford Publishing (UK) Ltd., Enterprise House, Wistaston Road Business Centre, Wistaston Road, Crewe
CW2 7RP UNITED KINGDOM
phone 01270 251 396 (local rate 0845 230 9601)
facsimile 01270 254 983; info.uk@trafford.com

Book sales for North America and international:

Trafford Publishing, 6E–2333 Government St.,
Victoria, BC V8T 4P4 CANADA
phone 250 383 6864 (toll-free 1 888 232 4444)
fax 250 383 6804; email to bookstore@trafford.com

www.trafford.com/robots/05-0615.html

10 9 8 7 6 5 4 3 2

For Robert S. Garnett, 1915-1998
Partner In This Project and Many Others for Forty-Four Years

Contents

LIST OF ILLUSTRATIONS AND CREDITS 7

CHAPTER I TWO UNEXPECTED DISCOVERIES 11

CHAPTER II SKYLIGHTS 21

CHAPTER III AN IMMEMORIAL WELL 35

CHAPTER IV BONES AND THE BOWL 39

CHAPTER V AN OUTVIEW FOR THE RIGHTHAND RECESS 47
     1. "W" 47
     2. Chevron Chain 48

CHAPTER VI AN OUTVIEW FOR THE CENTER RECESS 53
     3. Fan Sticks 53
     4. Fish Spine 54
     5. Disk 57
     6. "Ship Marking" 57

CHAPTER VII AN OUTVIEW FOR THE LEFTHAND RECESS 65
     7. Dot in Circle 65
     8. Counterclockwise Spiral 66
     9. Clockwise Spiral 67
     10. "Fern Frond" 77

CHAPTER VIII FINDING NORTH 79
     11. "Thumb" 80
     12. "Drinking Vessel" 83
     13. "Noose" 85

CHAPTER IX MOVING UPWARD 89
     14. Rungs with Triangle Sets 89
     15. Swastikas 91
     16. Saltires 93
     17. Reduction I: R12 Front 95
     18. Reduction II: R21 97
     19. Reduction III: K4 100
     20. Reduction IV: C8 104

CHAPTER X WATERDROPS 107
     21. Concentric Arcs 107
     22. Waterdrops 113

CHAPTER XI THREE-NESS: MOON AS TIMEKEEPER 121
     23. Triangles 121
     24. Triangular Stone as Sculptured Emblem 125

CHAPTER XII   COUNTING 127
    25. Three Rosettes 129

CHAPTER XIII   THE HOLE AT THE TOP OF THE VAULT 143
    26. Undivided Lozenge 143
    27. Boxed Lozenge 144

CHAPTER XIV   THE WHEELING SKY 149
    28. Lozengey Net 149
    29. Chequey net 151

CHAPTER XV   CELESTIAL AXES 153
    30. Facing Circle-Segments in Ellipse 155
    31. Tangents 162
    32. Paired circle devices 164
    33. Broken egg 164

CHAPTER XVI   TRACKING TIME 169
    34. Trio of cartouches 170
    35. Attached lobes 175

CHAPTER XVII   PLANETARY TRAVELERS 177
    36. Returning Arcs 177
    37. Seven Disks 178

CHAPTER XVIII   A FOREBODING IMAGE 181
    38. K1 as Emblem 181

CHAPTER XIX   K 52: A RADICAL SUGGESTION 187

CHAPTER XX   REGENERATION AND GNOSIS 201
    39. K1 plus K52 as an Emblem 201
    40. Sandstone Concretion 209

CHAPTER XXI   RAM, GOLD, AND SET-OF-POWERS 221

CHAPTER XXII   ANCIENT FAR-WESTERN LANDMARKS 229

CHAPTER XXIII   FAITH, AFFECT, AND PRACTICE 243

PARTIAL LIST OF SOURCES CONSULTED 253

LIST OF ILLUSTRATIONS AND CREDITS

Plates I-VI, VIII, XI-XIV, XVIII-XXIV, XXVI, XXVII, and XXIX are reproduced through the courtesy of the Irish Department of Works. Plate XXVIII is the work of Joanne Murray of Murray Studios, Seattle; she is also responsible for Plates XXVI and XXVII in which the Department of Works photographs of K1 and K52 have been set beside their reflected images: Plate XXV is the work of Barbara Green Post. The lighted globe in Plate X is a Scan-Globe A/S, ©1998 Scan-Globe Copenhagen (cartography by Karl-F. Harig). Plates VII, IX, X, XV and XVII are my own. Plate XVI is from an old set of tourist views: "Valentine's Snapshots" c 1928. The drawings and sketches are my own with the exception of Figures 6, 8, 10, and 14a, which are reproduced by permission from the drawings of Claire O'Kelly.

Plates

I	Overgrown Mound	10
II	Interior of Chamber	12
III	Restored Mound	15
IV	Midwinter Sunrise	22
V	Righthand Recess	23
VI	Top of Vault	24
VII	Newgrange Model:	25
	a. Outside of Vault	
	b. Inside of Vault.	
VIII	Boulder Cap	26
IX	Mirror in Bowl	36
X	Lighted Globe Showing Milky Way:	49
	a.Northeast to Southwest	
	b. East to West	
	c. Northwest to Southeast	
XI	Orthostat L22 in Passage	52
XII	"Ship Marking"	58
XIII	Lefthand Recess, C3: Counterclockwise Spirals	66

XIV	Lefthand Recess, C2: Clockwise Spiral	68
XV	Views of the Sky in Puddles	71
XVI	Old Baptismal Font, St. Giles Cathedral Edinburgh	74
XVII	Cockleshells	76
XVIII	Orthostat R21 in Passage: Rungs and Triangles	90
XIX	Righthand Recess Roofstone	129
XX	Bowl and Sockets	133
XXI	Kerbstone 67	145
XXII	Roofbox Lintel	151
XXIII	Kerbstone 52	169
XXIV	Kerbstone 1	182
XXV	Lakeside Reflection	184
XXVI	Kerbstone 1 and Its Reflection	185
XXVII	Kerbstone 1 with Kerbstone 52 and Their Reflections	202
XXVIII	Crabshell Relief Images:	
	a. Bes	214
	b. Naked Lady	216
	c. Fright-Mask	217
	d. Lion-Scalp	219
XXIX	Newgrange with a Cow	252

Figures

| 1 | Lefthand Recess Outview | 29 |

1 Lefthand Recess Outview   29
2 Center Recess Outview   30
3 Righthand Recess Outview   31
4 Snake-Wound Pole as Cross   63
5 North Celestial Pole of Newgrange Times, Circumpolar
   Constellations, and Three Comparable Devices   80
6 Claire O'Kelly's Drawing of Devices on Orthostat R12
   Face and Side   91
7 Formalized Version of R12 Side Device: 92
   a. Emphasizing Bipolar Swastikas
   b. Emphasizing Saltires
8 Claire O'Kelly's Drawing of Devices on Kerbstone 4   101
9 St. Brigid's Cross   105
10 Claire O'Kelly's Drawing of Righthand Recess Roofstone   130
11 Analysis of Ellipse Device   156
12 Sketch of Mound with Boulder-Cap Rim and
   Possible Sunset Passage   190
13 Sketch of Bes   204
14 Comparable Forms: 210
   a. Claire O'Kelly's Drawing of Sandstone Concretion
   b. My Drawing of Nine-Week Human Embryo

PLATE I. Overgrown Mound.

CHAPTER ONE

TWO UNEXPECTED DISCOVERIES

Newgrange is a stone-age passage grave located on a ridge above the River Boyne about 40 miles northwest of Dublin. It is a stone building of modest size that was originally covered by a huge symmetrical mound or cairn of river-rolled stones, shaped like a very shallow truncated cone which in the course of over four thousand years gradually collapsed and mellowed into an untidy green hillock.

Under the thick grass that had overgrown this mound there remained a great mass of loose cairn-stones. In the year 1699, some Irish workmen who had been sent here to collect material for road repair were digging into the bank and were taken aback to find themselves facing "a very broad flat stone rudely carved, and placed edgewise at the bottom of the mount. This they discovered to be the door of a cave, which had a long entry into it." (Lhwyd 1699).

The floor of the entering passage was two feet deep in loose dirt and stones, and the enormous orthostats which lined it had fallen forward so that they nearly met at the top. Early explorers had to crawl on their stomachs up the slightly sinuous sixty-two-foot passage, which gradually ascended about six feet to end in a large chamber.

Illuminated by candlelight and lantern, the chamber was found to be shaped something like a very asymmetrical three-leafed clover. It was about twenty feet from backstone to backstone of the two side recesses, and was roofed by a soaring twenty-foot stone vault. The lefthand and center recesses had been floored by large stone slabs. The lefthand recess slab had a little rim. The slab in the righthand recess was very much larger than the other two, was much more deeply hollowed, and when found supported a massive worked stone bowl. The chamber held a large quantity of bones, both human and animal. Both the interior orthostats and the stone kerb that surrounds the mound were found to be copiously engraved with rather geometrical-looking designs.

PLATE II. Interior of Chamber.

The passage into Newgrange was discovered by accident. The possible key to Newgrange faith and practice described in this book was also discovered by accident.

In 1949 I had taken a course on the sources of Mallory's Arthurian Cycle, with which the old Irish Ulster Cycle shares some themes. I wrote a thesis on one of the tales from this cycle, "The Sickbed of Cuchulainn," in which I suggested that Conchobar, the king of the northern region of Ulster, might have been associated with some figure in the northern region of the sky. His name looked to me as if it might have meant the "cabor" or "pole" of the dog, and there are many traces of dog names for asterisms around the north celestial pole.

Conchobar had an envious and bitter rival, Bricriu, who was powerful enough to challenge the king and the champions of Ulster. What center of celestial power,

I wondered, might have been figured as a formidable rival to a figure who had a special relationship to the polar point, around which the sky majestically revolves? The name Bricriu looks as if it might be related to an Irish word for "speckled," so I wondered whether there was any ancient trace of Irish interest in Cassiopeia, the constellation that ornaments the crest of the awe-inspiring, star-spangled arch of the Milky Way.

Some antiquarian plans and sections seemed to suggest that the Newgrange monument was so oriented and constructed that a person in its righthand recess could see Cassiopeia. Furthermore, as it was reported, this recess was decorated with chevrons, and Cassiopeia is usually recognized by its bright double chevron or W. Newgrange long antedated the Romans, but there was an old Gallo-Romano god named Cernunnos who wore antlers, a chevron-like outline. Both antlers and Roman coins had been found at the Newgrange site. As for Bricriu, there was a tale of a visit which he paid to Newgrange with Conchobar, at the time of the conception of Cuchulainn. Irish tradition was full of references to Newgrange, and the Roman coins, possibly votive deposits, were suggestive.

The cluster of facts about Newgrange which I had identified - one feature of its orientation, one detail of its ornament, and a few fragments of tradition - had some implications which I could see at once were both significant and far-reaching. There was the possibility that other Newgrange features might be linked to other engraved devices, and the even more electrifying possibility that there was a recoverable connection between Newgrange and still-existing traditions, both Classical and Irish, which could reveal something about the meaning of the monument.

In the 1950's Newgrange was not seriously engaged by linguists or folklorists, and archaeologists were reluctant to entertain ideas about stone-age astronomical interests. Many thought that it would have been impossible to see out of the top of the chamber because removing the capstone would destabilize the vault. Michael O'Kelly had not yet discovered that the monument had indeed one window on the sky, the so-called "roofbox," a sort of transom window over the passage entrance, narrowly focused on the point of the midwinter sunrise. It can now be argued that the vault was probably stable at every stage of construction, and O'Kelly eventually concluded that the solstitial orientation was an intentional feature.

It was obvious from early sectional drawings of the chamber that the top of the vault could not be seen from the back of the righthand recess, because its roofstone was too low. But it had been reported from the time Newgrange was first discovered that water often dripped into the bowl in the righthand recess and I believed that water in the bowl should have reflected the top of the vault. My husband and I went to Newgrange to verify the fact that a segment of the top of the vault could be seen reflected in a mirror placed level in the bowl. Had the capstone been removed a small wedge of sky would have been reflected to the eyes of an observer at the back of the recess. In fact, if the bowl had not originally rested on the slab but in the center of the chamber (a possibility that had presented itself to investigators) water in the hollow of the slab itself would have reflected a somewhat larger segment of sky. Archaeologists regarded the water as the result of a leak in the vault.

In the 50's the standard source on Newgrange was Coffey's *Newgrange and other incised tumuli in Ireland*. O'Riordain and Daniels's *Newgrange and the Bend of the Boyne* came out in 1964 and included a section of superb photographs which were very helpful. Then in the nineteen sixties, Newgrange was thoroughly and scrupulously excavated under the direction of the Irish archaeologist Michael O'Kelly. On visits to the site I obtained Claire O'Kelly's guidebooks and her monograph on the art of the Boyne valley. The O'Kellys' definitive *Newgrange: Archaeology, art and legend* was published in 1982, providing the detailed report of his excavations, along with Claire O'Kelly's drawings of all the then-known devices and her essays on the history of the monument.

Newgrange was the centerpiece of a spectacular row of at least four funeral monuments. O'Kelly's team excavated and reported on the nearly obliterated sites of three of the satellite mounds, from which it was possible to recover a great deal of information about their structures and the ways they were used. As these satellites were very close to and roughly contemporary with Newgrange, detailed information about them is important for the understanding of Newgrange itself.

I used the O'Kelly plans and sections to build a seven-eighths-of-an-inch-to-one-foot model in found stones, each one numbered and placed to conform with the interior position of each stone, and to make estimates of the azimuths and declinations that were involved in outviews through the top of the chamber vault. The drawings and values included in the book are the result of these estimates. A final determination would have to be made on the basis of a professional survey undertaken specifically for this purpose, as was done by Jon Patrick for the midwinter sunrise view through the passage roofbox.

O'Kelly restored the facade to its original quartz-faced splendor, straightened up the sagging orthostats of the passage, and added protective drainage features. Admission to the inside is now rigorously restricted, but a visitor's center provides information about the site.

Ever since the discovery of the monument, laymen and archaeologists alike have been puzzled and fascinated as much by the carved designs as by the nature and intent of the monument itself. Since almost nothing was known about either the identity or the beliefs of the people who built and used the site, there was little to guide the many attempts made to interpret either the building or the designs upon its stones.

It is plain that unless the engravings were purely ornamental they must have been related in some way to the beliefs of the builders. Various opinions about their meanings have been offered over the years. George Coffey, who produced the first full report on the Boyne tombs in 1912 remarked that "This question has exercised the minds of many fanciful archaeologists for a long time, but little more than absurd guesses have been the result." His own opinion was that the designs were chiefly ornamental.

PLATE III. Restored Mound.

The archaeologists O'Riordain and Daniels in their book *Newgrange* mention "with no enthusiasm" the suggestion that a carved device on R12 resembles human eyebrows and nose. Yet their book (completed after O'Riordain's death) describes an elliptical device in the center of the righthand recess roofstone as "...without doubt a motif representing in stylized form the oculi - goddess motif which appears so often in the mural and mobiliary megalithic art of France and Iberia."

Martin Brennan, the energetic and enthusiastic author of *The Stars and the Stones,* has worked out in great detail a theory that the petroglyphs reflect an interest in observing the movements of the sun and moon.

Thomas in his *Irish Symbols of 3500 BC* believes that the engravings show clear references to a sixteen-month calendar.

Liam MacCuistin, whose book *Exploring Newgrange* includes a good brief summary of competing interpretations, devotes a chapter to the engravings. He concludes that "The precise meanings of the engravings at the monuments will never be known," adding that "All in all, most people find in Newgrange what they want to find."

Claire O'Kelly, who was a partner in the excavation of Newgrange and who has studied and copied all of the designs on the then-revealed decorated stones has said (*Newgrange* p 147):

"It seems to me...that the symbolical meaning was the original inspiration for Irish passage-grave art, beginning with the random carving of motifs which had a meaning for those who applied them, or who caused them to be applied, and that it was only with the passage of time, as the tomb builders became more expert and sophisticated generally, that the aesthetic element in the carvings began to emerge and develop and designs and patterns began to be achieved, though perhaps this aspect never entirely overruled the symbolism, latent or otherwise."

One of the opinions that encouraged me in my attempt to link Newgrange features with Newgrange engraved devices was the monitory statement by the American ethnologist Garrick Mallery: "...No attempt should be made at symbolic interpretation [of petroglyphs] unless the symbolic nature of the particular characters under examination is known or can be logically inferred from independent facts." What was previously lacking in attempts to solve the puzzle of the Newgrange petroglyphs was the set of independent facts to which the particular characters could be related. Claire O'Kelly's copies of the hundreds of complicated devices themselves has now made them available for study. And Michael O'Kelly's work has now provided a set of independent facts from which the nature of the set of devices can be logically inferred.

Newgrange is uniquely suited to fulfill Mallery's requirement because the set of facts now known about the monument is so extensive and so diverse. The monument is very complex, had been almost miraculously well preserved, and has been thoroughly studied and reported, so that there is a wealth of features to compare and relate to the wealth of different engraved devices.

This means that we see in this site a diverse and abundant *set* of features that can be related to a diverse and abundant *set* of engraved devices, both of which reflect an integrated set of beliefs underlying the aim of the builders. We have long known one crucial element of this aim, for there were human remains found in the chamber: the builders and users went to this enormous trouble and expense of intellect and energy to achieve something positive on behalf of the dead.

I would like to submit that the designs carved on the stones of Newgrange should not be called symbols. They should be classed more rigororously as *emblems*. "A symbol represents; an emblem *resembles*." I am going to explain why the devices should not be seen as abstract, nor considered as ornamental, but may be recognized as simplified outlines or diagrams of certain aspects of various natural objects and processes that the builders had related to their faith. The aspects chosen are frequently not those we might have expected. This is surely partly because we have underestimated the intellectual sophistication of the men and women of Newgrange. The aspects which they wanted to refer to are pictured in a consistent, simple style which is as logical as the skillful engineering of the builders should lead us to expect. In fact, the set of emblems provides a kind of written text for the meaning of the main features of the monument, a text which may explain how these features were believed to help ensure an afterlife for the dead whose remains were brought here.

Ideally, my discussions and interpretations of the engraved devices should be compared throughout with the total corpus of ornament provided by Claire O'Kelly in Michael O'Kelly's *Newgrange*, a book which is absolutely indispensable for the serious student of the monument and the details of its history and features.

Newgrange is usually characterized as a funerary monument. We can infer that from the bits of bone found in the chamber and the burial deposits found in the nearby satellite monuments K, L, and Z. Whatever beliefs these people had, whatever pantheon or mythology they had inherited, must be sought at Newgrange in the terms in which they are left to us: the apparatus of what seems to be primarily, although not exclusively, a post-mortem practice. A pantheon or a mythology with its cult and ritual must have been part of the intellectual and spiritual world of the people of Newgrange, but the information which the monument can be expected to yield directly can most reliably be deduced from elements of the site understood as expressions of its funeral practice.

Newgrange cannot be understood as a simple resting place for human remains. The elaborate and costly provision for witnessing the solstitial event alone confirms this. Something in addition was done here, on behalf of the immaterial fraction of personhood that can be imagined to survive the death of the body and be able to achieve some kind of life beyond the grave.

We have three resources to guide us in understanding what may have been involved in the Newgrange post-mortem practice. We share with stone-age man the mortal experience of death and loss. We share the inexhaustible resource of the natural world, from which alone either we or they could build an image of an afterlife. And we have the complex physical apparatus preserved at Newgrange, thoroughly researched and fastidiously reported, including the stunning repertory of stone engravings or "petroglyphs."

In addition I shall show that the features and petroglyphs of Newgrange together may provide evidence that archaic survivals of its belief may have maintained themselves for centuries in traditions still available for study. Between ourselves and Newgrange there stretches back across a span of five thousand years a ruinous causeway of traditions about the supernatural. It is made up of a confused debris of ideas and usages, myths, stories and scraps of stories, names, superstitions and tags of folklore, as well as archaic survivals in living religions, distributed over a wide geographical area. But I would like to suggest that we might cautiously experiment with a working hypothesis that certain survivals may represent elements of a Neolithic faith: that what was believed at Newgrange was part of a very old belief system shared by a family of neolithic cultures. Thus because of the elaboration of its construction and engraving, the accident of its preservation, and the work of those who have studied it, Newgrange may open a window on a widespread neolithic faith, elements of which, I shall show, still live among us.

The study on which this book is based offers two contributions to the understanding of Newgrange, both of which were implicit in my original insight. First, I have shown that there is a straightforward relationship between physical features of the site and devices engraved on its stones. Second, I have described instances in which Newgrange's cluster of post-mortem transformational features, interpreted in the light of its engraved devices, can also be recognized in traditions preserved in verbal sources and superstitious usages from a wide range of times and places. Some of these traditions may help to explain not only the content but also, and very importantly, something about the style of thought that is expressed by the Newgrange monument and the set of emblems which constitute its written text.

CHAPTER TWO

SKYLIGHTS

In order to see how the Newgrange emblems are related to its features, and therefore what the people of Newgrange believed about the fate of the dead, it is essential to have a thorough grasp of the features the monument provided for its users. This involves paying minute attention to many of the details of its very thorough excavation.

When Michael O'Kelly and his team excavated Newgrange in the nineteen sixties, he discovered that there was a sort of narrow transom window, dubbed a "roofbox," built over the entrance to the passage. During the excavation, archaeologists had become aware of a venerable local tradition that at some time the sun shone into the cruciform chamber. The O'Riordain and Daniels book *Newgrange* published in 1964 mentioned a calendar current in Ireland in 1960 which contained the statement that "the rays of the sun at certain times of the year penetrate the opening and rest on a remarkable triple spiral carving in the central chamber."

Because the passage opened southeast, O'Kelly suspected that the rising sun might have shone into it at the winter solstice. After he had straightened up the leaning orthostats of the passage, he stationed himself in the chamber before the midwinter sunrise. The old tradition was spectacularly supported in the event: the beams of the rising sun did enter the chamber through the roofbox and shone all the way up the sinuous sixty-foot passage to splay a brilliant fan of light across the floor in front of the center recess. The sun also shines through the passage entrance.

PLATE IV. Midwinter Sunrise

Both the passage opening and the roofbox were equipped with fitted stone closures, so either or both could be closed, as could the opening over the chamber vault. The roofbox aperture had been fitted with two quartz blocks as closures, one of which was found in place, bearing scratches that showed it had been repeatedly withdrawn and replaced. Both apertures were found buried by cairn debris and vegetation.

It was clear, from that astonishing transom window that admits the rising sun for several days around Christmastime, that the structure of Newgrange revealed a second interest of its builders. There was the funeral function proper revealed by the presence of human remains, an interest in achieving an afterlife for the dead of the community. But there was also a second interest. The builders had provided a way to draw the rays of the rising midwinter sun into the monument, implying a belief that a particular heavenly power, the sun, or more precisely a particular event in the sun's cycle, could help to carry out the funeral aim.

The faith of the Christian like that of the Newgrangeman has attached special meaning to the winter solstice, the season when death begins to give way to life again. Midwinter was the date arbitrarily chosen to celebrate the birth of Jesus, whom the believer trusts can bestow everlasting life. The solstice has a natural relevance to the idea of resurrection. People have signed up for years in advance to be allowed to stand in the chamber of Newgrange around Christmas time to witness the sunrise.

But the midwinter sunrise was by no means the only focus of this complicated monument. In order to understand more about what the men and women of Newgrange believed we need to take into account many other important features provided by the chamber.

PLATE V. Righthand Recess

Although the midwinter sunbeam penetrates into the center recess, it is not this recess but the righthand recess that has struck most students as the possible ritual focus of the monument. This is because unlike the openings of the other recesses the portals of the righthand recess are curved inward a little like entrance-pillars, its floor is occupied by an enormous hollow stone basin which supports a great stone bowl, and its stones are more abundantly and more complexly engraved than those of the other two. Yet an observer in this recess cannot view the sky through the passage door or roofbox window. In fact its slightly convergent portal orthostats shield it a little from the radiance of the midwinter spectacle.

The righthand recess did however have a view on the sky which is only now beginning to attract proper attention: it was the view through the top of the chamber's twenty-foot stone vault.

PLATE VI. Top of Vault

PLATE VII. Newgrange Model: a. (top) Outside of Vault
b. (bottom) Inside of Vault

This used to be most frequently described as a corbeled vault. A corbeled vault is stable because the inner ends of the rising corbels that "oversail" the cavity beneath are held in place by leverage, the weight of stones stacked over their outer ends. Had this been the case at Newgrange it might be argued that it would have been impossible to open the chamber to the sky without somehow capsizing the vault.

However the ascending Newgrange corbels are now usually described as forming a series of compression rings or "horizontal arches," which were stable at every stage of construction provided that the builders always maintained a complete ring at the top as they built. The sides of the corbels in the ring were jammed together so tightly around the hollow core that they could not fall inward. However, they did slant down and out, and if not prevented would have slipped back outward and away from each other, loosening the rings. My model, which had no cover but the corbels themselves, proved this on a small scale. The stones of its vault gradually loosened and slipped outward.

PLATE VIII. Boulder Cap

O'Kelly's excavation showed how this was prevented when he uncovered the front segment of a cap of boulders, built around the front of the chamber vault and probably encircling it. (Only the front was excavated.) The boulder cap was built up tight against the outer ends of the corbels of the vault, and this prevented them from slipping down and out. The cap was faced with neatly fitted water-rolled stones, quite uniform in size and larger than those that compose the mass of the outer cairn. It formed a pleasing facade while it was uncovered.

The stabilizing boulder cap would have been raised on the outside step by step as the horizontal compression rings were raised ring above ring on the inside, safeguarding the integrity of the vault at every stage of construction, from bottom to top. The cap begins about half way up the height of the vault, resting on ordinary cairn material consisting of loose stones stabilized with layers of turf. Where it passes over the passage, the cap rests on a special cross- lintel that spans the gap below. O'Kelly states that "...it was clear that the boulders surrounded the chamber roof, and this suggests that the latter was built as a free-standing structure which had its own mini-cairn, the outside of which was held in place by the built cap or revetment of boulders."

Another stone-age vault whose dome is stable chiefly because of the way the blocks are jammed together laterally is the Eskimo snow-house commonly called an "igloo" (although in some of these domes the blocks are laid in an ascending spiral). This dome too is stable at every stage of construction. The snow- house resembles Newgrange in other ways, including an open "smoke-hole" at the top of the vault, an inclined passage with a transom window (the igloo often has an elegant translucent pane of ice or animal membrane over it), and raised platforms around the walls, reminiscent of the slabs that floor the three Newgrange recesses.

The Newgrange vault, then, was independently stable, and in any case the capstone itself never contributed much to its stability. When the capstone was tilted up, the aperture which it had covered provided the two side recesses with outviews of their own, each as impressive and significant in its own right as the midwinter sunrise.

The cloverleaf chamber is not at all symmetrical. The righthand recess is very much deeper than the left, and its axis is not quite at right angles to the passage. The top of the vault is much closer to the righthand recess than it is to the center of the chamber. These accomplished builders could certainly have made the chamber symmetrical if they had wished to do so. But just as the roofbox aperture, placed exactly where it is, furnishes the center recess with a focused outview on the sky, similarly, the position of the vault aperture, placed exactly where it is, furnishes the unsymmetrical side recesses, which are otherwise blind, with focused outviews on the sky. The vault aperture also provides the center recess with an overhead view similar to the one provided to the righthand recess, although the recess is much more open so the view is much less restricted.

Viktor Reisz has calculated and diagrammed the way the midsummer sun would have come into the chamber through the aperture in the vault. His diagram (see his website http://www.iol.ie/~geniet/eng/top.htm) shows that all planetary bodies would have shone into the center of the chamber when near the midsummer solstition. O'Kelly installed a protective concrete umbrella over the top, but if it were still possible to raise the capstone, all of the planetary bodies would still shine in as they traveled across the highest point of the ecliptic.

Five thousand years ago, if the capstone was raised, an observer standing at the back of the lefthand recess at the proper time could see stars of the Big Dipper (the "Plough") inching slowly around the celestial pole of that epoch. Figure 1 is a sketch showing a person standing at the back of the recess, not in the center, but close to the south side, looking up and out through the raised capstone. According to his epoch, he would have seen approximately the stars listed. Of particular interest are the three stars that form the handle of the Big Dipper, because they form a conspicuous asterism in the circumpolar sky. They are η or Alkaid, magnitude 1.9; ς or Mizar, magnitude 2.3; and ε or Alioth, magnitude 1.8. To Mizar, in the middle of the trio, is attached the unmistakable little "rider" Alcor, magnitude 4; it was once believed to be hard to resolve visually from Mizar although it is now quite easy to do so. If there had been water in the hollow slab, the observer would have seen circumpolar stars reflected in it. Because of the difference in the angle this reflected view would have been a little different.

An observer in the center recess had a view of the top of the Milky Way. and could also see the summer solstition, the highest point on the sun's path. Figure 2 shows three views obtainable from this recess. The direct view of the standing observer is pinched by an overhanging corbel, corbel 4 over C8 (there is a lozenge engraved on the west end of this corbel). A view reflected from water in the slab would have been very little crimped by this corbel. However, combining the supplied viewing options, the comparatively open recess permitted the observer to see a number of first magnitude stars. During the epoch that Newgrange was probably in use, these included Spica in the Virgin, Capella in the Charioteer, Regulus and Denebola in the Lion, and Deneb in Cygnus. He could also have seen the brighter V of Cassiopeia (α, β, and γ) and M44 Cancri, the Beehive Cluster.

LEFTHAND (SOUTHWEST) RECESS

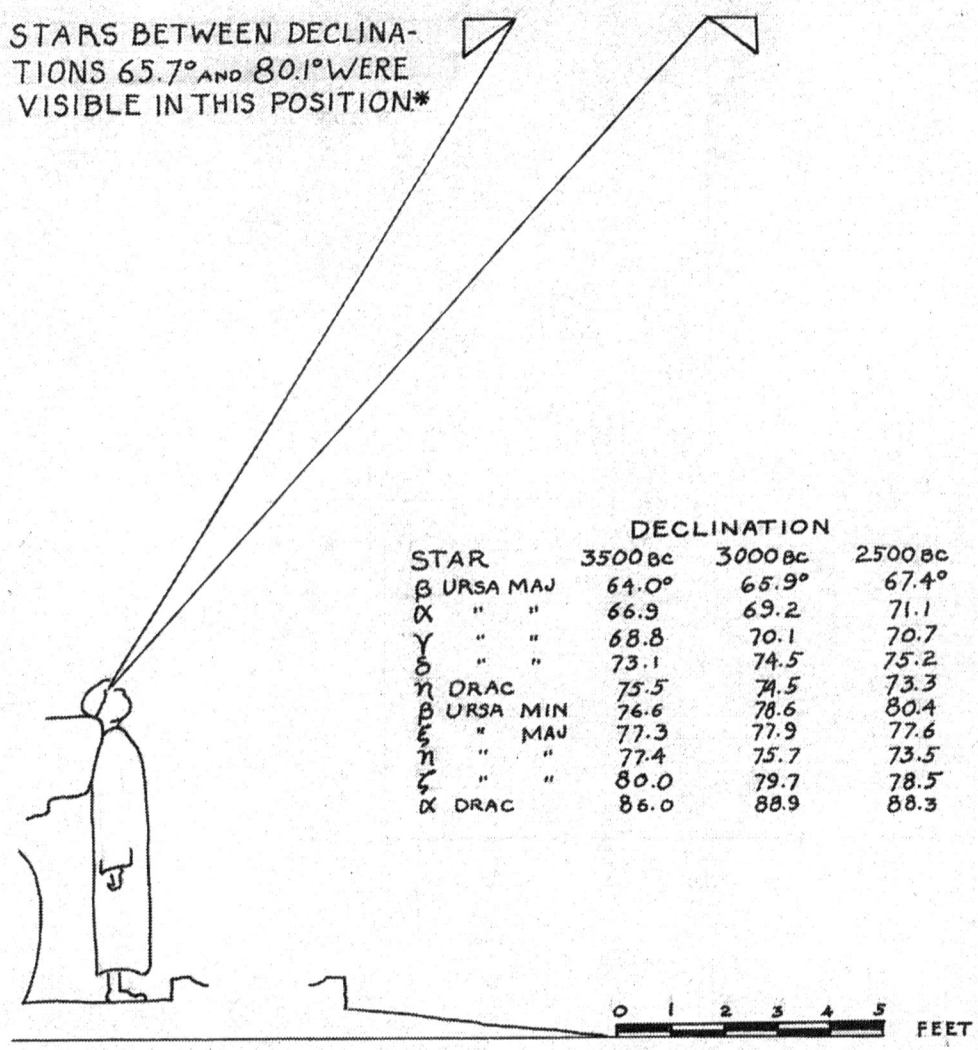

STARS BETWEEN DECLINA-
TIONS 65.7° AND 80.1° WERE
VISIBLE IN THIS POSITION*

STAR		DECLINATION		
		3500 BC	3000 BC	2500 BC
β URSA MAJ		64.0°	65.9°	67.4°
α	" "	66.9	69.2	71.1
γ	" "	68.8	70.1	70.7
δ	" "	73.1	74.5	75.2
η DRAC		75.5	74.5	73.3
β URSA MIN		76.6	78.6	80.4
ξ	" MAJ	77.3	77.9	77.6
η	" "	77.4	75.7	73.5
ζ	" "	80.0	79.7	78.5
α DRAC		86.0	88.9	88.3

0   1   2   3   4   5   FEET

*THE AZIMUTH of THE OBSERVER'S VIEW AS SHOWN IS 18° HIS SIGHTLINES, 31° AND 42° FROM THE VERTICAL, HAVE CELESTIAL DECLINATIONS 78.8° AND 77.3°, RESPECTIVELY. THE NORTHERN CORNER of THE APERTURE, ON HIS LEFT, HAS ANGLE 40°, AZIMUTH 15°, AND DECLINATION 80.1°. THE SOUTHERN CORNER, ON HIS RIGHT, HAS ANGLE 35.5°, AZIMUTH 42°, AND DECLINATION 65.7°.

FIG. 1 Lefthand Recess Outview

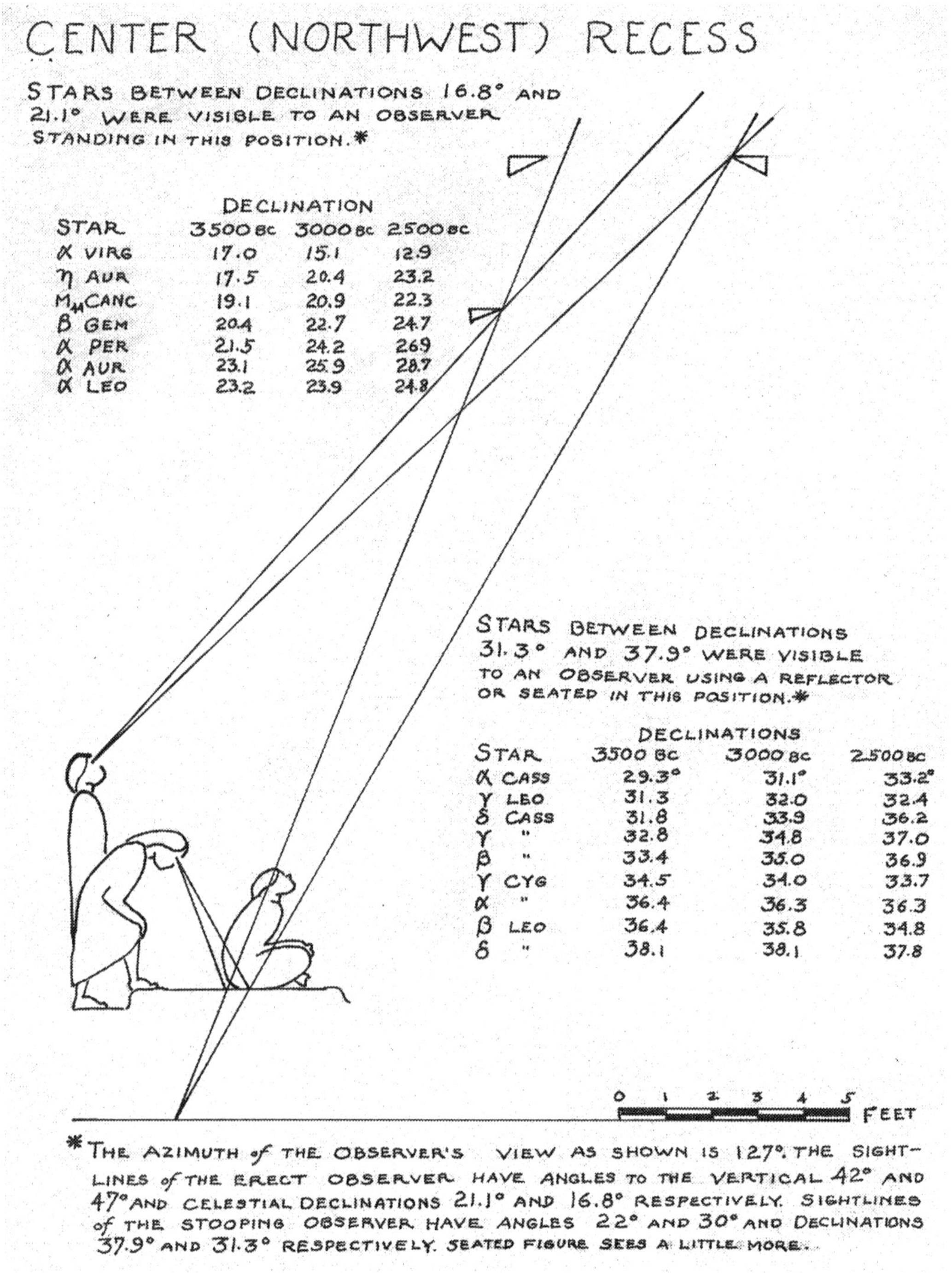

CENTER (NORTHWEST) RECESS

STARS BETWEEN DECLINATIONS 16.8° AND
21.1° WERE VISIBLE TO AN OBSERVER
STANDING IN THIS POSITION.*

STAR	DECLINATION 3500 BC	3000 BC	2500 BC
α VIRG	17.0	15.1	12.9
η AUR	17.5	20.4	23.2
M_MCANC	19.1	20.9	22.3

MₘCANC 19.1 20.9 22.3
β GEM 20.4 22.7 24.7
α PER 21.5 24.2 26.9
α AUR 23.1 25.9 28.7
α LEO 23.2 23.9 24.8

STARS BETWEEN DECLINATIONS
31.3° AND 37.9° WERE VISIBLE
TO AN OBSERVER USING A REFLECTOR
OR SEATED IN THIS POSITION.*

STAR	DECLINATIONS 3500 BC	3000 BC	2500 BC
α CASS	29.3°	31.1°	33.2°
γ LEO	31.3	32.0	32.4
δ CASS	31.8	33.9	36.2
γ "	32.8	34.8	37.0
β "	33.4	35.0	36.9
γ CYG	34.5	34.0	33.7
α "	36.4	36.3	36.3
β LEO	36.4	35.8	34.8
δ "	38.1	38.1	37.8

0 1 2 3 4 5 FEET

*THE AZIMUTH of THE OBSERVER'S VIEW AS SHOWN IS 127°. THE SIGHT-
LINES of THE ERECT OBSERVER HAVE ANGLES to THE VERTICAL 42° AND
47° AND CELESTIAL DECLINATIONS 21.1° AND 16.8° RESPECTIVELY. SIGHTLINES
of THE STOOPING OBSERVER HAVE ANGLES 22° AND 30° AND DECLINATIONS
37.9° AND 31.3° RESPECTIVELY. SEATED FIGURE SEES A LITTLE MORE.

FIG. 2. Center Recess Outview.

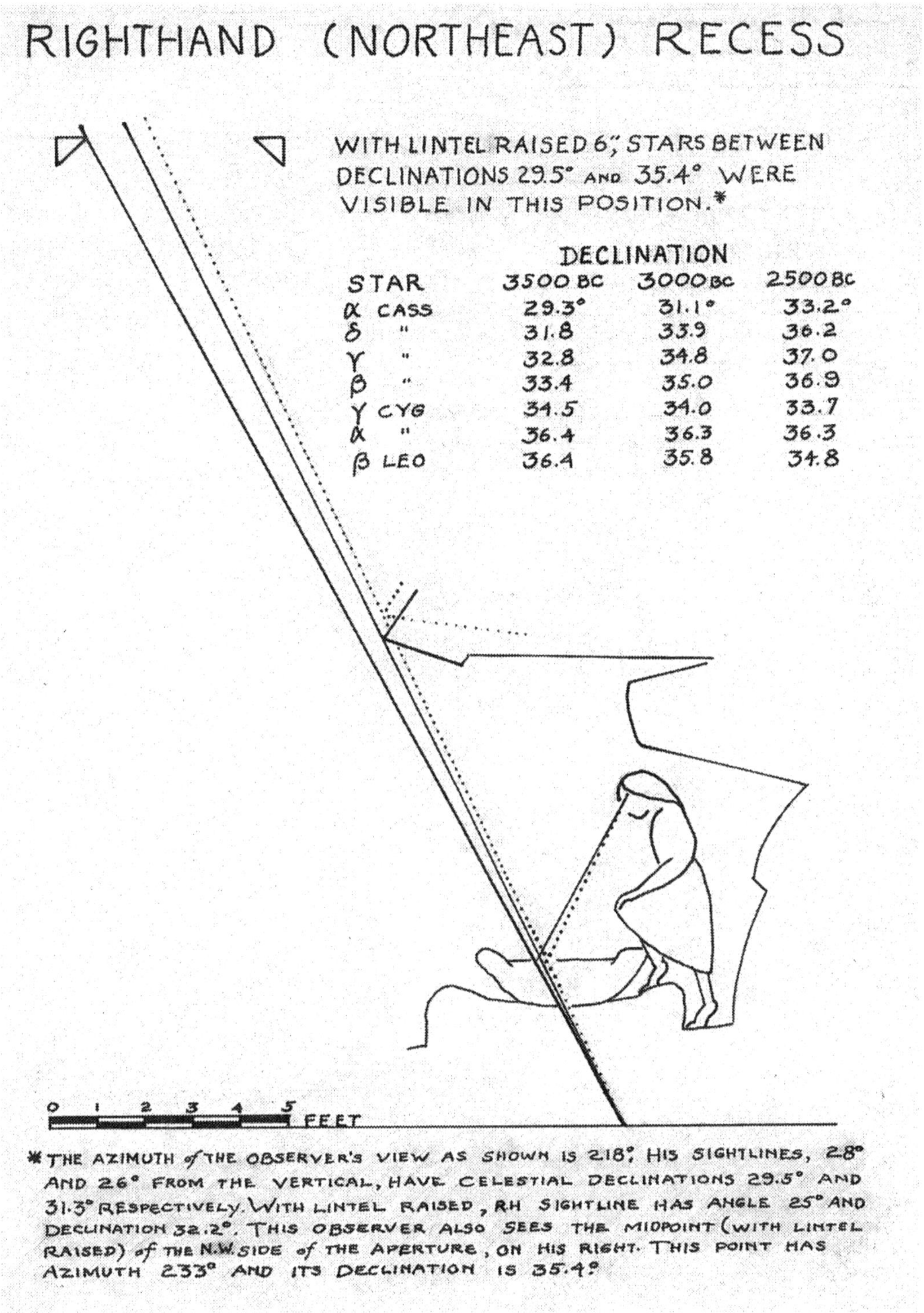

RIGHTHAND (NORTHEAST) RECESS

WITH LINTEL RAISED 6", STARS BETWEEN
DECLINATIONS 29.5° AND 35.4° WERE
VISIBLE IN THIS POSITION.*

STAR	DECLINATION 3500 BC	3000 BC	2500 BC
α CASS	29.3°	31.1°	33.2°
δ "	31.8	33.9	36.2
γ "	32.8	34.8	37.0
β "	33.4	35.0	36.9
γ CYG	34.5	34.0	33.7
α "	36.4	36.3	36.3
β LEO	36.4	35.8	34.8

0 1 2 3 4 5 FEET

* THE AZIMUTH OF THE OBSERVER'S VIEW AS SHOWN IS 218°. HIS SIGHTLINES, 28°
AND 26° FROM THE VERTICAL, HAVE CELESTIAL DECLINATIONS 29.5° AND
31.3° RESPECTIVELY. WITH LINTEL RAISED, RH SIGHTLINE HAS ANGLE 25° AND
DECLINATION 32.2°. THIS OBSERVER ALSO SEES THE MIDPOINT (WITH LINTEL
RAISED) OF THE N.W. SIDE OF THE APERTURE, ON HIS RIGHT. THIS POINT HAS
AZIMUTH 233° AND ITS DECLINATION IS 35.4°.

FIG. 3. Righthand Recess Outview

The roofstone of the righthand recess is so low that it cuts off the view of the top of the vault from the eyes of an observer standing behind the bowl at the backstone of the recess. An observer would have had a narrowly restricted view of the top of the Milky Way and Cassiopeia if he had lain down in the slab (the bowl may originally have stood elsewhere). Both bowl and slab were often found full of water, and the view presented in Figure 3 is the view as it would be reflected from the surface of water in the bowl to the eyes of an observer standing at the back of the recess. If the bowl stood elsewhere, water in the slab would have offered a somewhat wider view, as the slab extends farther toward the front of the recess than the bowl would. The reflection of the sky beyond the vault aperture would have appeared just in front of, as if attached to, the reflection of the elaborate engraving on the roofstone. (see Plate IX)

The roofstone is known to have sagged down over the centuries, and can be seen to have cracked under the pressure. The dotted line is an estimate of the minimum effect of this on the sightlines. The whole vault is believed to have subsided about a yard.

The brighter V of Cassiopeia is visible, as from the center recess, and Gamma of Cygnus, which marks the intersection of the "Cross," could be seen. The view will be described in the next chapter.

How might the Newgrange builders have set about to net these three outviews in one narrow frame? Here is one possibility.

The backstones of the lefthand and center recesses, and the righthand recess slab, were the cornerstones of the monument. A twenty-foot spar whose top would mark the eventual location of the top of the vault would have been erected. The first stone to be set behind the spar would have been the backstone of the center recess, which needed to face the midwinter sunrise point. It was also necessary for this backstone to be set far enough behind the spar that the midsummer solstition appeared behind the spar to an observer standing in front of the backstone.

The backstone of the *left*-hand recess then had to be set as a point from which an observer could see the Dipper stars at some point in their circle, behind the top of the same spar.

As for the right-hand recess, we know that the slab was present in the area of the recess before that recess was outlined with orthostats, for it is too large to have been inserted afterward. It is almost five by six feet, the longer dimension lying crosswise of the recess. The slab had to be placed so that an observer standing behind it could see a *reflection* of Cassiopeia (at some point in its circle) behind the top of the spar. The recess backstone had to be set behind the observer while he could see the reflection.

During the process of building up the vault, the view from each recess was secure as long as the top of the spar remained visible from all three recesses. (Any staging used during the erection of the vault must have remained clear of the spar.) The three sightlines converged on the top of the pole, and the stone vault was fitted around them so that all three always remained clear, each recess always preserving its target behind the top of the pole.

On the hypothesis outlined above, it was the needs of the three converging sightlines that so thoroughly skewed the symmetry of the chamber plan and placed the top of the vault so far from the center of the chamber.

Since all of the sky features were visible in the open air outside, and interest in them must have long preceded this monument, my interpretations of the devices does not depend entirely upon whether either the roofbox or the chamber vault could be opened. It could be argued that the targets of the three overhead views to which various devices seem to refer were elements of the religious system, regardless of whether or not they could be seen after the chamber was roofed. The case is simply that if it could be admitted that the chamber vault as well as the roofbox was designed to be looked through, this would not only provide additional support for the interpretations of certain devices as referable to outviews from side recesses, but also have the considerable merit of explaining the asymmetrical design of the chamber.

CHAPTER THREE

AN IMMEMORIAL WELL

Time and time again, from the rediscovery of the chamber in 1699 up until O'Kelly's installation of a protective concrete umbrella over the vault, water had been found to be dripping or trickling into the monumental slab and bowl in the righthand recess.

Precipitated water percolated through the porous mound in great abundance. Claire O'Kelly explains that conservation efforts had to be undertaken "...so as to stop a number of leaks in the chamber, principally one over the basin stone in the east recess." (*Illustrated Guide to Newgrange* p. 84) Michael O'Kelly remarks that "...In winter, water dripped through and frequently the basin stones in the east recess filled up, a circumstance obviously of long standing since in AD 1700 Lhwyd in one of his letters commented: 'We observed that water dropped into the right-hand Bason, tho' it had rained but little in many days...'" (*Newgrange* p. 113) The flow was so great that it probably contributed to the development of the serious crack that crosses the massive recess roofstone.

When the slab and bowl filled with water, and if the capstone was tilted up away from the vault, then on a clear night a person at the back of the recess could see a small wedge of starry sky through the chamber aperture, reflected in the surface of the water in the bowl in front of him. Except during the periods when they were blotted out by daylight, he could see the constellation Cassiopeia within the arch of the Milky Way as it wheeled above the monument.

Michael O'Kelly verified the fact that the builders were much occupied by problems of managing water. Passage stones were grooved to direct run-off away from the passage. The grooves were effective, for the passage remained dry. Caulking made of sea sand and burnt soil was found in abundance in corbels at the sensitive point where the passage and chamber roofs joined. Two samples of this material were used for radiocarbon dating. The chamber vault was not excavated, and although the archaeologists replaced small stones that had been used to fill the spaces between chamber corbels, O'Kelly did not report that any caulking was found there. Had caulking been found it would surely have augmented the very scarce material that was dated.

PLATE IX. Mirror in Bowl

O'Kelly's statement must be read very carefully, bearing in mind the details of his work and reports. "We have seen that every effort was made by the builders to keep the inside dry - the outward slope of the chamber and passage roof-corbels, the caulking of the roof-joints with putty-like burnt soil and sea sand and the cutting of water-grooves on roof-slabs and passage corbels." Neither grooves nor caulking is reported *within the chamber vault*. The part of O'Kelly's statement that refers to caulking can apply only to the caulking of the joints where passage and chamber met, and the part on the water grooves can apply only to the passage.

Almost all of the vault corbels do slant outward, shedding water out into the body of the cairn. But O'Kelly's sectional drawing shows that there is one corbel, and one corbel only, whose inside surface has been drawn as if it were slanted slightly inward, as far as was ascertained. This corbel is located at the back of the righthand recess. Since cairn pressure would have tended to weigh down the outer ends of the corbel, it seems likely that it may originally have had a steeper slope toward the interior of the chamber.

Considering the general purposefulness of the building, it is probable that just as the builders did not intend that water should enter the passage, and the passage stayed dry, they did intend that water should enter the slab and bowl, and water consistently filled these enormous receptacles. We ourselves waterproof our buildings, but pipe water into various tubs and bowls. The slab in the right recess did not need to be hollowed simply in order to hold the stone bowl, and both slab and bowl seem too massive to have been meant to hold anything but water. Water was certainly not intended to enter where it was found to enter in 1699 and afterwards. The gradual sinking of the whole vault, estimated at about a yard, had short-circuited whatever channel would originally have been devised.

The hypothesis that the bowl was filled by a source inside the chamber recess itself has perhaps some support in the odd fact that absolutely no ceramic was found in the building. The archaeologists did find that there was a small, winter-flowing stream under the passage orthostat R 8. This spring was not far from an original gap in the passage wall that had been closed by a wall built of small stones. Thus the builders might have obtained water from a source within the monument. A piece of a small stone bowl was found outside the entrance, but it was certainly too small to be practical for filling the large bowl, to say nothing of the slab. The builders probably intended to provide the bowl and slab with their own source of water, and in any event, water went on faithfully filling them for over five thousand years.

The boulder cap sheds an interesting sidelight on the builders' interest in providing water in the chamber. The cap is very expertly finished with selected stones. This was not necessary for stability, although there is a possibility that it was once uncovered, forming a decorative upper segment of the facade. But there is a device called an aerial well which makes use of the fact that dew and fog will condense on a stone-built pile or cairn and may be collected and led down for use. One famous example was located above Theodosia on the Black

Sea. Thirteen forty-foot cairns of loose rock delivered over 500 gallons of pure drinking water a day to the city by pipeline. This type of apparatus has attracted the interest of Unesco to help supply water in dry regions.

Passage graves were frequently remodeled. Site K west of Newgrange seems to have been remodeled twice. If in some former phase the boulder cap that was wrapped around the hollow chamber of Newgrange had been exposed, it would not only have created a pleasing facade, it would also have had a tendency to work as an aerial well.

The builders could hardly have planned better to insure the collection not only of rain and snow but also of dew. This is significant because from time immemorial, dew has been been thought to have supernatural properties. If these properties had some role in the Boyne funeral practice the cap would have provided a modicum of dew along with other atmospheric moisture.

The subject brings to mind a curious detail reported in an early and ruinously clumsy excavation of the nearby passage grave of Dowth: "In the Centre of the Mound a curious funnel or Air shaft was discovered, about 5 inches in Diameter neatly built with small flat Stones. This was reached about 17 feet from the datum line, & reached to the base of the Tumulus. It did not appear to have any connection with any Chamber or building which could afford any information as to the probable use for which it was designed." This funnel certainly conveyed not only air but a token amount of water into the body of the mound. Again, the presence of dew which condensed on the stone lining of the little shaft and ran down the sides may have been a factor that was regarded as hallowing the fabric of the mound.

CHAPTER FOUR

BONES AND THE BOWL

There is one serious objection to the theory that the righthand recess was planned to have and use the reflected outview through the vault, an objection which brings up some important considerations of its own. The objection is that the slab or bowl that occupied the recess would have contained human remains. Therefore, it has been plausibly argued, the builders cannot have intended water to enter the recess and fill the bowl as it did. So were human remains found in the bowl or slab when the chamber was first discovered?

There is a some confusion about this. Charles Campbell was the first person to enter the chamber after his workmen discovered the entrance to Newgrange in 1699. Although the bowl has been moved several times since then, the first report of the chamber places it on the slab. Will Jones was a draughtsman employed by the antiquarian Edward Lhwyd who visited the chamber shortly before December 1699. Jones reported on and drew a slender worked stone, about eighteen inches long and six inches in diameter, which he found under the stone bowl which he stated then rested in the hollow of the slab. He did not mention any bones in the bowl. Lhwyd stated that there was a great quantity of bones found in the chamber, but he did not say that they were human bones. He drew on reports of the discovery, presumably by Campbell, as well as his own observations, but he does not mention being told that bones were found in the bowl. Coffey comments that "It is not probable that if any information were given as to the finding of human remains, so careful an observer as Lhwyd would have omitted all reference to the matter."

In 1725, nearly a generation later, Thomas Molyneux published a report of his visit to the site. He describes the floor as "a rude sort of pavement, made of the same stones of which the mount is composed, not beaten or joined together, but loosely cast upon the ground only to cover it." Lhywd had described it as "nothing but loose stones of any size in confusion" adding that there were "amongst them a great many bones of beasts and some pieces of deer horns." Molyneux had also spoken with Charles Campbell, whom he may be citing when he says "Along the middle of the cave a slender quarry-stone, five or six feet long lies on the floor, shaped like a pyramid, that once, as I imagine, stood upright, perhaps a central stone to those placed round the outside of the mount: but now 'tis fallen down."

But Molyneux goes on to describe a sensational find: "When first the cave was opened, the bones of two dead bodies entire, not burnt, were found upon the *floor*...." [italics mine] At another time he gives a different version of this find, which he also attributed to Campbell: Campbell had reportedly said to Molyneux that he found "the skull and bones of a man in one of those *Cisterns* and the bones of another human body lying on the *ground* in another part of the cave somewhat remote from the cistern..." [italics mine] Campbell's conversation with Molyneux must have taken place thirty years after the monument was opened. Lhywd, a careful observer, neither saw nor heard from Campbell about these bodies, about whose locations Molyneux, as we see, gives two versions. Neither did Lhywd see the slender quarry stone Molyneux reported. Had someone else meddled with the site in the three intervening decades?

By the time O'Kelly began work, Newgrange had been open for over two centuries and there had been an enormous amount of interference with not only the contents but the very structure of the monument. It had been visited, shoveled out, tidied up, probably plundered of random finds, badly defaced with graffiti, violently propped up and energetically cemented together here and there, often unnecessarily.

Obviously whatever bones were present had not escaped the general roughing up. T. P. Fraher, O'Kelly's anatomy expert, who examined the fragments of bones that were found, stated that "Of the burnt material approximately 2200 fragments of burnt bone were found, weighing in all 1051 g" or less than two and a half pounds. In short the fragments were very tiny. He says that "The samples containing unburnt human material also included large numbers of animal bones as well as about 750 unidentifiable fragments. .....The unburnt material is likely to have been derived from a pair of skeletons, one of which is male and considerably larger and more heavily built than the other..." This would seem to support Molyneux's belated report of the presence of two bodies.

O'Kelly noted that remains were scattered in the chamber to such an extent that "the bones of the two [unburnt] skeletons identified were partly in the east recess and partly in the main chamber outside the recess. Teeth were also widely dispersed which, in the same way, were shown to have come from one individual." (*Newgrange* p. 107) Most of the remains were found in front of the two side recesses. The feet of visitors passing through the chamber must certainly have contributed to this pattern of distribution.

In fact, two hundred and fifty years of traffic, and a scandalous amount of meddling had made it almost impossible to judge whether the pattern of finds had anything to do with where the remains had originally been placed. O'Kelly's statement is "...it cannot be definitely established that [grave goods] were originally lying in the basins together with the burnt bone, though it is clear that both grave-goods and burnt material were concentrated around and under them, with the exception of the end recess where circumstances had made preservation of the remains impossible." (*Newgrange* loc cit) He concludes that "Though it is likely that several skeletons were involved, on the basis of the identified fragments it can only be stated with certainty that the burnt material included remains from three or more human skeletons, how many more it is impossible to tell." (*Newgrange* loc cit) Except for the implication of the words "lying in the basins together with the burnt bone" O'Kelly can not be quoted as stating that any of the remains were actually found by him in any of the basins, although he notes examples of this practice in similar monuments, and he did find and note human remains with a couple of artifacts in the rude stone basin of the almost obliterated satellite tomb Z just east of the Newgrange mound.

The remains of an average sized man, cremated in a modern reverberating furnace, occupy a container about the size of a small shoebox. There would not have been room for the burnt remains of many individuals in the bowl, nor in the slab, if the bowl was resting in it. Nor does it seem convincing that remains would have been divided in some way between the bowl and the slab.

At the time Campbell entered the tomb and saw (according to Molyneux) two entire bodies, the massive stone door that had been provided to fit exactly into the passage entrance was not in place. What Mrs. O'Kelly says is this. "The mouth of the passage had originally been closed by a stone which exactly fitted the aperture, but this was no longer in place in 1699. It lay tilted away from the entry with its top surface against the back of the entrance stone, and was so covered by stones and debris that the visitors of 1699 and later were not aware of its existence. It was first noted only in 1845. The question arises as to when and by whom the closing stone was levered back." (*Newgrange* p. 25) The stone that was "placed edgewise" (in the words of Lhwyd) must refer to the carved K1 and not to the stone door. Had anybody entered between the time the door was pried open, however long ago that was, and the time the workmen discovered the passage? If the two bodies were a later insertion, was the door already open before they were brought into the chamber?

There were later groups of people living in the area around the front of the mound at the time Newgrange began to collapse, completely burying the passage entrance, whether the door was shut or open. No evidence was found that would indicate that these people ever went inside.

Visitors to the site left Roman coins which were dated between the first and the fourth century after Christ. These coins were found lightly covered just beneath the sod in or on the mound at a time when it had collapsed all the way out to the so-called "Great Circle" of standing stones that partially surround the mound. The coins were presumably left during the stay of the Romans in Britain. It has been suggested that they may have been deposited as votive offerings, intended to win the favor of whatever supernatural powers the donors believed were still associated with the monument. There was an early report that coins were also found in the chamber, but this was not officially confirmed.

Norsemen were in the area in the ninth century, looking for valuables, but athough they entered many other gravesites, Newgrange is not mentioned by name as one of them. What is said is this: "The cave of Achadh Aldai and of Cnodhba, and the cave of Fert Boadan over Dubach, and the cave of the smith's wife , were searched by the Foreigners which had not been done before..." The names Cnodhba and Dubach are recognized as those of Knowth and Dowth, but the other two references have proved very vexing to identify. What was this "cave of the smith's wife"? The Dagda was a kind of all-purpose smith who once owned Newgrange, and he had an affair with Boann (a supernatural being associated with the River Boyne) somewhere in the neighborhood of Newgrange.

One reason the Norse are not thought to have been in Newgrange is that the passage entrance was then buried by the cairn collapse. But the possibility that the Norse entered the monument raises one intriguing possibility. O'Kelly found the capstone buried only about waist deep in cairn material, that is, loose stone, doubtless capped by a pad of turf. A Norwegian fairytale "The Three Princesses in the Mountain in the Blue" relates how the hero was told how to rescue them. "East of the manor there's a big mound. On top of the mound you're to dig loose a square piece of turf. Then you'll see a huge slab of rock, and under it is a deep hole. You must lower yourself down the hole. Then you'll come to another world and there you'll find the princesses with the Mountain Trolls. But it's deep and it's dark down there, and you must pass through both fire and water...." It was indeed pitch dark at the bottom, but the hero "...caught sight of a tiny glimmer of light a long way off, just like the dawn. He walked toward it, and when he had gone part of the way it started growing brighter about him, and it wasn't long before he saw a golden sun rise in the heavens, and the daylight was as bright and clear as in the real world."

The Newgrange chamber could probably always have been entered from above for the capstone was large but thin, and certainly not deeply buried. If the roofbox was not blocked, the sun shone into the chamber around Christmastime. O'Kelly had heard the local rumor that the sun shone into the chamber, and that rumor must have been circulating for some time. The roofbox opening was completely blocked until the excavation took place. The ages of fairy stories are impossible to establish.

To sum up, the users of the chamber must have intended the monumental bowl and slab to hold something. Since little beside human remains was found in the Newgrange chamber, it was natural to assume that it was these that the slab and bowl had held. The same reasoning had inspired the early guess that it was blood from some sacrificial rite. But although O'Kelly notes that remains were found in or on slabs in other monuments, including the nearby Site Z, he did not himself find them in the slab or bowl at Newgrange. *Unequivocal* evidence that they were found as an *original* deposit does not exist.

Remains were found in slabs in other sites, but it was only in Newgrange that there were two possible contents known to be present, bones and water. It seemed natural to assume that the two were mutually exclusive. If the bowl held bones, the water that dripped into it must have been accidental, an engineering failure.

Aubrey Burl once remarked (*Prehistoric Avebury* p 186) "...water has been an essential part of many religions although, like dancing or prayer, it leaves nothing for the archaeologist to find and its use can only be inferred." This is as true for the Newgrange recess as for every grave found with an empty "food" bowl or beaker in it. Many graves contain mirrors, probably for the same reason they contained these empty bowls or, more precisely, bowls that were found empty. Like a mirror, a water- filled container is a reflector. A bowl of water, like an up-facing mirror, brings heaven and its powerful presences down to aid and comfort the forlorn inhabitant of the grave. The water then vanishes. Without a trace.

Remains were not brought into the Newgrange chamber in handfuls. People carried them in some kind of packet. Why was a packet of remains brought into the chamber in the first place? Irish tradition had it that the monument was the resting place of three times fifty sons of kings. Yet although only a pitiful few remnants of bones were found inside there is no historical evidence for any wholesale removal of remains. Unless human remains were going to be permanently deposited within the chamber, why would they pass through it?

It is possible that the object was exactly to bring the packet of remains into contact with the solemn, numinous font whose water – perhaps mixed with dew – trickled from the heavens into the righthand-recess bowl. In fact, unless the entire monument had been built in order that one or two sets of bones could be laid in the bowl, the idea may well have been that it was somehow beneficial for the deceased that his bones should have an opportunity however brief to contact the water in the bowl perhaps by dipping or sprinkling.

For comparison, water has an important role in Christian ritual. Baptism is a major rite of this faith, and its intention is to assure the baptisand of a resurrection from death. "This is what [Christ] promised us: everlasting life." "None can enter into the kingdom of God, except he be regenerate and born anew of Water and the Holy Ghost..." The priest blesses the water in a special font and dips the baptisand in the font or sprinkles him with water from it. In addition, Christian funerals often include sprinkling the casket with holy water at various times during the service. Holy water is provided at the door of the church for believers entering the building. Water is usually mixed with the wine of the communion rite, accompanied by words that explain its significance. Taking the bread and watered wine of communion is expressly linked with a hope of life beyond the grave.

In the Christian rites water is usually blessed or hallowed by being made to accept the reflection of the religion's holiest emblem, the cross: the priest makes a gesture that imitates the outline of this emblem above the water, accompanied by an ancient liturgical formula. The formula invokes the presence of a supernatural power. The water is then understood to be supernaturally infused with the power of the emblem.

Two powers could obviously be attributed to the Newgrange bowl and basin. The builders had made certain that the water that filled the bowl came from heaven. And they had arranged the positions of the font and the openable skylight above it so that at night, in season, the water in the bowl was capable of holding a reflection of the crest of the Milky Way. The Milky Way has been believed from time immemorial to be a path of departed spirits. Human remains were certainly brought into the chamber, and it is not unreasonable to think that they were intended to be brought into physical contact with whatever special power their faith attributed to the mysterious font, hallowed by the image of a holy path or river, as well as water straight from heaven itself.

In conclusion, the capstone of the vault could be safely raised. It is enormous in relation to the small aperture beneath it, covering the whole narrowed upper part of the vault. It could be tilted or turned to cast a shadow for better viewing, and since the viewer was twenty feet below, it is possible that he could see first or second-magnitude stars through the narrowing "chimney" even when the sky was not entirely dark, as stars are said to be visible from the bottom of a well.

When the capstone was raised on a clear night an observer in the lefthand recess could see circumpolar stars, and if it was raised when water had filled the bowl, a person in the righthand recess could see a small wedge of the starry sky, reflected in the surface of the water. When the Milky Way was above at night, it was the reflection of the segment of the galactic arch that is ornamented with the five bright stars of Cassiopeia which was seen. As the water in this font came direct from the sky, and reflected a path believed to be walked by departed spirits, the contact would seem to favor an ascent to the heavens. It would be reasonable for a packet of wrapped bones to be dipped in or sprinkled with that water, infused as it was with the power of a great emblem of an afterlife.

If the reflection was intentional, there would have to have been some way to control the entrance of water into the bowl that did not involve rippling the reflected image.

I shall show that evidence of interest in the views from all three recesses, as well as interest in the properties of reflection, can be discerned in certain devices engraved on the stones of the monument. The devices are emblems, simple outline versions of ideas also revealed by the orientations of the monument and its recesses, and by the reflector and water-holder included in the chamber. They can be identified because they represent in understandable form certain aspects of ways in which both the astronomical features and the water features were believed to help those who had died to escape death and live in a bright realm above.

The relationship of all the outviews to adjacent petroglyphs is very straightforward. We shall find that in this respect the Newgrangemen's minds prove to be as reasonable as their engineering would suggest. The faith their stone engravings suggests seems equally reasonable.

In commenting on the way the various agencies were imagined to operate in this stone-age funeral practice I shall frequently compare, as I did above, what I judge to be relevant Christian beliefs and practices. I have no first-hand experience of primitive rites, but Christianity is a religious tradition with which I am familiar as both a student and a believer. Lacking hard credible evidence to the contrary, I assume throughout that in general what seemed reasonable to the Newgrange mourner as a believer in one version of an afterlife, would seem reasonable to me, as a believer in another version. It seems unlikely to me that these accomplished builders were either more childlike or more gullible in their religious faith than I feel myself to be.

My interpretations of Newgrange devices should not be extended to cover similar devices in other sites with other features. It is probable that some emblems may transfer in this way, but I have attempted to interpret Newgrange devices only as related to Newgrange features.

The numbered drawings of the devices inserted into the text are almost all sketches of the average outline of devices that occur more than once.

CHAPTER V

AN OUTVIEW FOR
THE RIGHTHAND RECESS

Five thousand years ago, when the vault was open at night and the bowl full of water, an observer at the back of the righthand recess could see (in season) the bright double chevron or "W" of Cassiopeia within the Milky Way reflected in the water. He could see it only as reflected, since the roofstone of the recess was so low that only a person lying within the bowl or slab could see the top of the vault directly. The W outline can be completed by the imagination of the observer in several ways.

1. "W"   **Possible Reference:**   **Related Site Features:**

                          Constellation Cassiopeia   Raisable Chamber
                                                          Capstone, Righthand
                                                          Recess Orientation

The double chevron could be seen as (for example) one set of branching antlers, two joined sets of V-shaped antlers, the horns of a pair of goats, or the pointed muzzles of a pair of foxes. Antlers were found at the site, although they were not thought to be part of the original deposit. This is significant because there was an important Romano-Gallic god called Cernunnos who is portrayed with antlers, and who pours a stream of small units, perhaps coins, from a sack. That Roman coins were found at the site might suggest some connection with this figure. Cernunnos may be flanked by two other divinities. One was sometimes Mercury, who as the god of commerce often carried a purse of coins. The other was Apollo, who by Roman times was virtually identified with the sun. The solstitial sunrise observation shows that the sun had a role in Newgrange religious thought.

On the second century A.D. Gundestrup Cauldron, a Celtic artifact, Cernunnos is pictured on one panel with antlers and a reindeer: the antlers of the pair touch each other so that each set makes up one V of a striking W. Female reindeer have antlers; Lapland legend relates how the great god Jubmel formed the cosmos from the body of his little vaja or female reindeer, including the bridge between heaven and earth.

Quite differently, the W is easily seen as the bent elbows of a standing human figure, a female figure because of the two milky streams that flow down from the area where the breasts would be. One old explanation of the Milky Way was that it was Hera's abundant milk, that spurted down in two streams when she nursed Heracles. Modern representations of Cassiopeia's Chair show the queen seated, a tortured configuration which is much less obvious and must be more recent; there is little agreement among celestial cartographers about how the stars are placed in the awkward seated form. The legs and feet of the more natural standing figure are now part of the constellations of Pegasus and Andromeda.

Cassiopeia has afterlife associations. The crux of the Greek story about her is the visit of her son-in-law Perseus to the underworld to fetch the Gorgon's Head, the terrible bogey whose sight turned those who looked at it to stone. Homer knew that the queen of the underworld held this fright-mask up to appall those who approached the gates of Hades' kingdom.

2. Chevron Chain	**Possible Reference:**	**Related Site Features:**
	Milky Way	Raisable Chamber Capstone, Righthand Recess Orientation

The galaxy itself is so irregular in shape and varies so much in brightness that it is impossible to draw satisfactorily. One of its common titles is the River of Heaven, and the simple double chevron of Cassiopeia is near the source or spring of what looks like a great double cascade. Its brilliance is completely lost to the modern city-dweller. The righthand recess is liberally engraved with chains of chevrons, those on the roofstone being drawn out into a long, broadly-redoubled band. Because it appeared near the top or apparent source of the streams, the familiar W may have been considered an emblem well suited to represent the Milky Way when replicated into a long chain, to indicate its length, and doubled or boxed, to suggest its breadth. It is worth noting that an Egyptian hieroglyphic determinant sign that signifies water in a special sense consists of a row not of curved wave forms but of linked chevrons exactly like some of the chains seen at Newgrange.

PLATE X. Lighted Globe Showing Milky Way:

a. Northeast to Southwest

b. East to West

c. Northwest to Southeast.

The appearance of the Milky Way is only intermittently symmetrical. From the northern hemisphere, the top of the arch, marked by the double chevron of Cassiopeia, is about 25° south of the north celestial pole. So as the top of the arch revolves around the pole and as its two limbs sweep around the entire horizon, each limb is shorter when it is cut by the northern horizon than it is when it is being cut by the southern horizon. The limbs are of equal length twice a day. When the top of the arch is due north of the pole the limbs, which are at their longest, extend equally southeast and southwest. When the top of the arch is due south of the pole the limbs, at their shortest, extend equally east and west.

The top of the arch revolves counterclockwise like the rest of the circumpolar sky. It moves eastward underneath the pole (that is, north of it) and westward when south of the pole. The advancing limb, decorated with Cepheus and Cygnus, sweeps the sky diagonally from northeast to southwest. Then as the top of the arch begins to dip back under the pole again, the trailing limb, decorated with Gemini and Monoceros, crosses the sky diagonally from northwest to southeast. The pale streamers crisscross the heavens like maypole ribbons.

When Newgrange was built, the top of the galactic arch was farther from the celestial pole than it is now, due to precession. Five thousand years ago, from the northern hemisphere, the whole galactic ring lay flatter in relation to the circle of the horizon. In those days, when the top of the arch was north of the pole it was only a little above the northern horizon in the latitude of Newgrange, so that the Milky Way could be seen to flow almost all around the southern horizon. At that time Cepheus was a little closer to the top of the arch than Cassiopeia.

The fact that the Newgrange carver has not tried to copy the outline of the Milky Way but has developed another quite rational way of showing it is important in itself. It gives an insight into an important characteristic of his method of representing things. He developed the astral device of the W at the source of the Milky Way into a device that can refer quite reasonably to the long, broad swathe of the Milky Way that flows from it.

The Milky Way has a firm link with the afterlife. The idea of the Milky Way as a path for departed spirits and supernatural beings is held very widely, and has a long history which has lasted into our own time. Both chevrons and chevron rows are common, ancient, widespread motifs on funeral ware. Interest in the Milky Way as a post-mortem feature may be very old indeed. Around 25,000 BC Paleolithic people decorated European caves with magnificent paintings of animals, and among these painted animals they placed a great many of their handprints, both positive and negative. Every Paleolithic handprint that was impressed upon the wall of a cave impressed against it the double chevron, inverted as an M, that marks the palm of every human hand. The presence of handprints in the caves may be a hint that these painted contexts, signed with personal M's, had some kind of supernatural association linked with the Milky Way, which looks so much like a pathway or river in heaven. The W form as suggesting bent elbows also suggests the great-breasted mother responsible for the abundant flow of supernatural "milk" suitable to nourish new life in the heavens.

As the celestial pole revolves around the pole of the ecliptic every 25,000 years, these paleolithic painters would have had our own pole star, Cynosura or Polaris. The bowl of the Big Dipper would have looked just a little more square to them than it does to us, because of the large proper motion of some of its stars.

However they were pictured and believed to act, the starry chevrons and the segment of the galactic stream that were reflected in the recess basin brought celestial agencies of great power into the chamber. Chevron devices and swathes of linked chevrons were engraved on many Newgrange stones, and were especially conspicuous in the righthand recess which was oriented toward Cassiopeia and the Milky Way. These devices would be frank references to the heavenly agencies which they resemble. They were emblems which invoked the aid of the supernatural powers of their agents in this funeral setting, as the emblem of the cross in a Christian setting invokes the power of Christ as the supernatural agent who can bestow eternal life.

I have noted that the boulder cap of Newgrange, through which precipitated water penetrated into the chamber, would also (if uncovered) have delivered a modicum of atmospheric moisture. Dew must have condensed upon its stones, and droplets of it would have trickled downward toward the chamber. Dew forms on clear nights, when the Milky Way is visible. The many little droplets of dew that materialize under many little stars, especially the dense, cloudy band of stars that make up the so-called River of Heaven, may have been understood to form part of the water in the bowl in the righthand recess, which reflected that heavenly river. Supernatural properties almost universally credited to dew would have had a natural place within a postmortem concept.

From the righthand recess the W could be seen only as reflected. When reflected, the double chevron becomes an M. Stone L 22 in the passage has a superb carving of an M, that is, a reflected double chevron, placed above a bold pattern of multiple wavy lines developed out of running chevron chains. This would be a logical way to represent the reflection of the W in the water of the celestial river which the righthand basin or bowl collected from the sky, specifically that part of the sky in which the chevrons lay, the galactic stream.

PLATE XI. Orthostat L22 in Passage

CHAPTER VI

AN OUTVIEW FOR
THE CENTER RECESS

Two Newgrange devices may be interpreted as references to the established interest in the midwinter observation. Their form is very unexpected. As in the case of the long broad chains of chevrons that may serve as emblems of the Milky Way, those two devices translate a certain aspect of the solstitial interest into simple and very rational emblems. These may be interpreted as diagrams of a method for determining the date of the solstice. They may be called the "fan-stick" and "fish-spine" or "offset" devices.

3. Fan Sticks **Possible Reference:** **Related Site Features:**

Noon Shadow as Openable Roofbox and
True North Indicator Raisable Chamber
  Capstone, Roofbox and
  CenterRecess Orientations

The sun at midwinter is at the most southerly point in its path, at the bottom of the very shallow, drooping arc or swag of the ecliptic, so the noon shadow cast by a standing stone or gnomon at that time is the longest noon shadow of the year.

The shadows cast by a standing stone in the course of a day may be pictured as a series that opens around the base of the stone like the sticks of an opening fan. The morning shadows shorten from west to north, the afternoon shadows lengthen again from north to east. The noon shadow, which is the shortest, points due north. It may be thought of as the midpoint of two graduated scales of shadow-lengths that are mirror images of each other.

The *time* of noon was presumably not known, so the noon shadow would have to have been identified by its other characteristic: it is the one that falls due north. Thus it was imperative to know the location of the north celestial pole, and we shall see in Chapters VII and VIII that locating due north is one of the concerns reflected by other Newgrange petroglyphs. After true north had been determined, the noon shadow could be distinguished.

Just to the right of the entrance of the Newgrange mound, excavation uncovered what is identified as an "oval stone setting," a feature believed to belong to the primary phase of the monument. It had been covered by a low mound of water-rolled quartz pebbles. This feature was an oval (or ellipsoidal?) enclosure made of thin slabs set on edge around a pavement "partly cobbled and partly flagged." One of the cobbles was described as a "highly polished piece of sandstone... displaying a fractured surface at one end and a blunt polished point at the other....It lay east-west, pointed end to the east." It was probably not meant for a phallus as suggested. At least we can say that the polished stone had a shape well-adapted for a gnomon, for which the oval enclosure would have served as a dial-face. Such an apparatus could have served to track the noon shadow.

4. Fish Spine	**Possible Reference:**	**Related Site Features:**
	Solstice- Determination	Openable Roofbox plus
	Tally	Center Recess Orientation

Once the location of due north is established and the lengths of the daily north-falling noon shadows have been marked, it can be determined which of those daily shadows is the longest of the year. Around the time of the solstice the sun is changing elevation so slowly that there is a whole series of noon shadows that are practically the same length. But suppose that on the day when the noon shadow stops lengthening perceptibly a person scratches a vertical line on a stone. Suppose that on each succeeding day he makes a horizontal mark, along alternating sides of the vertical line, until the day he can see that the shadow has begun to shorten again. Next year, this tally will reveal the number of days from the date the sun stops moving till the solstice occurs. It will be the number of days on one side of the line. The line with short lines attached on each side looks a little like a fish-spine. It is rare at Newgrange. Another device, which consists of slanted lines arranged on opposite sides of a spine, could serve the same purpose. It is possible that these are versions of the same idea, the idea of keeping a tally to determine the midpoint of a series.

This would be a very rough way indeed to determine the solstice, and devices engraved on the stones would not have been used for this purpose. As engraved, the tally device celebrates an intelligent insight into the *nature* of the solstice. The fish-spine illustrates the fact that the midwinter position of the sun is the midpoint of two (approximately) symmetrical series of stepped shadows, mirror images of each other. The series of lengthening noon shadows that approach the winter solstice matches (theoretically) the series of shortening noon shadows that leave the winter solstice. The two solstitial shadow series are symmetrical, like the shadow series of the fan-stick device that illustrates the middle position of the noon shadow.

Both diagrams have two special characteristics: symmetry and a critical midpoint. Each draws attention to a series of shadow-lengths which increase or decrease by measured *steps* to a null-point, noon or midwinter, and then decrease or increase back again in the same way. This results in matched pairs of items, graduated scales, incremental steps arranged symmetrically on either side of their midpoints. Although the solstitial midpoint cannot be identified visually, it can be reasonably deduced from the observation that the series on both sides of the midpoint are approximately symmetrical. If the fish-spine is considered to stand upright, the device could illustrate the fact that what is changing is the *elevation* of the sun (at either solstice).

Another way of determining the winter solstice is to watch the progress of the rising sun along the horizon as it swings from side to side of the solstice. This involves the same insight: noting the day when the rising sun appears to stop moving along the horizon toward its southernmost point, and then noting the day when it appears to start moving north again. In a rough way, the solstice is half the total number of the days the sun seems to continue to rise at the same point. Several examples of the fan-stick device and a few of the fish-spine with slant horizontals are found along the solstitial axis of the monument. The solstice, by my interpretation, is the feature that they refer to.

Interestingly, on a densely engraved corbel of the central recess there are two fan-stick devices. The smaller of them is off to one side of the larger, and its axis is rotated a little. The midsummer sun would also have visited the chamber through the uncovered vault, which had an outview that included the summer solstition. If the gnomon-like stone which was originally reported to have been found in the chamber had stood upright in the middle, the rising midwinter sun would have created (serially) a shadow fan on the floor in front of the center recess, while the morning sun of midsummer would have cast a shadow-fan on the floor off to the side of the passage axis.

Classical tradition reports that one of the inventions of the Classical smith Talos was the saw, which he made out of the spine of a fish. Talos was the nephew of Daedalus, the smith who made wings for Icarus to escape from Minos. The saw is a toothed tool for cutting something in two. The name Talos may be related to the word talanton, a scale balance, a device for evening up two quantities. Another Talos, servant of Minos, strode around Minos's island every day giving laws, also a way of evening things up. Minos himself became one of the judges in the afterworld of the Greeks.

Cadmus, the hero and inventor who built the famous walled city of Thebes with its planetary gates, did so with the help of the Spartoi or Sown Men. These fierce lance-bearing warriors sprang up from the ground in which Cadmus sowed the teeth of a dragon he killed, a dragon who guarded a spring with supernatural properties. To avert the wrath of the Sown Men, Cadmus threw *one* stone in the midst of them. The warrior who was hit lanced his neighbor, who lanced his own neighbor, and so on until only five were left: these five helped Cadmus build his city.

The lances borne by the dragon-tooth warriors can stand for the noon shadows around the time of the solstice. The image of the sown lancers is an emblem that has the same model as the fish-spine emblem. We may call it *self-canceling pairs*. It represents the symmetrical shadow-files on each side of the solstice: they cancel each other out except those right around the solstice, which all seem to be the same length and so are "spared." The solstice lies among them. The sun shines into Newgrange not just on the solstice itself, but for a number of days before and after it.

Cadmus was instructed to follow a certain specially-marked cow as she wandered and to build his city on the spot where she lay down. Newgrange was built on the banks of the Boyne - Bo Finda or "White Cow" - and its righthand recess had an outlook on the Milky Way. The citadel of Cadmus's city was called "The Isle of the Blessed."

5. Disk   **Possible Reference:**   **Related Site Features:**

Sun   Openable Roofbox,

Raisable Chamber

Capstone

The long redoubled chevron chains and the "tallies" were unexpected emblems of aspects of their models. In contrast, the disk or dotless circle probably refers forthrightly to the disk of the sun, as people have often assumed. It is not nearly as common at Newgrange as one would expect, from the elaborate provision for witnessing the midwinter sunrise. Claire O'Kelly reports the device (which she tallies together with a boxed or doubled circle) on around 40% of the decorated surfaces at Newgrange, roughly the same as the occurrence of the chevron and triangle/lozenge devices. This is a good deal less frequent than the occurrence of the same devices at the monuments of Dowth (76%) and Knowth (59%). One of the most interesting examples of the disk appears in connection with the so-called "ship marking."

6. "Ship Marking"   **Possible Reference:**   **Related Site Features:**

Solstice Tally plus Ecliptic   Openable Roofbox,

Dip and Solar Disk   Raisable Chamber

Capstone, Center Recess

Orientation

See Plate XII next page

The device that was early dubbed a "ship marking" appears on C4 in the chamber.

This device should probably be classed with the tallies. It looks like a rugged, very bold version of the fish-spine device, with a vertical spine. Most (perhaps all) of the parallel horizontal marks in the ship marking are discontinuous, not continued across the vertical axis. This discontinuity of the marks along the divider is a critical characteristic. The spine itself is not drawn, and from a logical standpoint this is correct: the solstitial dividing line cannot be seen.

The tally marks, if such they are, rise one above another within a little irregular panel, bracketed on the left and right by curved arcs like parentheses. Above the lefthand parenthesis the left margin of the tally marks curves upward in the opposite direction. Bracketing this opposite curve of the tally-marks is a crack on the stone, which on photographs can be seen as a continuation of the engraved parenthesis. Thus there is a continuous line, a triple curve: arcing leftward below, rightward in the middle, and leftward again at the top, repeating the curve made by the tally-marks. If the device was intended as a fish-spine solstitial tally with upright spine, the triple-curved line beside the tally might be interpreted as a visual reference to the double curve of the ecliptic itself, as it descends toward the winter solstice and ascends again on the other side.

Plate XII. "Ship Marking"

Placed just above the "dip" in the middle of the line is a small, clumsily hacked but emphatic disk. The tally-mark is missing to the right of this disk. It seems possible that the disk is intended to represent the sun, the shadow-caster, at the lowest part of its curve. The design would link three devices: the disk of the sun, the triple curve of the ecliptic, and a rather eccentric version of the fish-spine shadow-sequence, all three combined into one bold emblem. The striking, deeply engraved, conspicuously located emblem would refer to midwinter, the sun at the tally-determined bottom of its loop, just the event which the passage and roofbox aperture had been designed to showcase.

The slender stone or gnomon reported to have been found standing in the middle of the chamber would have projected its serial "fan" of shadows on the floor very close to the location of the "ship marking." The device's horizontal tally-marks would have been parallel to the shadows that fanned across the floor.

Now, in music, there is a simple relationship between length and pitch. If you halve the length of a vibrating billet, pipe, or string, you double the frequency of the tone it will produce. This must have been known from time immemorial. Stag's horn whistles or flutes were used even in Paleolithic times, and the Newgrangemen's hunting bows would have taught them the same musical law through the resonance of the plucked bowstrings. The graduated scale of lyre or harp strings or finger-holes in a pipe is a reasonable emblem of the graduated scale of shadows around the solstices. In the instrument you have two matched, related series: length and pitch. Similarly, in the shadow tally you have two matched related series: length and time.

Apollo, who was eventually identified with the deified sun Helios, was famous for both his lyre and his bow. He frequently accompanies the stag-horned Cernunnos on Gallo-Romano steles.

Newgrange was once owned by the Dagda, an old Irish supernatural being who was Good at Everything. One of the things he was good at was playing the harp. He owned a famous one. "That is the harp in which the Dagda had bound the melodies so that they sounded not until with his call he summoned them forth when he said this below:

Come Daurdabla!

Come Coir-cethar-chuir!

Come summer, Come winter!

"Now that harp had two names, Daur-da-bla 'Oak of two greens' [greens here means 'plains'] and Coir-cethar-chuir 'Four-angled music.'"

This tradition links Newgrange with the solstitial observations, through the interpretation of its fan-stick and fish-spine emblems as tallies. The Dagda's harp summons the solstices because their music is based on incremental changes in the length of its strings, which is how the shadow- fan and fish-spine refer to the daily "stepped" change in elevation of the sun from hour to hour and solstice to solstice. The four angles may be a reference either to the four solstitial and equinoctial colures or to the cardinal points.

The hero in an important class of fairy story is often released from the other world when he finds and blows a whistle or pipe. This gives him power over a supernatural being who is a kind of all-purpose artisan or smith often called "Lame and Crooked" or "Lame and One-Eyed." Lame and Crooked is a manifestation of the Weather God, whose musical instrument features blown sound, that is, wind. Classical tradition preserves many stories about the fierce strife between those who preferred the lyre, an emblem of the sun's path along the ecliptic, and those who preferred the flute, an emblem of the wind's song. This strife is based on the rivalry between a god whose personality is based on the sun and its cycle, and a god whose personality is based on the pole and weather phenomena. The conflict is seen in the fatal enmity between Apollo and a hero named Cygnus.

The brightest star of the constellation Cygnus is Deneb. In Newgrange times Deneb was very close to the winter solstition, a herald of midwinter, although far north of the ecliptic. The constellation is located in the Milky Way just below that of Cepheus "Drone," Cassiopeia's husband.

Cygnus is shaped like a cross with its head to the north, and has in fact another name, the Northern Cross. The long stem of the cross is slightly skewed and lies in what is called the Great Rift in our galaxy, a sort of starless island in the Milky Way. The Great Rift continues down to the constellation called Serpens Cauda, the Serpent's Tail. If the constellation is considered to extend down the Rift, Cygnus's outline suggests one of those snake-men we find in myths, which have a human head and arms, but a lower body formed by a long snaky tail. Cernunnos is frequently pictured sitting cross-legged, so that he has only half the stature of a man, and when he holds a snake, the combined emblem equals the half-man-half-snake we might call either "halfman" or "snake-man."

One of the snakemen in Greek tradition was Apollo's son Asclepius, the great physician. Athene gave him two vials of Gorgon's blood: the vial from the left vein killed, but that from the right brought the dead to life. Another famous snakeman was Oedipus, whose father nailed his feet together and mummy-wrapped his lower torso. The old East Indian Naga is a snakeman. Several Egyptian gods, including Osiris and Ptah, have mummy-wrapped torsos. An asp often decorates an Egyptian crown.

Cygnus is now pictured as a swan, with its tail to the north marked by Deneb and its long neck extending southward. But the emblem of the Greek hero called Cygnus was not a swan but either a lion or a snake. His name is probably related to the element "can-," a ringing musical sound, which appears in the Latin cano " I sing." The name of the hero may link him with the emblem of the graduated scale.

Classical writers preserve fragments of tradition about the connection of the swan with music, living for us still in the expression "swan song." Pausanias wrote "The swan is a bird with a reputation for music, because, they say a musician by the name of Swan became king of the Ligyes [from ligyz, "sharp, sweet, piercing, thrilling"] on the other side of the Eridanus beyond Celtic territory, and after his death, by the will of Apollo, he was changed into a bird."

Aelian reported that "the ancients" believed that when the swan had sung its swan song it died, and that it sang because it was cheerful at the approach of death. Socrates said swans rejoiced to go away to the god whose ministers they were. Aelian also described two Hyperborean (that is "far Northern") priests of Apollo named Calais and Zetes, the sons of Boreas "North wind" and Chione "snowy." At the time appointed for their ritual, clouds of swans swooped down from the Rhipaean "windy?" mountains, circled around the temple, and descended into the precinct, "an area of immense size and of surpassing beauty." The swans accompanied the singers and harpers in unison.

Do swans sing? - Swans' customary notes are striking enough. "They fill the air with sounds that range from deep bass notes to shrill tones like those of a clarinet...and utter loud trumpet-like notes...[their] call sounds clear and shrill" (writing of various kinds of swans, De Schauensee in *World Book)*. As for singing, most ornithologists do not believe they sing, and at least one says that anatomically they cannot sing. But in his monograph "The Birds of British Columbia," C. J. Guiguet quotes this account of a "Dr. D. G. Elliot (1898), a reliable observer and celebrated naturalist":

> I had killed many swan and never hear aught from them at any time save the familiar notes that reach the ears of everyone in their vicinity. But once, when shooting in Currituck Sound over water belonging to a club of which I am a member, in company with a friend, Mr. F. W. Leggett, of New York, a number of swan passed over us at a considerable height. We fired at them and one splendid bird was mortally hurt. On receiving his wound the wings became fixed and he commenced at once his song, which was

continued until the water was reached, nearly half a mile away. I am perfectly familiar with every note a swan is accustomed to utter, but never before nor since have I heard any like those sung by this stricken bird. Most plaintive in character and musical in tone, it sounded at times like the soft running of the notes in an octave, and as the sound was borne to us, mellowed by the distance, we stood astonished and could only exclaim, 'We have heard the song of the dying swan.'

The name Orpheus occurs as a title of Cygnus, and also, in connection with the adjacent constellation Lyra, as the name of its player. Other lyre-players linked with Lyra are Apollo, Hermes or Mercury, Amphion, and Arion. The name Hercules has been attached to the old constellation Kneeler abutting Lyra, and he played the lyre himself. Lyra has an old title Testudo, that comes from the shell of the tortoise that forms the body of the lyre. Hercules was cradled in a tortoise shell and the original lyre was made by Hermes from a tortoise shell. Apollo obtained it from Hermes.

The constellation Lyra does not look at all like either a lyre or a tortoise. On the other hand Cygnus is easily seen as two well-matched pairs of triangles – Allen cites The Triangles for the upper pair. They could well have suggested a frame supporting strings of regularly graduated lengths. The name Lyra may have been moved from Cygnus.

Cygnus is not a famous figure in Greek mythology. Most versions of his story are preserved in odd fragments. Yet the Greeks named three great gods as his father: Apollo, Poseidon and Ares; and Heracles needed help from Zeus, Athene and Hephaestus to kill him. It was Apollo who instigated his murder.

Newgrange is called a *cruciform* passage grave, and in fact its outline resembles that of the Christian emblem, the body of Jesus attached to the crucifix, and drooping to the side. The passage and three-lobed chamber may have been to some extent modeled on the outline of the constellation Cygnus as snakeman. This outline in its funeral setting would have been an agent of the afterlife purpose of the monument. Similarly, Moses was supposed to have raised a serpent on a staff to save the Jewish people from death by snakebite, an emblem that John's gospel refers to Christ, raised on the cross as an agent of everlasting life.

FIG. 4. Snake-Wound Pole as Cross

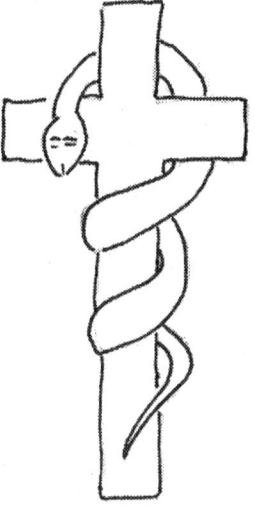

Snake-Wound Cross

Snake-Wound Cross as Tree

The upper drawing is from a rubbing of the baptismal font in Seattle's First Presbyterian Church, and the unambiguous inscription around the device reads "Christus Exaltatus Salvator." The lower drawing is from a photograph of an uninscribed roundel very high in the apse of St. James (Roman) Catholic cathedral in Seattle, above a panel of windows honoring the virtue of compassion.

The dwelling of the Norse underworld goddess Hel was made of snakes' backs, and had a smoke-hole, that is, a skylight, which dripped venom. The interior orthostats of Newgrange have been treated with an all-over picking that looks like scales. The passage itself makes a slight, snaky double curve. Many spirals and winding serpent-like devices appear among the petroglyphs in the interior as well as on the kerbstones around the mound.

CHAPTER VII

AN OUTVIEW FOR THE LEFTHAND RECESS

If the capstone of the monument had been lifted, the left recess, like the center and right recesses, would have had an impressive outview. This was a view of the part of the sky where the circumpolar stars execute their stupendous nocturnal circle.

7. Dot in Circle

Possible Reference:
Celestial Pole and
Circumpolar Path

Related Site Features:
Raisable Chamber
Capstone plus Lefthand
Recess Orientation

The circle with center dot accurately pictures the outline of a star circling the celestial "pole." In Newgrange times there was no conspicuous star that occupied the location of the north celestial pole itself, although it was plain that there was a point center of rotation. The direction of true north was important to both navigators and builders with an interest in astronomy. The circle-enclosed dot is a good emblem for the focus of the firmament's rotation. This idea of a supreme power that inhabited the apex of the north sky tended to take the form of a weather god, master of the lightning and thunder bolt. Stone-age men made fire by rotating a vertical stick or a bow in a socket, perhaps thought of as analogous to the celestial fire that originated in rotation of the sky.

8. Counterclockwise Spiral 	Possible Reference: Direction of Circumpolar Rotation	Related Site Features: Raisable Chamber Capstone plus Lefthand Recess Orientation

When an observer looked upward from the backstone of the lefthand recess through the opened chamber vault, he could not see the polar point itself. What he saw was some circumpolar stars that circled counterclockwise around the vacant north celestial axis of neolithic times. The backstone of the lefthand recess is dominated by three fine large counterclockwise-unwinding spirals of different sizes.

PLATE XIII. Lefthand recess, C3: Counterclockwise spirals

These counterclockwise spirals may reasonably be interpreted as a reference to the circumpolar outview.

A circle with a center dot represents the celestial pole with the circular track of a circumpolar star around it and many such devices occur at Newgrange. Stars go around the pole in circles, not spirals. But a circle can indicate neither the direction of rotation nor cyclic repetition. The choice of the spiral rather than the encircled dot as emblem shows that it was direction, that is, polarity, that was significant for the engraver's purpose. It was this characteristic that he wanted to emphasize.

If it is agreed whether spirals should be read from inside out or from outside in, they can indicate polarity, or direction of rotation. I am assuming that Newgrange spirals read from the inside out, the way a snail shell almost always grows. Quantities of land-snail shells were found at the site. Also, it is easier to draw a spiral from the inside out and probably much easier to engrave it.

The famous three-spiral device in the center recess is a counterclockwise-opening double spiral whose double end splits to enclose a linked, reversing pair of counterclockwise-opening double spirals.

The spiral is a representational device, but it refers to an unexpected aspect of its model, its polarity. This is also true of the fan-stick and fish-spine devices, which refer to unexpected aspects of their models, as the midpoint of two symmetrical, graduated scales of shadow-lengths. The counterclockwise spiral is an emblem of circumpolar rotation. Why was it important to emphasize its polarity?

9. Clockwise Spiral	Possible References:	Related Site Features:
	Circumpolar Rotation Reversed by Reflection as Clockwise. Also, Planetary Movement.	Raisable Chamber Capstone, Recess Orientations, Hollowed Basin Stones, Water in Chamber, Low Righthand Recess Roofstone

Spirals of both polarities are carved at Newgrange. There are about equal numbers of each, but the way they are combined and the way they appear with other devices should always be considered significant.

It is important that examples of *reversing* spirals are very numerous and very well made. On the lefthand orthostat of the left recess there is a fine clockwise spiral. This is a double spiral, one in which the lines are all doubled so that if you follow the spiral from the outside in, it twists back in the middle forming a yang-yin figure, and goes back out in the other direction.

Some spirals reverse by rolling up the free tail of the spiral in the other direction; these might be dubbed reversing or "breathing" spirals. Furthermore, separate spirals of opposite polarity frequently appear in the same panel. At Newgrange *pairs* of spirals are almost invariably clockwise. This could be modeled on the orbits of the sun and moon, a natural pair, disks of the same size, both moving clockwise with respect to the counterclockwise diurnal movement of the stars.

PLATE XIV. Lefthand Recess C2, Clockwise Spiral

If counterclockwise spirals refer to circumpolar rotation, to what do clockwise spirals refer? As noted, they might refer simply to the direction of planetary movement, and in the case of clockwise pairs that might well be the case. But the facilities of the chamber expose another possibility. When a person in the northern hemisphere looks up at the night sky he sees the stars revolving counterclockwise. But if he looks down at their reflection in a film of water or in a mirror he sees them revolving backwards, that is, clockwise. Their polarity is reversed by reflection.

Both water and reflectors were available in the chamber. The flooring stone of the left recess was slightly rimmed and a film of water in it would reflect circumpolar rotation as clockwise. If the now shattered basin in the center recess had had a rim and a film of water, it would also have reflected circumpolar rotation clockwise. So from the back of the lefthand recess and perhaps from the center recess too the stars could be seen either directly, moving counterclockwise, or as reflected, moving clockwise. Both recesses do contain clockwise spirals, a large and well-made multi-coiled doubled spiral in the lefthand recess, a rough, informal spiral of a coil and a half in the center recess.

In contrast, the viewer at the back of the right recess *only* sees reflected stars, because the roofstone had been built so low that he could see them only as reflected from the surface of water that filled the bowl. For him, the stars were seen to circle only clockwise. Like most arrangements at Newgrange these arrangements and the spiral devices that seem to refer to them were probably intentional. If this is true, the righthand recess had an additional power to help the dead on the journey into the afterlife. Beside the reflection of the sky-traversing Milky Way and the chevrons of the nurturing Cassiopeia, there was the fact that from the back of this recess stars could not be seen to revolve counterclockwise at all. The spirals of both polarities carved on the right-recess roofstone were of course all reflected backward in the mirroring basin beneath them.

Time is a problem for the seeker of everlasting life. Even without other interference, age by itself leads to death. Time is measured out by the invincible revolution of the heavens. But reflection reverses the direction of that revolution. And on the plane of reflection itself the celestial clock is stopped. If a packet of human remains was dipped in or sprinkled with the water in the bowl, the remains were signed by an emblem of eternity.

A striking feature of K1 in front of the passage entrance, one which has always occasioned speculation, is the broad groove in the middle. Because the position of the stone as found puts the groove directly in front of the passage entrance it has been supposed that the groove was intended to direct attention to the entrance, and this is probably true. But the groove refers to something else as well. It originates from the pair of clockwise spirals on the right, it separates them from the trio of counterclockwise spirals on the left, and it leads directly into the chamber with its reflecting bowl and slabs.

This corresponds to the contrast in the functions that were suggested for the righthand and lefthand recesses. The lefthand recess had an outview on the majestic time-linked, counterclockwise rotor of celestial rotation. The three counterclockwise spirals on the lefthand side of K1 correspond to the three counterclockwise spirals on the backstone of the lefthand recess. At the very entrance to the interior of the monument, K1 makes a statement about one way in which agencies captured by the monument help defeat death and win an afterlife. It is the lucky, death-defeating clockwise spirals that pour themselves into the groove which points to the passage entrance.

A wide variety of almost universal traditions relates counterclockwise movement, the left side, or left-handedness, to bad luck and general badness. Opie's *Dictionary of Superstitions* lists many of them. Seeing the new moon over the left shoulder (usually) means bad luck. Putting on the left shoe first brings bad luck. Drinks must not be handed around counterclockwise. The bad are placed at God's left hand. The word sinister means on the left. There is a traditional prohibition against going around a church "widdershins" or counterclockwise which was carried over to (or began with) prehistoric sites. A version of this idea appears in a story involving Newgrange: Boann, mother of Angus (who once owned Newgrange), was destroyed because she went around Nechtan's well counterclockwise. On the contrary, clockwise movement, the right side, and right-handedness are generally regarded as lucky and good. The good stand at God's right hand.

The celestial clock which drives time has a permanent contract with death. The chariot of Oedipus's father Laius "Leftward" was driven by Polyphontes "Welcomer of Many," one of many flattering titles which people used to avoid saying Death. Oedipus, the "snake-man," destroyed them both. He did it by entangling Laius's chariot in its own reins.

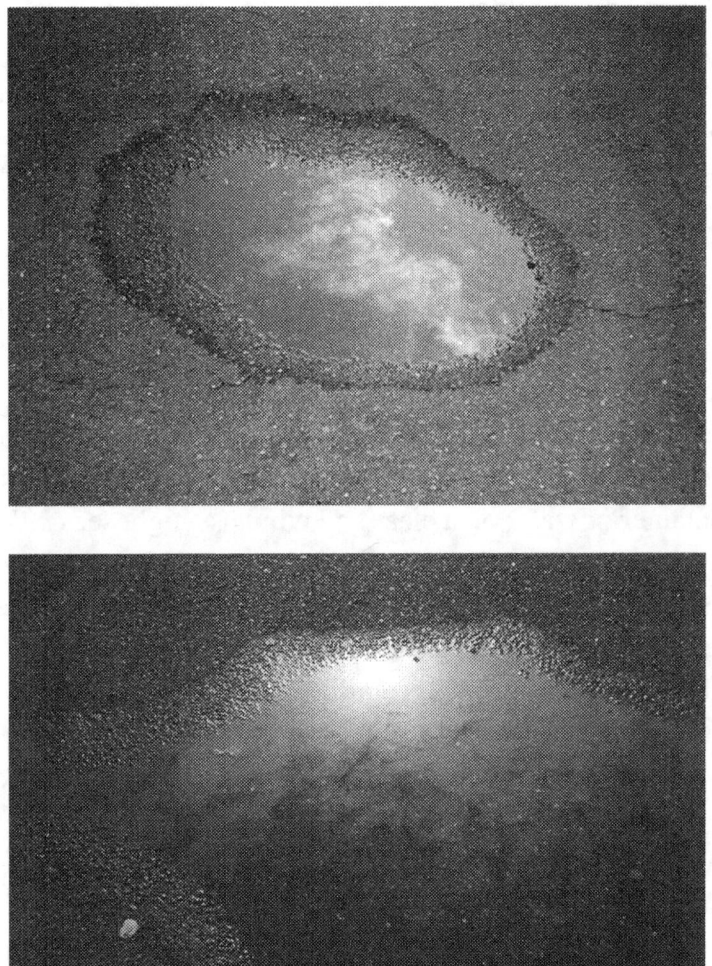

PLATE XV. Views of the Sky in Puddles

The plane of reflection is an intimation that there may be a mysterious water-linked place where time seems to be magically defeated, a vision of eternity. A jeering, comic version of the idea of water tied to the march of time appears in the Greek story of a far Western paradise, described to Midas by the satyr Silenus, a land where the fruit of trees watered from one stream caused a person to grow older and older and die, while fruit watered by the other made him grow younger and younger till he disappeared entirely....

Another fact which would make people associate clockwise rotation with luck is that the sun and other planetary bodies move in the opposite direction from the celestial clock. The users of Newgrange must surely have thought that the sun, which they went to infinite pains to invite into their chamber, was a power that was well disposed toward man, or at least could be persuaded to show good will, probably, as usual, by prayer or gifts. The same may also be true in a different way for the moon, which visited the chamber much oftener, on its monthly circuit of the heavens.

Reflection has one striking and beautiful aspect which would help give the clockwise direction a supernatural advantage. A person looking down into a puddle or container of water on a clear and windless night sees *below* him what seems to be a view through a black hole into a sky shining with stars. Like a space traveler he seems to stand in space. Heaven, an emblem of the afterlife, is almost universally located in the skies above us. The reflector visually lifts us there in a moment of insight. This would be another reason why mirrors and empty pots are found in grave sites: virtual space-travel.

This concept, or experience, of reflection as a supernatural carrier to heaven, or heavenly *steed*, is graphically pictured in the constellation Pegasus which appears just below Cassiopeia, and in fact utilizes one or two stars of the standing figure. As almost always shown, this famous supernatural horse is rising half out of the water, that is, its body is cut by a plane of reflection. The name Pegasus comes from a word for spring water. The water-horse is usually shown with wings, which shows that it carries its rider to the sky.

The idea of the half horse, incomplete, cut in two, "not all there," gives rise to the familiar emblem of the "Sorry Nag" which figures so often as the hero's steed in fairy stories. The hero must choose the shaggy colt, or the worst horse in the king's stable. Sometimes the hero's horse is cut in two by a closing gate. The ass in myth and Bible story, seen as not a real horse because it is in a way genetically incomplete, is another version of the half horse. The ass is the traditional mount of the judge, a decider or divider.

A remnant of the importance of the horse emblem persists in the custom of putting a horseshoe over the door for "luck." A confused relic of the water source that was involved in the original emblem remains in the argument over whether the shoe should be open-side-up to prevent the luck from running out.

A dramatized emblem of clockwise and counterclockwise rotation still lives: dancing around a maypole while holding colored ribbons, weaving and reweaving them clockwise and counterclockwise around the pole. The modern date for the celebration is May first, about fifty days before the summer solstice. In Newgrange times this would have seen the sun just entering the zodiacal constellation of the Crab. It would have been visible from the chamber through the opened vault.

One peculiar and important spiral form which with one or two doubtful exceptions does not appear among Newgrange petroglyphs is the "heart." The classical heart-shape is created by juxtaposing the inmost half-coils of two spirals of opposite polarity. The outline is relevant because the ground plan of the mound has the outline of a very plump heart. The passage enters the mound at the indent of this heart on the southeast side of the monument. On the other side of the mound, almost but not quite opposite the indent, there is a slight, original, somewhat crooked "point." The emphatic "point" of the human heart is also skewed slightly to the left.

Many emblems important in other traditional contexts have cardial outlines. Among them is the matched pair of valves of the cockle shell, an emblem of Aphrodite, and of the Christian pilgrim. The Christian baptismal font is sometimes shaped like a cockle shell.

The face-plate of the barn owl, an emblem of Athene, is heart-shaped. The hazelnut, important in the tradition about the source of the Boyne, is shaped very much like a heart, and is of a ruddy color. The ram is an important emblem in a number of religions, including Egyptian, Jewish, and Christian. Its horns are juxtaposed spiral-beginnings, the lefthand horn spiraling counterclockwise from the skull, the righthand, clockwise.

The Newgrange mound could only be considered ovoid because the entrance stone lies across the indent, and in fact the point opposite the indent, which is original, shows that the outline was not conceived as ovoid. As the passage was provided with a stone door to control access it is plain that the builders intended both to provide entrance and to be able to prevent entrance into the passage by means of the door. In order to retain K1 in front of the entrance as it was found, wooden stairs had to be installed around and over the kerb. K1 was not needed to deter entry, and it might be questioned whether this was its original position.

The groove which points to the passage as the stone now stands pointed into the mound wherever it stood, and this is also true for the groove on K52.

PLATE XVI. Old Baptismal Font, St. Giles Edinburgh

It has been suggested that many Neolithic enclosures could have been constructed with ropes, stake lines and scribing methods, and that ovals often originated as heart-shapes, filled in by a third pivot.

"Since the top arc smoothes over the indentation in the cardioid, one might guess that the builders dismissed this shape because it served as merely an auxiliary figure. There is evidence from other megalithic structures, however, that this was not the case, and indeed the cardioid may have been regarded as quite exceptional. The structures in which cardioid shapes seem to be important are the numerous passage tombs found throughout Britain and Ireland. Examples include the chambered tombs of the Severn Cotswold culture. One of these, the tomb at Parc le Breos Cwn at Glamorgan, is obviously cardioidal, albeit misshapen." ("Megalithic Rings: Their Design and Construction": Cowan, *Science,* 168: 321-325 1970).

The first phase of site K on the Newgrange ridge was unequivocally cardioid. It was reported that "One very weathered fragment of cockle shell was found with the cremated bone deposit at the outermost end of the passage extension" in the second phase of site K. Cockle-shell fragments were also found in the chamber of L. One reason for discussing the cardial shape as an emblem is that the cockle shell was used early and often to decorate funeral vessels. Cardial ware was being used at least a millennium before Newgrange was built. The shell was pressed into the clay to make the design. Sometimes the whole valve was imprinted on the clay, sometimes just the zigzag edge.

This is not a feature of the ceramic associated with the class of monument to which Newgrange belongs. The ceramic associated with this class is Carrowkeel ware, extremely rough-looking pottery decorated by stabbing the clay with some pointed object. Bird bone has been suggested. The stab marks often form patterns, and one common pattern is the zigzag or chevron chain also found at Newgrange. It should be noted that clay of this ware is often gritted with a substantial amount of ground seashell. (However most of the pottery found in association with the satellites - there was none inside Newgrange itself – was gritted with stone, not shell.)

The cockle is an edible marine bivalve, common on the Atlantic coast. The shell is ivory to reddish in colour. It consists of two matched valves joined by a hinge. Just ahead of the hinge are the raised umbos, the bosses or "beaks" of the valves. Looked at endwise, they are two elegant little mirror-image spiral-beginnings. As they are the oldest part of the shell, the umbos are finer in texture and ribbing, and may be a little deeper in colour. From the umbos, the ridges of the valves fan out to the edges of the shell where they form zigzags that interlock to close it. The shell displays three outlines found among Newgrange devices: (1) paired clockwise and counterclockwise spirals, (the valves) (2) "fan-sticks", (the ridges) and (3) zigzags (the locking edges of the valves).

The Cardium Aculeatum is about two and a half inches across and has a long, reddish foot. The Cardium Rusticum has a pale- red body, and a bright red foot about four inches long. The cockle contracts its foot and then suddenly expands it to execute a startling leap of several inches. Leaps of as much as a yard have been claimed. The animal is supposed to have been collected for purple or crimson dye, though the dog whelk (a spiral form) seems to have been the preferred source in the British Isles.

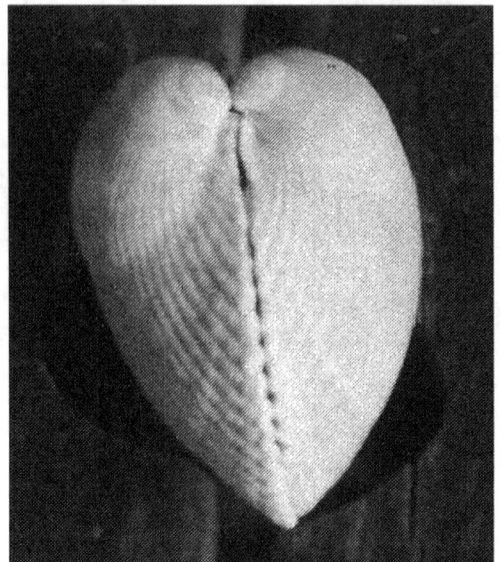

PLATE XVII. Cockleshell

The cockle did not look like a romantic valentine to classical eyes. It had a firm association with Venus, explained, rather late, as occurring because this animal *"toto corpore simul aperto in coitu misceatur."* The wildly energetic red foot, sticking out of the fleshy pink mass within the shell, contracting and extending as it propels the animal in convulsive spasms through the water, suggests coitus in no uncertain terms. The whole animal imitates a detached, uncannily vigorous male member. The two stories of Aphrodite's birth, from the cockle and from the severed genital of Uranus, are frank doublets.

Another tradition makes the conch, here the bivalve, sacred to the Cnidian Aphrodite, because it delayed a ship which was transporting boys to Periandros for castration. The foot extended between the two sharp-edged valves is a hint at castration. Aphrodite was married to Hephaestus, the smith. There was some monument in the neighborhood of Newgrange that was called the Cave of the Smith's Wife.

The cockle is also related to Aphrodite through the emblem of the dove. The "kissing" beaks formed by the valves of the shell are short and stubby like those of the dove, and the finely ridged umbos resemble the colored gorget around the dove's neck. Most doves have red feet, like the cockle. Doves are supposed to be amorous, and the behavior of the cockle has been described above.

A heart-shape is created when the inmost coil of a spiral is cut by a reflective surface. The opposed or "married" spirals arrest each other. This is what happens when the revolving sky is mirrored. Uranus is castrated, "Time" stops.

10. "Fern Frond"	**Possible Reference:**	**Related Site Features:**
	Circumpolar Rotation as Spiral	Lefthand Recess Orientation plus Raisable Chamber Capstone

The so-called fern-frond on the side of C4 looks like a naturalistic depiction, very unusual for Newgrange. The frond lacks the central spine, but otherwise it is almost exactly like the "palm branch" usually depicted in the hand of the classical figure of Cassiopeia, whose reflection was visible from the opposite recess. A credible starry branch may be outlined either by the curved row σ,ρ,τ AR beside β Cassiopeiae or by one of several distinct arcs of small stars above α.

The device has been placed right above the righthand end of a horizontal row of chevrons that runs back into the picked area on the chamber face of C4. This row suggests that the engraver intended the device to be associated with the constellation. We have no idea what figure the builders saw in Cassiopeia. The double chevron is however a recognizable imitation of the asterism's outline, and the coincidence that Cassiopeia's traditional palm-branch is found facing the recess that gave a view of her is intriguing. Someone has suggested that the nearby "ship marking" may be a later addition, and the same could be argued for the fern frond. As palm frond, it suggests a Classical reference. Roman coins were found at the site, and the (unverified) report of coins in the chamber itself might mean that some tourist familiar with the Classical depiction of Cassiopeia actually entered the chamber. As noted on page 18, the chamber could probably always have been accessed from above.

The classical palm-branch was traditionally associated with victory or triumph. As a matter of fact, the constellation was rising out of the chamber so that every generation the chevron pair was a little higher. Eventually, the W was free of the recess, finally escaping triumphantly from the chamber, a possible model for the "fern frond's" ascending series of chevrons, placed just above the chevron row.

There are other possibilities. The date palm is a tree with a tall straight trunk bearing enormous clusters of succulent dates. The tree might have been developed into an emblem of the celestial pole with clusters of stars around it, astral clusters under whose aegis dew formed. In this case the association with Cassiopeia would show that the figure of the queen went back to the concept of the swarm: stars as celestial bees, or little winged beings associated with the afterlife, like those shown fluttering around cinerary urns under the protection of the spirit-guide Hermes. Cassiopeia's husband is Cepheus "Drone."

But the palm did not grow in Ireland, and at Newgrange the most probable interpretation of the device is that it is really a fern frond. This would associate the device with the spiral that dominates the lefthand recess rather than with the chevrons that dominate the right. All ferns unroll in spirals. Thus the fern frond in proximity to the W would express the same idea as the snake in the hand of the antlered Cernunnos on the Gundestrup Cauldron, where Cernunnos, the persona developed on the model of the celestial double chevron, was master of the agency of the spiral. The little Mycenaean goddesses or votaries holding snakes show a similar relationship. At Newgrange the righthand recess, focused on the chevron, is more elaborate and numinous than the lefthand recess, focused on the spiral.

CHAPTER VIII

FINDING NORTH

Locating true north was important to the Newgrangmen, who were probably navigators as well as builders. The noon shadow, a factor in determining the solstice, was the one that fell due north. But these people had no pole star. The star nearest to their celestial pole was located under the Dragon's tail, but was of only the 5th or 6th magnitude, close enough to the border of visibility to require very good viewing conditions. Nor was this little star located in any easily recognizable asterism. But there are three different asterisms that would have been useful for locating the pole. I will call these asterisms "Thumb," "Drinking Vessel," and "Noose." Three peculiar categories of outlines, resembling each of these three objects, appear several times among Newgrange engravings, and faint traces of all three images may be discernible in later traditions.

Figure 5 shows circumpolar stars which may have served as polar locators in Newgrange times, for the location of the celestial pole of the epoch.

Thuban passed closest to the celestial pole about 2796 BC. Thuban is lettered α Draconis, magnitude 3.7 but perhaps is now dimmer than when the letter was assigned. Iota Draconis, Al Dih or Edasich, west of it in the tail, is magnitude 3.3. The name Edasich means Male Hyaena (Allen says that the designation Hyaena also appears for Thuban, for ζ, and for η). The Newgrange polar point was about a third of the distance from α to ι and about that same distance below a line connecting them, as indicated in the drawing. Examples of the three devices which may have served as polar locators are drawn near the star groups they refer to on the star drawing, oriented to correspond to the positions of the asterisms as they appear there. One should bear in mind that relationships are better shown on a celestial globe than on the flat projection of the map.

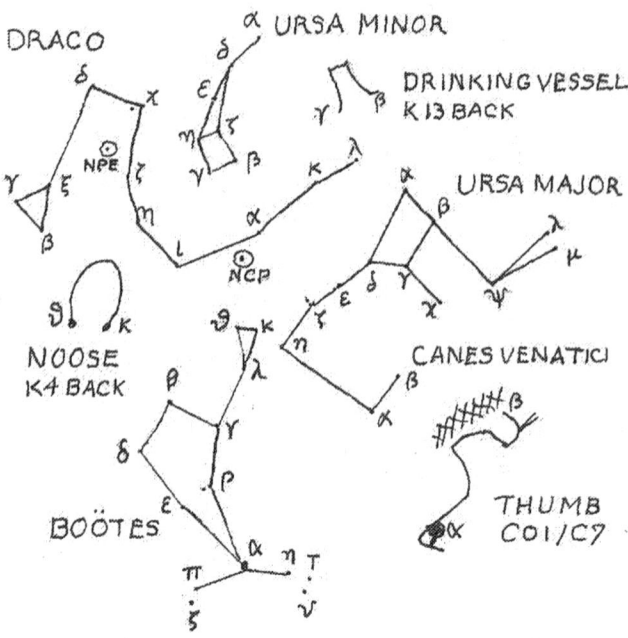

FIG. 5. North Celestial Pole of Newgrange Times, Circumpolar Constellations, and Three Comparable Devices

11. "Thumb" | **Possible Reference:** | **Related Site Features:**
Celestial Pole Locator | Raisable Chamber Capstone plus Lefthand Recess Orientation

An odd device which appears several times at Newgrange is a vertical line from whose top a 90° arc extends clockwise, to the right and down as far as the bottom of the vertical. The figure could be seen as the end of a toe or thumb in profile, the vertical representing the straight nail and the arc representing the rounded pad. More or less similar outlines can be seen on K67 (scratched faintly), K3, K6, K9 (possible), K13, K54, K88 (possible), K95, L13, and Co1/C7. As in the case of the solstice-determining diagram, the shape would not be intended to be exactly accurate; it would simply be intended to be recognized as the emblem of the special pole-finding asterism.

There is a very conspicuous, absolutely unmistakable (though not too evenly curved) arc in the sky around the celestial pole. It forms the long handle of the

Big Dipper. Let us assume that this bright circumpolar arc would be the most natural place to start in identifying the thumb-shaped device. The arc of the Dipper handle, continued down to χ Ursa Majoris magnitude 4, would be the rounded pad of the Thumb. A vertical line drawn from η at the outer end of the Dipper handle down to α in Canes Venatici "The Hunting Dogs" (mag 2.9), would be the straight nail of the Thumb. If the base of the nail is connected by a line to the base of the pad, that line and the nail would make an angle of roughly 90°. The stone age pole was halfway between the top of the thumbnail, η Ursae Majoris mag 1.9, and Ferkab in the Little Dipper mag 3.1.

The thumb device on K13 Back suggests another way to locate the pole. This device has a circle in the middle of the Thumb, from whose center a vertical line goes up through the arc or "pad" to a dot. A vertical line drawn from the *middle* of the Thumb asterism through ζ Ursae Majoris, pointed fairly accurately to the pole. Zeta Ursae Majoris is unmistakable because of its small "rider" Alcor. The remarkable deep-red variable called La Superba in the middle of the Thumb is also unmistakable: its magnitudes and period are variously given, but may be about 4.8 to 6.3 over a 160 day period. This star has unusual physical characteristics which may suggest that it was more conspicuous five thousand years ago. Thumb devices on K6 and K88 also suggest, by small vertical lines, a pointer through the position occupied by ζ in the arc of the thumb-pad.

The example of the Thumb device shown on the star map in Fig. 5 is that seen on Co1/C7. This is the most detailed of the engraved Thumb devices I have mentioned. I have chosen it because in addition to the Thumb itself, this device includes three features that may indicate special interest in the blazing red-orange star Arcturus in Bootes, which at magnitude −0.04 is the fourth brightest star in the heavens. The device consists of a thumb-like outline that bulges out on the left of the long base-line that runs from front to back of the corbel, although it is not quite straight. The base-line outlines the thumb-like shape without cutting across the base of it, and in fact only three of the ten examples which I have proposed have a line across the base; two of these three emphasize the right angle at the base of the thumbnail. Toward the front of the recess, the base-line bends right at an acute angle within which is a large picked circle.The bent angle is joined to the circle by a little stub. The thumb-pad slopes out and back toward the base-line, which it meets at an angle of about 115°. Behind this junction a perpendicular to the base-line runs up into an area hidden by Corbel 2. The position of the corbel is indicated on the map by a hatched area. The base line ends beyond the perpendicular in a small, very marked split. Four features of this device seem relevant to its relationship to the position of the stone-age celestial pole and its nearby stars.

(1) Arcturus has a very large proper motion in the direction of Spica: 2.29 seconds of arc a year, so that for the Newgrangemen the star appeared approximately 3° north of its position on our map, which is about equal to the distance between ζ and η in the Little Dipper. A straight line from χ Ursae Majoris, near the end of the thumb's pad, to the stone-age position of Arcturus, would have run right through α and β Canum Venaticorum. Thus the large picked circle crowded against the right side of the long base line of the Col/C7 device is positioned about right for Arcturus in relation to the Thumb device.

(2) A little below Arcturus in the sky, arranged quite symmetrically on either side, are two matching vertical pairs of fourth-magnitude stars: π and ζ Bootis on the left and τ and υ on the right. A line drawn through the top of each pair makes an acute angle with the base line through ψ Urs Maj, located just beyond the end of the thumb-pad below χ, and Arcturus. As we saw, the long "base line" on the corbel device bends back and right below the pecked circle at an acute angle, and a small stub from the bent segment is attached to the circle.

(3) Near the end of the long base line, closest to the back of the recess, we noted that there is a line that extends left at a right angle from the base line of the thumb-pad. Psi Ursai Majoris marks an outward-slanting extension of the thumb-pad, below the line that connects χ Urs Maj, α and β of Canes Venatici, and Arcturus. In the sky, a line extending up from ψ Urs Maj through α and β Urs Maj, the pouring edge of the Dipper is nearly parallel to a line from χ Urs Maj to γ in the bottom of the Dipper. It is possible that the perpendicular line that disappears below the upper corbel referred to this relationship; the location occupied by α Urs Maj (mag 1.8) would be hidden under the upper corbel.

(4) We noted the small split with which the long base line ends, beyond the perpendicular. It is in the right position to refer to λ and μ Urs Maj, a striking pair of stars called the "Second Spring of the Gazelle" which lie on the line between Arcturus and ψ Urs Maj. However, since that line is not quite the same as the line between Arcturus and χ it is possible that this is not the right reference.

The importance of the interest in Arcturus and the Dipper lip is that both furnished *conspicuous* clues to the location of the elusive stone-age pole. A line drawn between α Urs Maj and ι Draconis crossed a line between Arcturus and β Ursae Minoris very close to the pole.

On K67, L13, and K95 there is a small open square in the vicinity of, or attached to, the righthand side of the Thumb. The square occupies very roughly the position of the Dipper Bowl, the quadrilateral formed by δ and γ in the pad of the Thumb with α and β outside the pad; the pad would be extended below the quadrilateral to χ and perhaps on to ψ Ursae Majoris. Five thousand years ago the quadrilateral was very slightly, probably just perceptibly, more square that we see it, because of the large proper motion of some Dipper stars in the direction of the end of the handle.

Absolute accuracy is not a must for average needs; our pole pointers currently point to a spot one degree (or two lunar diameters) from the celestial pole and our Polaris is now about the same distance away from the celestial pole, but both serve popular needs.

The recognition of a circumpolar toe- or thumb-like outline may be the basis of a peculiar scrap of Norse tradition. Orion was was supposed to have been known to Norse sky-watchers as Orwandil, and Alcor at the top of the arch of the Dipper-handle was supposed to be his toe. In the Old Icelandic collection called the *Elder Edda*, Groa was Orwandil's wife. Thor told her "that he had waded from the north over Icy Stream and had borne [Orwandil] in a basket on his back from the north out of Jotunheim...that one of [Orwandil's] toes had stuck out of the basket, and became frozen." Thor broke it off and threw it up into the heavens, making a star called Aurvandill's Toe. The big toe has about the same profile as the thumb. This odd story locates a starry "toe" in the northern sky, close to the thumb- or toe-shaped asterism I have described, perhaps relating the asterism to the striking little star Alcor in its curved pad.

12. "Drinking Vessel"	Possible Reference:	Related Site Features:
	Celestial Pole Locator	Raisable Chamber
		Capstone plus Lefthand
		Recess Orientation

Another distinctive device which occurs several times in the Newgrange repertory is an outline that suggests a small beaker or tumbler. The sides of the figure begin to rise almost straight, but gradually flare outward a little. Considered as a beaker, a consistent feature is the narrow, flat bottom, which is usually about one-third the length of the left side. Outlines of this kind appear on K52, K93, K95(top), L13 (twice), L15, and L20.

I suggest that these devices may refer to the four stars in the bowl of the Little Dipper. I have noted above one way in which the Little Dipper may have been involved in locating the neolithic pole. The polar point lay about half way between η Ursae Majoris and γ Ursae Minoris.

Although other star references are possible I have picked the four Little Dipper stars as the probable model for the "Drinking Vessel" because the asterism has a beaker-like outline, and part of it is known to have been called the "Horn," a name Dante knew for the whole constellation. Considered as a drinking horn, the drinking vessel asterism would be extended past η and ζ in a curve whose tip is marked by our Polaris. It is very graphic. In centuries succeeding Newgrange times the location of the celestial pole moved in an arc past Thuban (polar around 2800 BC) toward Cynosura "Tail of the Dog," our Polaris.

Ursa Minor as a horn recalls the many representations on Norse funerary steles of a horn of this shape offered as a stirrup cup by a woman to a man on horseback. This drinking horn, a real horn or based on this shape, is slightly spiral-formed. As filled with liquid it is also a reflector, tying in with the interest in the polarity of the circumpolar whorl and its reversal by reflection and also with the reflection emblem Sorry Nag that may be the model of the rider's mount. The stirrup cup would have been a supernatural safeguard for the rider on his journey into the afterlife. The Christian custom of receiving the eucharistic chalice at the last rites has a similar affect.

The name and shape "horn" might have referred to a wind instrument as well as a drinking horn. Allen cites a Spanish name Bocina, a bugle. The watchmen of the Norse gods, Heimdall, had a horn called the Gjallarhorn "Shrieking Horn." He guarded the god-built bridge called Bifrost. Bifrost is commonly identified with the rainbow, although some of the stories attached to it seem to fit the Milky Way as well or better. Heimdall was to blow the horn to summon the gods to the last battle. Until that time, the horn was hidden under the root of the cosmic ash-tree Yggdrasil.The ash was associated with bees because they love the honey-dew which forms part of its tradition. This horn is also associated with water: the dwarf Mimir, who took Odin's eye in exchange for supernatural knowledge, continually pours from the Gjallarhorn a mighty stream of water over the tree. The cosmic tree itself may be a pole emblem.

13. "Noose"

Possible Reference:
Celestial Pole Locator

Related Site Features:
Raisable Chamber
Capstone plus Lefthand
Recess Orientation

A third peculiar device which occurs three times among the petroglyphs looks like a very small, compact open loop, or noose, whose free ends are emphasized by dots. It appears on the back of K4, the back of K13, and K54.

There is a group of three or four small stars that may be the model for this little device. In traditional pictures of the constellation Bootes, this compact little group marks the arbitrarily high-stretched hand that is holding the leash of the "Hunting Dogs," Canes Venatici. The stars are θ and κ Bootis, with ι just a little below them and λ below this. The group is a couple of degrees across, two-thirds the length of Orion's Belt. Lambda is a fourth magnitude star and the other three are under the fourth magnitude; ι is a triple star, a visual double. This group of stars was recognized as an independent asterism in some systems; Allen cites Aselli, the Little Asses. The ass, we remember, is a Sorry Nag emblem.

Although it is small and dim, the trio θ, κ and ι is easy to find, because the group forms a right isosceles triangle with η (Alkaid) and ζ (Mizar), the two last stars of the Dipper Handle. There is also a small straight line of three evenly-spaced fifth magnitude stars extending out from Mizar and pointing directly at Bootes's hand. As noted above, Mizar is impossible to mistake because of its little rider Alcor.

The trio in Bootes had an interesting relationship to the stone-age celestial pole. A nearly straight line can be drawn from Arcturus through λ and right between θ and κ; through the stone-age celestial pole; continuing on past that pole through 5 Ursae Minoris in the flared lip of the "Drinking Vessel" as far as α Ursae Minoris, our Polaris. The old celestial pole was located on this line at a point about as far above θ and κ as the distance between Alkaid and Mizar.

The constellation Canes Venatici, the Hunting Dogs, is a modern constellation. The astronomer Hevelius placed this image here. But hunting dogs are seekers and pointers. Stone Age people needed pointers in the long centuries between pole stars. There is some evidence that the two Dippers themselves were once seen as dogs. Allen writes: "...at one time on the Nile the Wain [or Dipper] stars seem to have been the Dog of Set or of Typhon. This may have given rise to the title Canis Venatica that La Lande cited, if this be not more correctly considered as the classic Kallisto's hound [Kallisto "most beautiful" was a title of the Great Bear]; and the same idea appears in the Catuli, Lap-dogs, and Canes Laconicae, the Spartan Dogs, that Caesius cited for both of the Wains."

The Arabs gave several stars in Draco hyaena titles, including α, η, ζ, and ι. According to Allen, β Bootis formed with γ, δ, and μ a trapezoid figure called the Female Wolves or Hyaenas, and of particular interest in connection with the Noose figure is his statement that θ,χ, and λ, formed an Arabic asterism called The Whelps of the Hyaenas. Thus we have an example of one culture which grouped together in a significant way stars of both the Noose and the Dragon, which seems also to be a possibility for the Newgrange culture.

In nature, the four types of hyaena form a family of their own. In the very early stone age at least, the hyaena's range included Europe. The animal looks rather dog-like although it is supposed to be more closely related to the cat. It is rather tawny, marked with spots or stripes, has a mane, and like the cat vocalizes in a terrifying manner. The hyaena is a good hunter, but it is also a carrion eater. The Arabs have identified these hunters with an appetite for carrion with stars once useful for locating the north celestial pole. At Newgrange, dead bodies and an interest in locating the polar point are found together.

We are fortunate in having a good bright pole star, the second-magnitude Cynosura "Dog's Tail." The name Dog's Tail fits only if the curve of the Big Dipper handle is taken as forming the fore-quarter and throat of the dog. This fore-quarter completes itself as an enormous, very graphic dog, of which β and γ form the short hindquarter (the hyaena is also distinguished by the fact that its front legs are much longer than its back legs). Zeus was supposed to have had a golden mastiff made to guard him by the divine smith Hephaestus.

The noose outline, like the chevron chain, has an Egyptian parallel. The sign for "hobble" is very similar to the Noose, the only difference being that the sides of the Egyptian loop are straight and parallel to each other.

In her *Sacred Signs*, Wilson says that "The Egyptian word for their pictorial writing was 'medu netjer,' which means 'words of god,' and it seems that this was recognized as the primary function of the hieroglyphic script, to communicate between Egyptians and their gods." This may perhaps have been the function of the Newgrange text.

Several circumpolar constellations have shapes that may have suggested names they bear or may once have born. The bear, the dog, wolf, fox, or hyaena, the plough, and the cart or chariot are among them. These constellations were circumpolar for people of Newgrange as they are for us, although they were differently placed in relation to the celestial pole. Not a single one of these can be recognized in the petroglyphs: the engravers avoided animal outlines as scrupulously as the Muslims. It is possible that the outlines I have dubbed Toe, Horn and Noose were named differently or even not named at all by people who used the outlines as polar locators.

CHAPTER IX

MOVING UPWARD

14. Rungs with	**Possible Reference:**	**Related Site Features:**
Triangle Sets	Earth/Sky Ladder	Carved Rungs Beneath
		Overhead Stair, Ascending
		Passage, Fused Swastikas
		as Rotors of Opposite
		Polarity

See Plate XVIII and Fig. 6.

Inside the gently ascending passage, underneath the monumental flight of stone steps created by the tops of the ascending roofslabs, there are two passage orthostats which have great horizontal grooves carved across their faces. These grooves might be thought of as the rungs of a massive stone ladder. The first section of the ladder appears on R12, and contains three rungs. The second section appears on R 21 and has six rungs. The rungs are not identical in size in either set. Because the passage rises as it approaches the chamber, the lowest rung of the set on R 21 would be just above the highest rung of the set on R 12. The two sets are similar in style and scale, and together make up two parts of the same feature. R 12 is located under the midpoint of the flight of stone steps above it, and R 21 is located beside the chamber entrance.

PLATE XVIII. R21, Rungs and Triangles

For the very complicated device on the side of R12 I have relied upon Claire O'Kelly's drawing in *Newgrange*. The device is constructed of twelve or thirteen picked triangles which can be read as either two meshed swastika-forms of opposite polarity or as six locked saltires. I will describe the "swastikas" first.

Most of the surface of R 12, like much of the rest of the interior, has been subjected to an all-over scaly-looking "pick-dressing." This consists of thousands and thousands of little chipped pockmarks laboriously hacked out with a flint point. The rungs on R12 and R21 have all been subjected to this pick dressing.

The righthand side of this orthostat, facing toward the entrance, is not picked. There is a nearly vertical crack or groove, presumably natural, near the middle of this surface, and attached to this crack, almost on a level with the groove above the highest of the three rungs, is the device which I am going to explain here. I consider this inconspicuously located device one of the most important in the site.

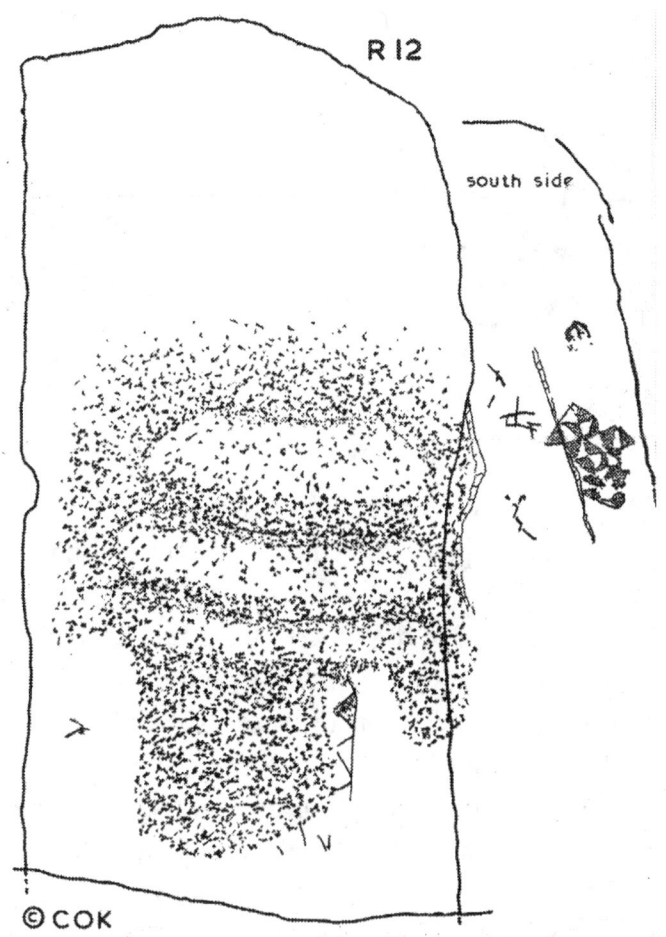

FIG. 6. Claire O'Kelly's Drawing of Devices on R12 Face and Side

Mrs. O'Kelly's permission to use her drawing of the device on R12, and also her drawings of R12 Face, K4, and the righthand recess roofstone, reproduced in Figures 13, 14, and 16, does not in any way imply that she agrees with my interpretations of her drawings of these devices.

15. Swastikas   **Possible Reference:**   **Related Site Features:**
Time-Linked Lifters   Rungs, Solstitial Orientation

See Fig. 7a

I have drawn a version of what I believe may be the import or intent of this very small, very dense device by straightening out the lines in the original.

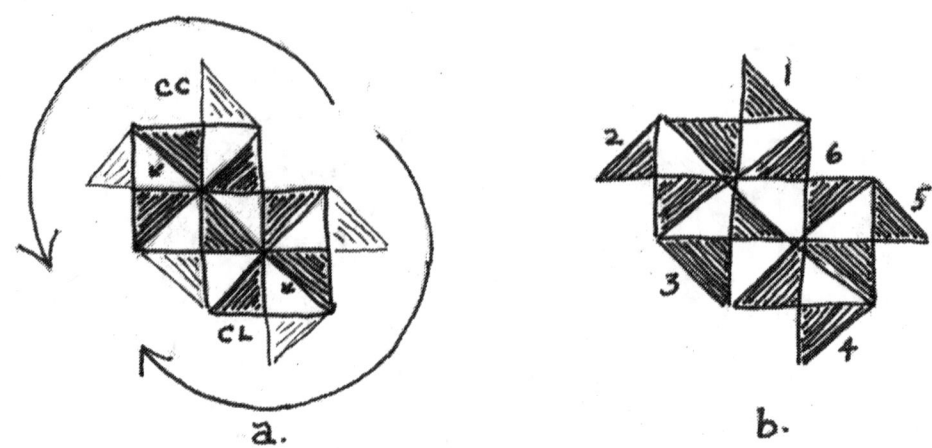

FIG. 7. Formalized Version of R12 Side:
a. Emphasizing Bipolar Swastikas. b. Emphasizing Saltires

Some of the triangles I have drawn are shaped more like crescents in Mrs. O'Kelly's drawing. My discussion is based upon the formalized version of the device, which the reader needs to compare carefully with Mrs. O'Kelly's drawing.

The upper half of this device is a three-inch square, which I am going to name Square I. Square I is divided into four equal squares, and divided again from corner to corner, so that the four small squares are all divided diagonally, producing eight isosceles triangles. Every other triangle is picked, so that picked and unpicked triangles alternate around Square I. The outer points of all of the picked triangles point counterclockwise. Although there is a diagonal line drawn from the end of each arm back through the center of the device the result can be seen to be a form of counterclockwise swastika. It rotates in the direction of the circumpolar stars.

A second swastika, constructed in the same way, of alternate picked and unpicked triangles, can be made out, with some effort, in the very much less regular triangles of Square II.

Square II overlaps Square I. It uses the lower righthand quarter of Square I as its own upper lefthand quarter. Thus the centers of these swastikas are located on opposite ends of the same diagonal line. But picked and unpicked triangles in this device must alternate. The picked triangles of Square I lie on the clockwise sides of its diagonals but the picked triangles of Square II lie on the counterclockwise sides of its diagonals. The outside points of the picked diagonals of Square I point counterclockwise: those of Square II point clockwise. While Square I is effectively a counterclockwise swastika or rotor, with the polarity of the circumpolar stars, Square II is effectively a clockwise swastika or rotor, with the polarity of the *reflected* circumpolar stars (or alternatively of the paths of the planetary bodies). As a reflection, Square II is properly connected with Square I, and properly placed below it. Square II is dependent upon Square I as the reflection upon its object.

The one diagonal which the two squares share has the same effect as the plane of reflection. It reverses the polarity of the linked lower swastika. It does so because when an observer traces first the direction Square I is moving and then the direction Square II is moving, his position, or point of reference, has moved from one end of the diagonal to the other. Just so, the reflective plane seems to move the observer from one position to another, so that instead of seeing a starry vault overhead he sees a starry abyss underfoot. The idea of ascent expressed in the rungs has been translated into an emblem of rotation by the bipolar swastikas.

To this pair of meshed bipolar swastikas there has been added another important feature. This is a set of vanes that has been attached to each swastika. Each *vertical* divider of each swastika is extended on past the side of its square, as far again as its distance from the center. The end of that extension is connected by a diagonal line back to meet the pointing-corner behind it. This makes a picked vane that sticks out from each edge of each swastika. The straight edges of the all of the vanes face in the same direction as the points of the all of the picked triangles.

16. Saltires	**Possible Reference:**	**Related Site Features:**
	Couplings, Generation, Reversal	Solstitial Reversal, Fused OpposedSwastikas, Reflective Surface as Generator

See Fig. 7b

The device on the side of R12 may be interpreted as meshed swastikas, "rotors" of opposite polarity. But there are indications that the engraver was conscious as he worked that he was also producing a nest of saltires. The vanes were superfluous to the swastikas but they are essential elements of the saltires.

Because each of the four picked vanes in Square I lies against an unpicked triangle of its swastika, it is therefore point to point with the nearest picked triangle. Each pair of picked triangles, lying point to point, forms a picked saltire.

The four saltires that belong to Square I meet point to point in the middle of it, with the base of each saltire spanning one open side of its neighbor. As before, the same arrangement can be made out, with difficulty, in Square II. (The position of the bottom vane of Square II is occupied by an almost indecipherable blot, and beneath the design described above, an extra triangle and another device which I cannot identify touch the vertical line on the stone.)

Since their bases lie on the diagonals of their squares, all of the saltires are rotated 45° from the verticals and horizontals of their Squares.

The total number of saltires in the design on R12 side is six. The reason there are not eight saltires is that Square I and Square II share one quarter. Half of Square I's righthand saltire is formed by one of Square II's shaded triangles; half of Square II's lefthand saltire is formed by one of Square I's shaded triangles. Those two middle saltires lock the design together, transforming it from the dynamic of the two rotor-like swastikas to the stasis of the blocked saltires.

The famous design on the roofbox lintel is composed of a series of eight framed X's. If the resulting triangles were picked alternately, there would be a row of eight saltires, the axes rotating alternately, vertical and horizontal. If you imagine the whole design on R12 rotated 45° from the vertical, the saltires would be arranged in two rows, one above the other, all their axes alternating between vertical and horizontal.

The importance of the saltire outline is made clear by the two large picked saltires which occupy the extreme upper right corner of C8, the backstone of the center recess. This device is discussed below as the fourth of the shorthand versions.

The design on R12 is very small, and the shading has been done by picking with a flint point. It must have been very hard to engrave and very hard to copy. The device, which as I understand it has a great deal of intrinsic fascination, cannot originally have been worked out in stone. It must have had a long history on other surfaces, such as skin, bark, sand or clay before it was painstakingly chiseled into the very inconspicuous, comparatively inaccessible surface of R12. The device on R12 is a key to several others that are located in much more conspicuous positions, like the saltires on C8, and the fact that it is placed as it is is intriguing and probably significant.

17. Reduction I: R12 Front <u>**Possible Reference:**</u> <u>**Related Site Features:**</u>
                              Lifter   Rungs, Dependence on
                                                       R12 Side Device.

See Fig. 6

In the light of what can be learned from the complex device on the side of R12, we shall see that the small device attached to the lowest rung on the face of this stone is an abbreviation, a reduction or shorthand version of the device on the side. But the position of this reduction explains the significance of both the complete device on the side of the stone and the set of carved rungs themselves.

On the surface of R12 that faces the passage there is a small, straight-sided area which has been spared the general picking. This unpicked area is located just below and to the right of the lowest of the three massive stone "rungs" that extend over most of the face of R12. Inside the smooth area is a seven-and-a-half-inch vertical line, with a vertical zigzag attached to the left-hand side of it. The projecting right angles of the two zigzags form two touching right triangles; the upper triangle is picked, the lower triangle unpicked. Below the lower triangle, is a slanted line, parallel with and the same length as the upper sides of the two triangles, and that line extends leftward to the picked area. The whole device runs up against the lowest of the three ridges or "rungs" of the ascending set on this orthostat, and it is unmistakably attached to the lowest rung by another short slanted line attached to the top of the vertical. In short, the triangles are intended to refer to the rungs.

The triangles plus the extra slanted line coming off the bottom of the vertical form three slanted steps, their tops parallel like those of a tipped stair. They would refer to the three sculptured ridges or rungs which mount the vertical rock-face above the device. The meaning of the little device is explained by the design on the right side of this orthostat, of which it is an abbreviation or shorthand version.

In the small device, two right-angled triangles are attached to the left side of a vertical line. The upper triangle is picked. Referring to the device on the side, we can identify the two right-angled triangles as a shorthand reference to Square II. The triangles belong to a swastika standing on its corner, that is on one of its diagonals. Although nothing is left of it but the diagonal and the triangles on one side, the polarity is identified by the fact that the upper, *picked* triangle is on the *counterclockwise* side of the diagonal. Its acute angle points clockwise. Thus, this is a shorthand version of a clockwise rotor like the lower rotor on the side of the stone. It has the polarity of the *reflected* circumpolar stars or of planetary movement.

This clockwise "reflecting" rotor is attached to, as if supporting, the lowest of the ascending series of rungs. In short, the device refers to the rungs as a lifting agent, a stone escalator. The device is a written text explaining what the sculptural rungs do.

The rungs are a dramatic model of ascension. But those swastikas on the side of R12, rotating in opposite directions, explain what the real agent of ascent is: in the last analysis what powers the escalator is the reflecting water surface. It is the water reflection which is the lifting engine, the self-moving stair that gives a taste of the experience of being moved from a place under the stars to a place among them, the experience that stops time and escapes death.

Both the stone rungs and the engraved texts illustrate the important fact that the men and women of Newgrange shared the almost universal concept of the sky as the realm of the afterlife. The Milky Way has commonly and very naturally been pictured as the path of departed spirits. Its southern extremities touched the earth, turn by turn, as they swept across the horizon on the other side of the Boyne, and at night they could be seen through the passage as they passed. But the summit of the galaxy, ornamented by the bright chevrons of Cassiopeia, was the visual focus of the righthand recess. The recess was provided with a water source and a massive container suitable as a reflector, and the whole arrangement was carefully contrived to make sure that from the backstone the stars could be seen *only* as reflected. I would submit that human remains were brought into the chamber because within this dark tomb there was a spectacular moving picture, as well as a stone model, of conquering time and being borne up to heaven.

The double swastika design on the side of R12 is a complete expression of an idea that appears in shorthand versions not only on the face of R12 but also on several other stones. The design on R12 is small and inconspicuous, deeply shadowed and almost hidden by R11, and it could be argued that the owners of Newgrange did not want to call attention to it simply because it is a working key that unlocks devices on more public stones.

18. Reduction II: R21 **Possible Reference:** **Related Site Features:**
Reflector as Lifter Rungs, Dependence on
R12 Side, Clockwise
Swastika Quarters Set as
Stair, Adjacent Bowl and
Water

See Plate XVIII

One of the most striking of the shorthand references to, or reductions of, the text on R12 is the design on R21. (Plate XVIII) This design is bold and large; it is placed on the facing surface of the orthostat that stands just before the entrance into the chamber; and it is just adjacent to the numinous righthand recess that housed the water-holding, star-reflecting slab and bowl. Like the surface of R12, the surface of R21 is almost entirely picked over. Into it there has been carved a set of six rungs, also picked, which with the three on R12 completes a set of nine.

Set into the all-over picking of R21 is a bold design of six squarish lozenges, located just above the topmost rung. This device is a little over a foot high altogether, and in contrast to the very small design on the side of R12 it is most certainly intended to be seen. The sixth or top rung has been extended just far enough to the right to define an unpicked corner into which the design fits.

The three smallest squares or lozenges are set in a vertical row at the left side of the device. They are point-down, are divided horizontally, and are not connected with each other. Their bottom halves are picked.

Below this row is a pair of larger horizontally-divided lozenges, side by side, touching each other point to point. The upper half of the right-hand lozenge is picked, and the lower half of the left-hand lozenge is picked. That is, this pair may be interpreted in accordance with what we have seen in Square II on R12. The picked triangle lies on the counterclockwise side of the diagonal so that its acute corner points clockwise, exactly like the reduction on the face of R12. It is part of a clockwise swastika. It refers to the reflection of the sky, and in fact there is a reflector adjacent to it, the container of water in the recess just behind it. The lozenge on the left of the line is balanced on the topmost rung of the carved set that extends rightward below it, making it clear that like the abbreviation on R12 this abbreviation too refers to a climb upward.

The lowest of the three small divided lozenges on the left touches the lefthand lozenge of the larger bottom pair. This lefthand lozenge is picked on the bottom, as are all the ascending row of three, so we can logically infer that we are to consider them together. On the bottom of the design is the polarity-determining linked pair, with a definite indication that the pair and the three ascending lozenges above the pair are intended to be read as a group. The horizontal pair determines the polarity, and the lefthand lozenge is also intended to be read as the fourth member of the vertical group of three above it, as it is attached to the lowest of the three.

The shorthand reduction of the clockwise swastika design on the face of R12 was made to touch the bottom of the three-rung series. The shorthand reduction of a clockwise swastika that is implied by the group of divided lozenges on R21 is made to touch the top of the six-rung series. The design on R21 has introduced a graphic addition to the pictured concept. That is, the set of four clockwise-determined lozenges is a version of the four divided lozenges of Square II, the clockwise rotor, but to emphasize the point, which is ascension, the four picked planes of the lozenges have been turned so as to rise vertically, as four ascending steps. There is a different, sketchy version of this in the reduction on the face of R12, the three parallel slanted "steps" that ascend to the bottom rung.

Now, above the *right*-hand lozenge of the polarity-determining pair at the bottom of the device on R21 is the sixth and largest lozenge of the panel, and this one is different. It is much larger than the three "ascending" lozenges on the left of it, does not share a diagonal with them, and is not attached either to them or to the clockwise-rotating lozenge beneath. The lozenge is divided horizontally, and the top half is picked. Attached to its unpicked bottom half, on the left, is a picked vane. What is the meaning of this vaned lozenge, which has been inserted boldly but with obvious awkwardness into the spaces between the other four lozenges?

An answer is suggested, as before, by the design on R12. All of the vanes on R12 are picked. The picked vanes attached to each square are attached to the unpicked triangles of the square. Their edges always face in the same direction as the points of the picked triangles. The direction of the vane depends on the polarity of the swastika. Therefore it can always indicate the polarity of the swastika by itself.

I will accept the convention I adopted for the meshed swastikas on R 12 as definitive for the large lozenge on R21. The vane will be considered to be attached to the outside of a lozenge which would be one quarter of a four-lozenge square. The swastika to which this lozenge must belong is standing on its corner, as in the shorthand reduction on the face of R12. The flat side of the vane on this lozenge is nearly in line with the edge of the unpicked side of the lozenge. (The reason it is not in line is that there is not enough space between it and the picked triangle of the lower pair.) This means that the center of the implied swastika has to be on the right. The vane faces counterclockwise and the position of the vane shows that the large lozenge in the middle of the device on R21 belongs to a *counterclockwise* rotor.

Interpreted in this way, R21 includes the defining elements of the complete design on R12, arranged differently, but not unrecognizably.

The fused clockwise and counterclockwise swastikas on R12 have been taken apart on R21. The four quarters of the clockwise rotor, each quarter rotated to put its picked half on the bottom, have been stacked into a flight of four steps. We have already seen this interest in taking the original fused pair apart expressed in the two little bisected lozenges on the front of R12. The interest in reducing an emblem to its lowest common denominator is a very important characteristic of the engraved devices at Newgrange. On R21, the great time-measuring, unlucky, counterclockwise rotor of the circumpolar sky is expressed by a bold, single compact vaned lozenge. The whole device is "supported" by the top rung of the complete set of nine as the reduction on R12 supports the bottom rung of the complete set.

It is intriguing that the nine rungs are divided into a set of three and a set of six, while the divided lozenges occur in two sets of four, overlapping in one quarter, on the side of R12. Each swastika has three unshared lozenges. There are only seven independent divided lozenges in the complete device, although each swastika must possess four. There is some sort of wizardry about the shared square, which in theory must be moving simultaneously in opposite directions. There is something of seven, something of eight, and perhaps some supernatural aspect of nine about it.

As noted above, the reversing diagonal within the shared square performs the same function as the reflective plane. It reveals the relationship between the rungs and the reversal of reflection shown in the swastika device. The ascent to heaven was related to reflection. As it was the direction of circumpolar rotation that was reversed, the ascent was related to time. The fact that the devices are built entirely of triangles would suggest that the moon was the timekeeper for the ascent. The triangle, and the nine rungs divided into a set of three and a set of two threes, both suggest that the ascent was related to the number nine itself as a power of three.

We have deduced from the device on R12 that the picked vanes are a determinative element by themselves. They are also important because of how they combine with the interior picked triangles of the swastikas into picked saltires. Both spirals and swastikas refer to circumpolar rotation and its reflection. Saltires add an additional element to the concept.

This element is stability. Within each swastika, the four saltires are locked together in a rigid frame. The addition of the saltire-building vanes to the swastikas keeps them from rotating.

The builders were much interested in the difference between counterclockwise or time-linked rotation and clockwise rotation, as modeled by reflection. They took advantage of the power of reflection to cancel out time. But they would not have wanted there to be any doubt about the end result. They would not want the process of turning back time to end in the comic debacle which Silenus described derisively as a feature of the far Western paradise, where time was reversed and the subjects of the process got younger and younger and finally disappeared altogether. The best result would be to live for ever, young but not too young. This would mean that the crux of the transformation was the actual plane of reflection, the infinitely thin layer of water where the magical transformation took place. One possible interpretation of the saltire is that it was meant to refer to the plane of transformation as a null-point of time, a concept of eternity.

The symmetry of the saltire suggests a double reference, combining two prime agencies that promoted an afterlife: the cyclic regeneration of life that is suggested by the two solstices as "null-points" on the sun's path, and the path upward that is powered by the null-point of the reflective plane.

19. Reduction III: K4	**Possible Reference:**	**Related Site Features:**
	Milky Way, Midwinter,	Galactic and Solstitial
	Rotor as Lifter,	Orientations, Rungs,
	Sun/Rain Phenomena	Water Drip in Chamber,
	Reflection Phenomena	Potential Reflectors,
		Reference to R12 Side

See Fig 8

The devices on R21 and the front of R12 can be seen as shorthand versions of the device on the side of R12. This development provides an insight into an unexpected aspect of the intellectual style of the people of Newgrange. Experimenting with reduction or abbreviation of an emblem tends toward the development of writing. A panel on Kerbstone 4 shows still another arrangement of the elements which we recognized on R12 and R21, exhibiting another striking example of reduction.

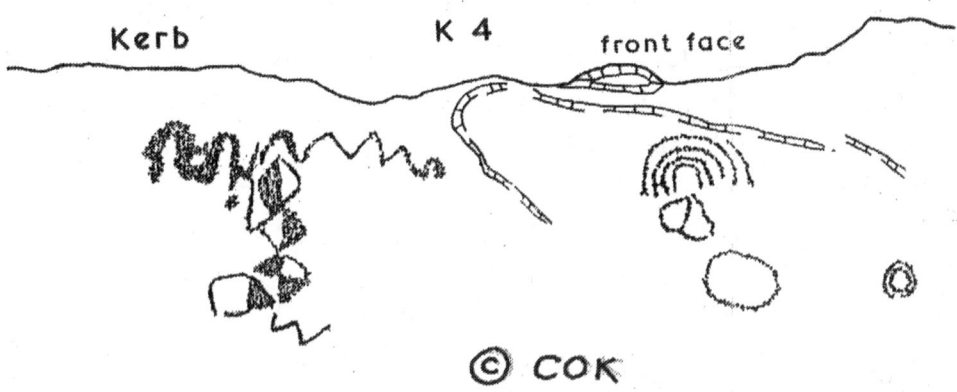

FIG. 8. Claire O'Kelly's Drawing of Devices on Kerbstone 4

Kerbstone 4 is located about twenty-eight feet west of the passage entrance. Near the top of the stone, there is a deeply picked wavy line which forms two steep arches with rather straight legs. In the low bight or loop of the line between the arches is what looks like a small picked disk. Except that these arches are very steep and the line is horizontal rather than vertical this arrangement recalls the disk in the shallow dip of the double-curved line at the left of the "ship marking" in the chamber.

Near the foot of the righthand arch, a horizontal line extends to the right and splits. Its short branch ascends vertically, not quite touching a longer, fainter, snaky, horizontal line. Its long branch descends vertically, passing a joined pair of lozenges balanced on their points. The vertical line attaches itself, by means of a purposeful little stub, to the left angle of the lower lozenge. The upper lozenge is fitted into the hollow space formed above by the first arch of the wavy line. That arch is a little more deeply engraved than the rest of the line.

The two lozenges are divided vertically. The counterclockwise half of each lozenge is picked, so that in compliance with the convention established in the discussion of R12, the outer points of the picked triangles point clockwise. These two lozenges are, then, one half of a clockwise swastika.

Below this swastika-half, and clearly attached to its vertical axis, is a saltire. Just as in the case of the saltires on R12, its axis is rotated 45° from the vertical. A small slightly arced line joins the right-hand points of the saltire.

A little to the left of the saltire is an undivided lozenge to which a picked vane is attached on the side adjacent to the saltire. Now within a divided lozenge, like the ones on R12 side, the axis of a saltire composed of a picked vane and the picked triangle it is touching is always parallel to a diagonal through the swastika to which it belongs. So the position of the vane shows not only the polarity but the orientation of its swastika.

In the case of the undivided lozenge on K4, the lower side of the vane must be attached to a horizontal side of a swastika, so that the center of its swastika must be at lower left of the lozenge. This swastika, like the half-swastika that is balanced on its diagonal, rotates clockwise. The saltire of which the isolated vane would be one half must be rotated 45° from the base of its lozenge. Thus it will have exactly the orientation of the bottom locking saltire on R12 side. The complete saltire attached to the half-swastika that is balanced on its diagonal does not belong to that swastika, because the axes of the saltires that would belong to that would lie horizontal and vertical. The complete saltire on the other hand is rotated 45° from the vertical, and so it is oriented in conformance with the isolated undivided lozenge to its left. Thus that complete saltire has exactly the orientation of the upper locking saltire on R12 side. The two saltires on K4, complete and incomplete, are placed adjacent to each other there in exactly the same relative positions as the locking saltires on R12 side.

The half-swastika on K4, half of a clockwise swastika, is balanced on its point like the half-swastika on the front of R12, where its upper planes create a sort of stair. There, the relationship to the climbing rungs is made plain by the lines that connect the device to the rungs. A stair-like series has also been created on R21 in the same way, by deconstructing the lozenges of the clockwise rotor or swastika and arranging them in an ascending series.

On K4, the isolated undivided lozenge below is also part of a clockwise swastika. The vane itself shows that. But this swastika must be lying on its base like the swastikas on the side of R12. The upper half-swastika is an emblem of ascent. But the complete saltire must be read together with the half-saltire attached to the ghost-swastika below. These two saltires, whose swastikas have been purposefully omitted on K4 are reduced to emblems of two critical occult midpoints which the site suggests were involved in attaining life beyond death: the transformational plane of reflection and the transformational instant of the winter solstice. In this respect they are similar, although not identical, to, the pair of saltires on C 8, adjacent to what may have been an access to a possible sunset passage. The C8 pair have for some reason been permitted to rotate 45° according to their polarities.

The whole device has some characteristics that may suggest that some far-sighted engraver saw that the intention of this minimalist device needed to be made more explicit, so that perhaps he altered or glossed it a little. The isolated lozenge to which the picked vane is attached seems, comparatively, rather informally engraved. The little slightly-curved line that spans the righthand points of the saltire also seems comparatively sketchy. And placed just to the right of the vaned lozenge on K4 and nearly touching its point is another outline of importance at Newgrange, the "W," which, like the undivided lozenge and line across the saltire, seems less carefully or at least more informally drawn.

The W is the starry emblem that marks the top of the galactic path. This was the astral emblem which the builders had provided with a reflector. Like the rungs, the point-balanced half-swastika produced two steps of an upward path. The saltire's model was stopped time, an element of everlasting life. But the Milky Way, whose source was engraved with a double chevron of stars, has been seen as a path up to or through the sky, or as a heavenly river, or as the milk of Hera, foster-mother of the hero Heracles. All three were emblems of a supernatural life above and beyond this world.

We noted that above the two lozenges on K4 is a serpentiform with a disk in the bight. This serpentiform is of the variety in which the curves seem to be confined within imaginary parallel lines. The model for this device might be the ecliptic. The placement of a circle in the bight may be comparable to the circle that appears in the bight of the very shallow curve left of the so called ship marking on C4. Both disks are placed in the bottom of the "ecliptic" curve, if that is what it represents, and this might be the element of the K4 device that refers to the important role of the midwinter solstice in the afterlife thought and practice of the Newgrangemen.

At the top right of the device on K4 there is a rather deeply cut arch over the vertical lozenge-row, but the arching line continues to the right as a much less deeply-cut row of three irregular chevrons opening downwards, and finishing with a more deeply cut miniature arch. This prolongation of the serpentine line does not give the impression of having defined limits for its maximum and minimum heights. It is a cross between a serpentiform and a chevron row and may have been meant to represent the Milky Way. The chevrons are in much the same style and of much the same size as the W beside the vaned lozenge. This feature, as well as the undivided lozenge and arc over the saltire, might permit one to conjecture that the design as it stands may be the work of two people with slightly different emphases and styles.

20. Reduction IV: C8 Possible Reference: Related Site Features:

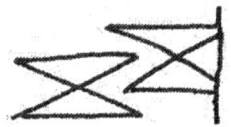

Possible Reference: Twin Rotors, Solstice Based Regeneration

Related Site Features: Reference to R12 Side, Rungs, Placement by Possible Second Passage

C8 displays the most radical of the reductive versions of the device on the side of R12. The device consists of two bold saltires with vertical axes. These saltires are pulled out a little horizontally, so that unlike those in the device on R12 their central angles are not right angles. The upper triangle of the lefthand saltire is fitted into the angle between the touching triangles of the righthand saltire.

The device on the side of R12 is locked in place by the two saltires they share, a result of their sharing one quarter. If however you imagine that the two interlocked swastikas are pulled apart so that they are separated vertically in space as the object and its reflection are separated in nature, each will have its proper four quarters, and each will be free to rotate as in nature. When both swastikas are rotated 45° according to their opposite polarities, the upper or circumpolar swastika rotating counterclockwise and the lower or reflected swastika rotating clockwise, the two saltires in the middle of the design will approximate the position occupied by the two saltires on C8.

If this was the intention of the engraver, one of C8's saltires belongs to the astral swastika, the other to the reflected swastika.

This device is superbly executed and dramatically emphasized by its central location. It seems significant that these saltires are deliberately crowded as far as possible against the righthand surface of C8, very near the area where Captain Keogh said in 1893 that he could see into another passage behind C10, opening a possibility that I will discuss later.

All of the devices I have discussed in this section except the one on K4 have been placed on the solstitial axis of the monument. So is possible, if not probable, that they were intended to refer in some way to the solstice. One saltire belonged to the clockwise rotor, and this is the direction followed by the sun. If it is true that the tallies express an interest in the two solstices as the midpoints of symmetrical series, the saltires might refer to the symmetry of the shadow series on each side of both solstices. It is noteworthy that the saltires on C8 are pulled out along their *horizontal* axes. In addition, the reflection across the vertical axis suggests reflection by a water surface. Both reflective planes suggest generation, a critical agency in a post-mortem setting.

The remarkable reduction seen on C8 presupposes a familiarity with the swastika as an independent rotor. There is an Irish precedent for such an object. The St. Bridgid's cross is an emblem woven of straw which has clockwise or counterclockwise polarity depending on which side you are looking at.

Fig. 9. St Brigid's cross

The cross does not have a stem. The vanes are the projecting arms of the cross, each of which is flush with one side of the woven "swastika." The same idea is translated into stone on some old interlaced crosses. These applications of the device suggest that they had an ancient pedigree as emblems of supernatural power in another religious system also featuring escape from death.

Swastikas of both polarities, along with saltires, horses, fish, and both chequey and lozengey nets, are all staples of Greek Geometric art, beginning around 900 BC. Pieces of swastikas such as detached arms are often seen, another manifestation of the interest in reduction I have remarked at Newgrange. What is significant is that on countless ceramics so many of these devices appear together in the same panel. They appear as a set, and they are elements of the same set of concepts I have identified at Newgrange. The model for the little emblem-set horse- plus- fish is the same as that for the winged half-horse Pegasus and the Sorry Nag: the reflective surface: water as transport to the skies. The linked swastikas and the water-cut half-horse are references to two ways in which a reflector suggests the possibility of attaining an afterlife in the heavens: stopping time and inversion.

CHAPTER X

WATERDROPS

O n the right of the complex of devices on K4 described above is an excellent boxed arc or set of concentric arcs. An obvious natural model for a set of concentric arcs is the rainbow. (Mayer advances the view (Roscher *Lexicon* "Iris" 320, line 30) that it is the fact that the bands in the rainbow are *concentric*, not their colors, which has inspired Homer to compare one detail on Agamemnon's armor with a dragon.)

21. Concentric Arcs	**Possible Reference:**	**Related Site Features:**
	Rainbow, Sun/Rain as Producer of Water- Bridge and Dewdrop Spectrum	Boulder Cap, Water Drip in Chamber, Views of Midwinter and Midsummer Sun Through Openable Apertures

Good sets of concentric arcs also occur on RS7 and and K52. There are three sets on the right of the groove on K1; one against the lower edge of the stone and two which are upside down against the upper margin.

There is a possible example on the right side of the righthand recess roofstone, which because of its position would be of great importance if one could be sure of it. Toward the chamber edge of the roofstone there is a set of four concentric lines that run back under supporting orthostats. The whole right side of a large counterclockwise spiral has been made to stop short in order to spare the outer line of this partially-obscured device. One argument in favor of identifying that device as a set of arcs is that there were already both an excellent clockwise and an excellent counterclockwise spiral on the roofstone.

A rainbow is created by a marriage of sun and rain. At Newgrange, features and engraved devices reveal roles for both sun and precipitated water in the funeral practice, so the rainbow that combines them might well have had special significance. There was a rainbow cult on the Greek island of Delos, and it has been observed that the Delians probably sacrificed not to the rainbow itself but to the power of the formidable goddess who concealed herself in the bow. This bow would have been a mysterious and magical manifestation of the benevolent and nurturing sun, who blessed the earth with comfort and plenty.

It has been said that the bow in the sky did not give the Greeks the impression of the heavens smiling through tears after a storm, nor a covenant between god and man. To them the rainbow was a kind of monstrosity arousing anxiety, a *teras*, defined as "sign, wonder, marvel, portent...an omen: a monster, strange creature." Although most rainbows are ethereal, there are rare, blazing rainbows which fully merit the Greek designation. The colors burn like a neon sign, and the rainbow may overarch the sky for a long time, like a solid, brilliantly enameled bridge. Such rainbows have a solemn, eerie effect.

Boyer in his *The Rainbow: from Myth to Mathematics* has collected a large number of folk beliefs and traditions about the rainbow. There is a common belief that to point at the bow risks being struck by lightning, or losing the finger, or that passing under one causes a change of sex. The rainbow is frequently linked in some way to death or the danger of it. The rainbow may be thought of as the bridge to the otherworld like the Milky Way. Lithuanian children "stamp" at a rainbow.

To the Jews the rainbow was an emblem of god's oath: Jehovah swore to Noah by the rainbow never again to wipe out mankind by a flood. However, Boyer cites a Jewish tradition that depicts the rainbow as an object of worship: "Following the example of Ezekiel before the throne, certain of the Hebrews believed that one should prostrate himself before the rainbow; but others enjoined the custom as savoring of heathenism, and approved instead the repetition of a benediction: Praised be the Lord our God, the King of the Universe, who remembereth the covenant and is faithful in His covenant, and maintaineth His word." (*op. cit* p. 26)

The rainbow was also involved in the oath-keeping of Greek gods. The rainbow goddess Iris traveled on this bridge to fetch from Hades the water of Styx, so holy that if a god broke an oath sworn by this water he lost all his power for a time. Iris carried the caduceus or herald's wand which was also borne by the spirit-guide Hermes. The emblem of the winged rainbow goddess with caduceus has the same significance as the swarm of small winged female figures shown hovering over cinerary urns in the company of the caduceus-bearer Hermes. The afterlife aspect is of course of interest here. Iris has been pictured with a child in her arms, which would mean that she had the function of nurturing young children, a function that was characteristic of the figure of the supernatural mother who protected the new regenerated life. Styx was an Oceanid; all Oceanids had the title "Nurturer of Children." At Newgrange some similar aspect of the sun may have been one motive for the solstitial observance.

The Finnish scholar M. Kuusi collected nearly three thousand of the expressions that people use when the sun shines during a shower. He gathered examples from a great many places, as far apart as Finland and Japan, Turkey and Ireland. The expressions people use for a simultaneous occurrence of sun and rain are very striking. Many of Kuusi's sun-rain expressions refer to events or celebrations in the afterworld. The devil, a witch, or a troll is marrying, baking, churning, bathing, or bleaching; the people in Hell are celebrating a "church festival"; or those who have drowned are drying their clothing, or the dead are celebrating a wedding, or the old maids are being buried, and so on. (My mother said "The devil is beating his wife.")

In general the expressions that refer to the weddings of animals, quite often of different species, are the most numerous and the most widely spread. Sun and rain together suggest a marriage of unlike partners. Beliefs that involve the actions of animals are the commonest in Asia, Africa, around the Mediterranean and northwest of the Baltic.

Sayings about the marriage of fox and vixen, and to various activities of the dead seem to belong among the oldest. Kuusi believed that the very oldest of these expressions, from which most of the others may have developed, was the fox wedding. In his opinion the forms of the thousands of expressions and the great distances over which they are spread must have been the result of a thousand-year, perhaps a several-thousand-year process of development and dispersion. This would mean that the fox-wedding expressions, and probably also the wedding-of-the-dead expressions, might go as far back as the Stone Age. Kuusi's opinion cannot be the only explanation of the wealth of fascinating material he collected, but it is worth considering. If it is true that the concentric arcs at Newgrange are rainbow emblems, patterns of belief revealed by Kuusi's study might contribute some insight into the afterlife concept here.

Both of the Dippers can be seen as short-legged, long-tailed animal forms. The fox is a short-legged animal whose magnificent tail is as long as its body. The sun-rain expressions would involve the fox because of the location of these conspicuous forms so close to the celestial pole. Fox would be a possible emblem of the weather god. Its ruddy color would associate it with fire, already a feature of the weather-god because of the relationship with the celestial fire-stick or bow drill and lightning. The dog emblem associated with the circumpolar stars would be later, for the emblem indicates an interest in tracking, a feature of the interest in locating the polar point, not in the location of the weather-power.

Opie's *Superstitions* cites a charm used to dismiss the rainbow which is almost identical to the common charm for dismissing a ladybird: "Rainbow, rainbow, haud away hame, A' your bairns are dead but ane, And it lies sick at yon grey stane, And will be dead ere ye win hame: Gang owre the Drumaw and yont the lea, And down by the side o' yonder sea, Your bairn lies greetin' like to die, And the big tear-drop is in his ee."

What do the ladybird and the rainbow have in common? Both have a link with the sun.

The solar power that produces the glory of the rainbow produces a far more unsettling manifestation, also characterized by a unique display of color: the apparition of the solar eclipse. The ladybird has a round body like the solar disk, but more significantly it shares the color fieldmark of the solar eclipse: the red of the chromosphere, the white of the coronal rays and the ebony of the eclipsing lunar disk. The fox, who figures so prominently in Kuusi's study of sun-rain phenomena, and may have been a totemistic emblem of the weather-god, also has this black-white-red fieldmark of celestial fire.

One example of a sun "goddess" whose description reveals a clear relationship to eclipse phenomena appears in the traits and titles of the great Egyptian goddess Hathor. Hathor is a radiant being of light, many of whose titles reflect the beneficence and beauty of the sun, such as The Golden One, The One Who Shines Like Gold in the Sanctuary of the Golden One, The Female Solar Disk Equal to the Aten. But at the behest of the sun-god Ra, who wished to destroy a disobedient human race, she took the form of a lion and like the sphinx she devoured her victims.

The lion emblem is attached to Hathor because of the (male) lion's distinctive mane. The model for the mane is the halo of golden filaments and tuft of polar bristles surrounding the disk of the eclipsed sun. This is the feature that suggests Hathor's titles "The One Who Creates the Rays of the Sun" and "Lady of the Tresses."

As solar disk, Hathor has titles that can be recognized in the fundamental concept behind the figure of the Greek Kore "Maiden." Two of the definitions of the word Kore are "a puppet, doll, Latin pupa," and "the pupil of the eye, from the small images seen in it." One reasonable model for Kore, and for Hathor is the eclipsed solar disk: "The One of the Beautiful Face Who Penetrates the Orb of the Sun in the Sky, The One Whose Images are Hidden and Whose Manifestation Is Sacred, Mistress of Transformation in Front of the One Who Created Her, and The Female Soul With Two Faces." These titles expose the idea of a hidden "maiden" or miniature image of a supernatural solar being, who is imagined to be contained in the inky pupil of the solar "eye" as it appears when the radiant sun is blacked out by the lunar disk.

Some titles of Hathor have as model the fiery red chromosphere seen around the black disk in a solar eclipse: "Great Flame, Mistress of the Sanctuary of the Flame, The One Whose Fire Is Great, The Uraeus on the Brow of Atum, The Uraeus on the Head of the Master of the Universe, The Uraeus of Ra in Dendera, The One Who Inspires Great Fear." Some of the larger bursts of flame around the disk have a snaky appearance, and the thin solar crescents at the beginning and end of totality often seem to waver. The Uraeus was a fire-spitting cobra with extended hood.

Hathor's titles "Lady of the Red Headband" and "Mistress of the Fillet" suggest features in descriptions of two supernatural beings who loved the old Irish hero Cuchulainn. One of these beings was Fand "Tear," the beautiful daughter of Aed Abra, a name which was said to mean "fire of the eye's fringe, the pupil of the eye." "Tear" is a waterdrop. The other was the smith's daughter, the gruesome Dornolla "Big Fist." an infatuated admirer who had a "Face like a bowl of jet... Hair very wild, very red, below the headband around her head."

"The One Who Takes Wing as the Female Falcon" and "The Divine Female Falcon" suggest the coronal wings, or perhaps the tenuous extended wings of the zodiacal light that can sometimes be seen shortly after sunset. In the old Irish story called the "First Wooing of Etain," the beautiful Etain was turned into a bowl of water and then into a scarlet fly.

Heracles always wears the skin of the Nemean lion, his face framed by its scalp and mane as the figure of the maiden Kore was imagined to remain within the eclipsed solar disk. He wears the lion's scalp because in some religious revolution the "hero" had won the power of a suppressed pre-Olympian feminine solar divinity. In the mature Olympic pantheon only the figure of Iris betrays obliquely a former feminine solar persona.

Moon, Lion, Water, and Iris are linked together in a tradition cited by Graves that the lunar goddess Selene made the archetypical Nemean Lion out of "sea foam enclosed in a large ark; ....Iris, binding it with her girdle, carried it to the Nemean Mountains." The Virgin in the zodiac is preceded by the Lion. On his rump there is a star Zosma, from a form of Zona "Girdle," and Allen notes the incongruity of the name in this position. But this name, in this position, may be the remnant of the tradition that the caduceus-bearing Virgo, like the caduceus-bearing Iris, held the supernatural astral lion on a leash made of her own girdle. The model of these fragmentary traditions is the feminine solar persona who controls the bright-maned lion. As for Selene, the solar "mane" is exposed by the moon's eclipsing disk. Iris leads the lion by her girdle because the phantasm is created by the "encirclements" around the eclipsed solar disk, the chromosphere and corona.

Gold is consistently linked with the rainbow. The pot of gold at the end of the rainbow is a cliché. Other traditions maintain that if you throw a shoe over the rainbow it will be filled with gold coins. Or the shoe will be turned to gold. The Irish leprechaun, who makes just one shoe, was supposed to own a pot of gold. Both the single shoe and the pot belong to the concept of the reflector, being carried upward by reflection, setting foot on a reflective surface, or "stamping" to create a supernatural spring. The pot and the shoe have the same model: the inverting reflective surface. We shall see that at Newgrange gold may be a feature of an interest in tracking astronomical cycles. Heimdall, an important Norse god thought to be of Celtic origin, guarded the approach to the rainbow. Norse traditions used the name Bifrost for both the rainbow and the Milky Way, as if both might have played the same role, and the Milky Way has consistently been visualized as a pathway to or through heaven. Heimdall had gold teeth.

The boxing or concentricity which occurs in a number of Newgrange devices is an effect that water characteristically produces. Concentricity is a signature of water, appearing not only in the rainbow or halo but whenever a water surface is disturbed.

Claire O'Kelly lists eight examples of the concentric arc device at Newgrange, occurring on 8% of decorated surfaces. The device also occurs on 8% of decorated surfaces at Dowth. This is a great contrast to the occurrence at Knowth, where she finds 39 examples in the kerb and 45 in satellite sites 2, 3, and 4, 54% of decorated surfaces.

The Database of Irish Excavation Reports adds to the Newgrange examples the following note on kerbstones cleared and examined since the O'Kelly work: "Most of the kerbstones show evidence of random pockmarks with a few examples of formal art. The latter consisted of cup and circle, chevron, concentric semicircles, zigzag and crude spiral motifs." Those concentric semicircles would be references to the rainbow, and these examples are described as being set among references to the Milky Way and polarity-specific circumpolar rotation.

22. Waterdrops	**Possible Reference:**	**Related Site Features:**
	Waterdrop or Dewdrop as Agent or Manifestation in of Supernatural Power	Boulder Cap, Water Drip in Chamber, Milky Way Orientation, Concentric Arc Devices

Just a little below the concentric arcs on K4 is a device that looks like two waterdrops fused together. These drop-shaped forms are nearly the same size as the arc device itself. A rainbow is a mass of waterdrops, each diffracting sunlight like the diamond-flashing dewdrop. The minute waterdrop supports the magnificent celestial arc. Spray from waterfalls and ocean breakers also display rainbows, as does steam from a boiling pot. It is frozen water crystals that form the concentric rainbow-circles called haloes and the pairs of bright rainbow-segments on either side of the sun called sun dogs. Since the bow depends on a fusion of individual drops, it is possible that what looks like a fused pair of waterdrops under the banded arcs on K4 is modeled on the way the waterdrop supports the rainbow. It is the single waterdrop that is the operative agent.

There is a deep cupmark on each end of the set of concentric arcs on K52. Rainwater or dew would have run down the arcs into these two cupmarks. When the sun shines into a wet, concave depression it fills it with golden radiance. K52 faces north, but had it faced in a southerly direction this pair of cupmarks on K52 could have periodically displayed a peculiar sun- and water-linked effect at the ends of this set of concentric arches.

There is what looks like a very large waterdrop or dewdrop-shaped device near the north edge of the righthand-recess roofstone. If the identification is correct, this would be another example of the great distortion of scale noted in the "waterdrops" on K4 and perhaps the cupmarks at the ends of the arches on K52. As a waterdrop, this device located in the recess with an orientation to the galaxy might be a reference to the Milky Way, under whose aegis dew forms.

As shown in sketch # 15 above and in Claire O'Kelly's drawing of the roofstone, there is a definite line making an arc or perhaps a right angle, curving from the drop-shaped device toward the chamber side of the roofstone, ending quite close to the large rosette. Whatever it means, the line is certainly intended to be read with the drop-shaped device. I cannot offer any interpretation of it, but it must certainly be significant.

The waterdrop has many uncanny powers besides the miracle of refraction that produces the rainbow. It miniaturizes the entire world and imprisons it in a minute sphere. It magnifies whatever lies under it. It is also plainly related to the mathematical miracle of the snowflake, the witchery of the frost dendrite, and the many forms of the stinging hailstone.

Water that collected in the stone bowl at Newgrange was delivered from the sky as water drops, chiefly rain, but if the boulder cap was exposed, there must have been some minimal component of atmospheric moisture, especially dew. Dew forms under clear, windless skies when the temperature falls below the dew point, forcing the air to release its moisture in the form of droplets. Thus many little drops of dew tend to form when many little stars are out.

The significance of this is that stars form a kind of swarm. The idea of the stars as a multitude with a single origin is reflected in our own word for star, which comes from a root meaning "to strew." A swarm is "A large number or body of insects or small living things of any kind, especially when each individual is in irregular motion." Individual stars glow and pulse as if they were many little energized living powers. Shooting stars and comets reinforce the impression of star life.

Stars as little airy powers under whose influence is bestowed the almost supernatural gift of dewdrops might be compared with bees, who bestow the almost supernatural gift of honey. A good hive of bees has from 80,000 to 100,000 workers. When they swarm they form a dense, buzzing column in the air to which one might compare the dense, glittering column of the galaxy. Both dewdrop and honey drop are magically linked with color: the spectrum is dissolved and exposed in a dewdrop, the flower-meadow is dissolved in a drop of honey.

The intelligence and organization of the two aerial swarms, bees and stars, may have linked them in people's imagination. The father of Orion was Hyrieus "Beekeeper," he loved Merope "Honey Mouth," and her brother was Euanthus "Fair Flower." The mother of Cygnus, a midwinter herald for Newgrange, was Hyrie "Beehive." The name of Cassiopeia's husband, borne by a constellation adjacent to Cygnus, is Cepheus "Drone." The name Uranus, usually interpreted as "mountain," may be a secondary development from the root yr- "swarm," the idea of a height or mountain having developed secondarily from a concept of the celestial vault as home of the starry swarm. The tradition that makes Hyrie Cygnus's mother makes his father Apollo.

The miniature winged maidens who are shown on classical jars hovering over cinerary urns with the spirit-guide Hermes are Danaids, one of the many names containing the water-linked element dan-. They killed their bridegrooms on their wedding night with pins, as worker bees sting the useless drones to death. The worker bees are all unmated females like the Danaids. The Danaids were punished in the afterworld by being forced to fetch water in perforated jars or sieves; they bring water in many little drops as the maiden bees bring nectar in many little droplets. When people pick up pins or throw pins in wells, they are acting out part of the complex of folk-beliefs that honor bees and wells *together* as supernatural agents: the pin is the emblem of the stinger. The well is Hyrie "Beehive," the generative womb of the snake-man Cygnus, the transformational plane of the *reflected* starry swarm whose emblem is the clockwise spiral.

Hampe and Simon remark in their book *The Birth of Greek Art,* (p. 324) that "In general the bee is rather to be placed among the entourage of mother-goddesses, such as Demeter and Rhea, and for that reason in Crete it was regarded as one of the nurses of the infant Zeus....In the Greek oral tradition melissai (bees) was a general term for nymphs, whose characteristics as pure, nourishing and prophetic beings were equated with those of bees....people were convinced that bees emerged from the bodies of the dead, and therefore saw in these creatures symbols of immortality..." In the story of Samson's slaying of a lion, in whose carcass he later found that bees had hived and made honey, the swarm generated from carrion belongs to this cluster of afterlife emblems.

Both the swarm of many little bees and the swarm of many little stars are ruled by queens. Cassiopeia rules near the summit of the galactic column with her husband Cepheus "Drone". On the other hand, as a feminine persona, the sun might well be considered as the queen of all the heavenly bodies. Her husband would be the all-powerful weather-god at the zenith of the heavens. Newgrange shows evidence of interest in the sun, the celestial pole, and Cassiopeia.

A link between sun, winged maidens, and waterdrops is reflected in the classical story of Memnon, the son of Eos. Eos means dawn, although "Dawn of the Year" or Midwinter Dawn would better suit some of the very dramatic narrative modules in which she figures. After Memnon's death, a flock of phantom birds or troupe of girls formed out of the funeral blaze and circled his pyre, sprinkling his grave with their tears. In one tradition Eos wept tears of dew every morning. At Egyptian Thebes, a statue which the Greeks called Memnon emitted a musical note at dawn; this musical note suggests the Graduated Scales agent that is associated with the determination of the solstitial sunrise, a Newgrange example being the Dagda's harp. Eos had an affair with Orion after his rape of Merope.

In some cases a special aspect of the solar persona seems to have been developed around the sun's intimate relationship to the rainbow, which is linked to the waterdrop. In such a case the primary emphasis is not on the sun's agricultural role but on the magic powers displayed in the sun-struck waterdrop and the rainbow, and probably also in the eclipse. I remarked above that there may be a set of concentric arcs on the other side of the roofstone from the "waterdrop." Both devices may refer to powers of the sun, here linked with the emphasis on water.

Graves cites a tradition that at Delphi they said that the first shrine was made of bees' wax and feathers, the second, of fern-stalks twisted together. The "shrine made of bees' wax" is an emblem of a faith based upon the very archaic concept of the heavenly host as a swarm of bees with a supernatural role in an afterlife concept. Involved also is the emblem of the wings of Icarus, made of feathers which were glued together with wax: he was warned not to fly too high, and when he did the sun melted the wax and he fell.

The second shrine was made of fern-stalks twisted together. Bees depend on flower nectar, so ferns are of no interest to them. Fern fronds always develop in spirals, and this is especially notable in the fern-brake, which unrolls in the shape of a cross, each of whose arms unrolls in a spiral. This is a type of fern which is characterized by especially long strong stalks. The shrine made of fern-stalks twisted together is an emblem developed out of a concept based on the spiral as an emblem of circumpolar rotation, involved with time. The snake is a natural spiral emblem. Other examples of combinations of W and snake may be the bare-breasted Mycenaean female figures holding serpents, and the antlered Cernunnos holding a snake on the Gundestrup cauldron. It may indeed have been such snakes as these that Patrick drove out of Ireland.

The Greek king Minos's son Glaucus was drowned in a jar of honey but was revived with the aid of a snake. This is an emblematic narrative scrap dramatizing the same sequence described in the Delphic tradition.

The same sequence of swarm and spiral may be discernible at Newgrange. The righthand recess is focused on a view of the Milky Way, and is constructed and oriented so that the heavenly swarm was seen reflected, rotating clockwise. This pool would have been generative as well as transformational. Cygnus's mother Hyrie "Beehive" was turned into a lake named Beehive: this was the generative womb. Bees suggest the shrine made of wax. Just as the righthand recess seems primary in the chamber, preserving the oldest and holiest part of its synthesis, the bee emblem is remembered as the oldest in the Delphic tradition.

The lefthand recess displays a "fern stalk" beside the W of Cassiopeia. The outview of this recess is focused on a view of circumpolar stars, which rotate counterclockwise. It is dominated by spirals, chosen because they can differentiate polarity of circular movement a feature that suggests a relationship with the emblem of the "shrine made of twisted fern stalks." This emblem is remembered as the next-oldest in Delphic tradition.

The lower half of the constellation Cygnus is just above the constellation called Serpens Cauda, "Snake's Tail." Cygnus's emblem was the snake (or lion), not the swan. The form and concept of the constellation may be a reference to an emblem of regenerated, transformed life. The upper torso of the new man, his supernatural being, is imagined as supported on a snake, the clockwise spiral of the starry reflection. The shape of the constellation Cygnus is very similar to the elongated cruciform interior of the Newgrange building. In addition, the interior walls look rather scaly, because of the all over picking. At Newgrange "bee" and "fern" emblems had been combined in some kind of working synthesis which was probably reflected in some narrative tradition.

A beehive functions with great discipline and organization.: "As a forcible illustration of the manner in which a colony of bees was recognized as the embodiment of government by a chief or ruler, in the earliest times of which there is any existing record, it may be mentioned that on the sarcophagus containing the mummified remains of Mykerinos.... dating back 3633 years B. C.... will be found a hieroglyphic bee representing the king of Lower Egypt." (*Ency. Brit. XI* "Bee")

From the middle of the second millennium, a number of images are preserved which should be referred to the emblem Bee. For example in Hampe's *Birth of Greek Art* a famous mid-second- millennium Mycenaean ring from Tiryns (Plate 299) shows four respectful "demons" bearing "jugs" to a seated female figure. Their bodies, shown in profile, resemble those of lions standing on their hind feet, their backs covered by what look like the carapaces of insects, with well-nipped waists like those of wasps or bees. The tips of their ornamented wings trail down to touch the ground behind their clawed feet. Another combination of lion with bee is found in the figure of the Sphinx, a lion with wings and human face. The name Sphinx is probably derived from sphex "wasp," the carnivorous lion of bees, a hostile reading of the emblem in a context in which Oedipus, the snake-man, overcomes her.

It is extremely important that the bodies of the jugs which the bee-lion demons carry are spheres, equipped with geometric looking spouts and handles. The outline is simply that of a waterdrop. Other plates in the book show gems of about the same era, that feature bee-lion figures with similar spherical "jugs." The jugs are equipped with slightly different handles and spouts: what is constant is the spherical shape.

These jugs are intended to be recognized as waterdrops. Plate 263 shows a "Talismanic" example from the sixteenth century, where the sphere has neither spout nor handle; it is crowned by a symmetrical device of arcs and/or arches. Some of these examples feature a conspicuous "palm branch." A very much later gemstone from the Roman spa at Bath which was dedicated to Diana shows a discus-thrower, with a dewdrop-shaped flagon that holds a palm. The spa at Bath may have been popular at the time Roman coins were left at Newgrange. The form of these "palm branches" closely resembles the form carried in the hand of the constellation Cassiopeia and the fern-frond device in the Newgrange lefthand recess. The combination of waterdrop and snake or fern emblems is the same as that noted in the Delphic tradition.

One possible interpretation of the globular cluster that decorates the front of the Ephesian Artemis is that these globes too represent dewdrops or waterdrops, the succulent cluster that nurtures all life. In ancient cult Artemis seems to have been a goddess of fertilizing moisture. Since her link with the moon was very late, she may originally have been linked to water through a relationship to either Cassiopeia and the Milky Way or to the sun. Artemis is closely related to the Cernaeian Hind, which was probably a form of the goddess herself. This hind is always portrayed with antlers, like a female reindeer.

The palm branch may also have been used as an emblem for the waterdrop-yielding sky. It may have originated because the date-palm has a long straight trunk and produces an enormous cluster of small succulent fruits. This is a possible emblem of the celestial "pole," as the trunk of a cosmic tree whose fruit is myriads of waterdrops.

As described above, the stars as a swarm of little aerial dew-fetchers may suggest bees, which often hive in trees. But the shape of the Milky Way suggests a stream as well as a swarm. It was often called River of Heaven. Because the stream has a milky color the imagery was also developed in a different direction. One story is that the streams came from the breasts of Hera as she nursed Heracles.

Further, milk produced from many little founts in the form of many little succulent drops suggests the many-teated sow, bitch, or vixen, and all three, particularly the pig and her piglets, have appeared in old afterlife contexts. The name of the Hyades cluster in Taurus was often popularly related to water, but the constellation was associated by the Romans with sow and piglets. The word could mean either. Pig and dog were taboo to the Jews, which may show a strenuous rejection of an original involvement with this very archaic emblem, centered on a many-teated female animal. Such an emblem would be an earthy totemic version of the idea behind the majestic many-breasted Ephesian Artemis. Her breasts are drop-shaped.

Tertullian says that new Christians were given a drink of milk and honey before baptism, and that both milk and honey were added to the wine of the first communion. The "promised land" is traditionally a land of milk and honey. The *Encyclopedia Britannica XI* ("Honey") notes that in India honey is a ceremonial offering to a guest or to a bridegroom, and honey is placed in the mouth of a male newborn. In Madagascar honey was put in the lustral water used in blessing a child before circumcision. The Greeks presented honey with milk or water as a libation to the dead. The sex-specific usages belong to the same concept that dictated dressing male infants in female clothes, to prevent the little boy's being snatched away prematurely by the amorous queen of heaven. This is a result of the archaic regeneration module " She runs away with her son" of which the story of Prince Ivan's rescue of his mother Goldentress from the power of Whirlwind the Whistler is an example; the Oedipus story is a late and hostile reading.

Opie's *Superstitions* quotes numerous modern examples of the belief that bees must be notified of the death of a member of the family, and also of a wedding, as well as beliefs that the actions of bees foretell the future or respond to certain important events. They are supposed to love virtue and hate bad behavior.

Newgrange seems to have been built in a countryside which would have been ideal for bees. The pollen and seed analysis included in O'Kelly's *Newgrange* showed that "...the landscape around the Boyne must have been opened up by men to a considerable extent because of the large variety and high number of herbs." A note in the *Enc. Brit. XI* article "Honey" (p653) remarks that "...curdled milk (A.V. "butter") and honey as exclusive articles of diet are indicative of foreign invasion, which turns rich agricultural districts into pasture lands or uncultivated wastes."

CHAPTER XI

THREE-NESS: MOON AS TIMEKEEPER

The moon could enter the Newgrange chamber through the opened chamber aperture every month, and could be seen through the roofbox aperture on the rare occasions when it happened to pass the winter solstition near its node. What emblem would refer to this celestial traveler? The shape of the moon changes constantly, and the disk itself was already in use as an emblem for the sun.

23. Triangles	Possible Reference:	Related Site Features:
	Moon as Timer, Phases and Cycles	Openable Roofbox, Raisable Chamber Capstone, Solstitial Orientations

It is possible that the triangle, a literal emblem of three-ness, represented a special interest in one striking aspect of the moon, its connection with the number three. The moon has three phases, new, half, and full, or perhaps, since true new moon is invisible except during an eclipse, waxing crescent, full moon, and waning crescent. The crescents face in opposite directions, so the moon has a left and right side as does a triangle. An unpicked or bright triangle could indicate the waxing east-pointing crescent, or perhaps the full moon; and a picked or dark triangle could indicate the waning west-pointing crescent, or perhaps the new moon. A lozenge or square combining two triangles, one picked and one plain, could be used as an emblem of the moon in all its phases. The device might also have served as an emblem of a period measured by the moon, a month, rather than the physical body of the moon. The fan-stick and fish-spine devices also refer to elements of time-keeping: noon and the solstice.

The lozenge sets on R12 and R21 that are arranged so that they refer to the rungs in the passage are composed of picked and unpicked triangle pairs. According to the interpretation of triangles in the present chapter this might indicate something about how the ritual was related to time and season measured by the moon as well as by the sun. The division of the set of nine rungs into a set of three and a set of six might have memorialized dates, perhaps counted from the solstice. The moon probably did have an important role as measurer of time. The upward climb of the departed spirit may well have been conceived as requiring a definite period, perhaps counted out in lunar months. The funeral observances of several cultures involve ceremonies carried out at specific intervals after the death occurs.

As an emblem of the moon, the triangle would have been developed to stress a special interest in one of its characteristics, the number three. Similarly the spiral seems to have been developed to stress a special interest in one of the characteristics of circumpolar rotation, its polarity. In both cases the rather abstract-looking emblem itself may then have acted as a model that spun off more concrete emblems of itself. The spiral spun off the snake, and the triangle may have spun off such emblems as the clover.

The three leaved clover (in some varieties) is marked with conspicuous chevrons, and the dome of florets is a succulent cluster of nectar droplets beloved of bees. The shamrock is an important Irish emblem. St. Patrick supposedly used it to illustrate the doctrine of the trinity. The rare four-leafed shamrock or clover is a symbol of luck. The *Handbook of Irish Folklore* cites the curious belief that the four-leaved shamrock grows where an ass has foaled three times, or where a mare drops her first foal, or is the spot where the true mare was born. This little cluster of emblems links the clover with the supernatural steed that is an emblem of reflection.

Both lozenges and triangles are common at Newgrange. In her *Passage Grave Art in the Boyne Valley* Claire O'Kelly shows the number of examples of each device along with the total number of decorated surfaces at Newgrange, Dowth and Knowth. She does not separate triangles and lozenges, but triangle/lozenge devices appeared on 43% of Newgrange decorated surfaces. This proportion is over eight times that recorded for Dowth and about seven times that recorded for Knowth. If these devices are related to the moon or perhaps more properly to lunar periods, this might indicate unusual emphasis at Newgrange on a supernatural lunar agency of a special kind or special attention to observances based on lunar cycles.

The ascent to a heavenly afterlife might have been timed by, or partially modeled on, cycles of the moon. Easter celebrates an afterlife event, Jesus' resurrection, and is celebrated by the Western church on the first Sunday after the first full moon after the spring equinox. Baptism, whose ultimate aim is everlasting life, has often been celebrated at Easter. At Newgrange the afterlife ritual may also have been enacted at a religious celebration linked to the cycles of both sun and moon.

Frequently a fairy-story's hero is the youngest of three sons. This might be intended as a reference to the moon's three phases, or simply to the importance of the youngest, or "new" moon. Often the hero is an only son, protected and helped by his mother. This might reasonably be modeled on the way the new moon is hidden within the sun's radiance, as if she were defending him or preparing him for his destiny. A familiar example is Parsifal, whose mother secludes her young son to protect him from the perils of a warrior's life.

The young soldier in the Norse story of the "Mountain in the Blue" is the son of an anxious widow. In the Russian story of "Whirlwind the Whistler," Ivan's queen-mother Goldentress, whom he is trying to rescue from her kidnapper, hides him under her robe, and tells him how to overcome Whirlwind. Thetis, the mother of the great Greek hero Achilles, begs help for him from Zeus, and persuades the smith Hephaestus to make him his armor - especially his greaves or leg armor. Thetis dipped Achilles in the Styx, a river flowing in the afterworld, to make him immortal, all but the heel she held him by, an inversion of the idea of stepping on a water surface to gain heaven, also seen in the idea of the leprechaun or one-shoe-maker.

Newgrange was set up to view the midwinter sunrise, so the users must have had a way to keep track of the solar year. If midwinter was their New Year's Day, this was another reason why keeping track of the exact day of the solstice was important. But keeping track of the moon must have been of great interest. To prepare for seeing the midwinter sunrise, people must have spent at least part of the night awake and watching, a favored few in the chamber itself. It would have been important to be able to predict the phase and position of the moon at both solstices.

The moon crosses the solstitial colure every month as it completes its eastward circle of the skies. But because its orbit is tilted about five degrees from the ecliptic, it intersects this path only twice a month. These intersections are called its nodes. The roofbox is a rather narrow slit, and the moon can be seen through it only when the lunar nodes are very close to the ecliptic. To make matters worse, the nodes are in motion. It takes them 18 years and 219 days to make a complete westward revolution around the ecliptic, so they require two or three weeks to move one degree. But the moon, the fastest planetary body in the heavens, moves about thirteen degrees eastward each day, so that it is close to its node for only a few hours.

If the roofbox had required all the conditions to be met exactly, the moon could have been seen only when its node lay exactly at the point where the midwinter colure intersects the ecliptic. There was a little leeway in the dimensions of the roofbox, but to see the moon through the narrow slot would obviously have been fraught with complications. Fortunately, the highest point of the ecliptic, the summer solstition, was visible from the center recess through the aperture at the top of the chamber vault. Viewing conditions there were not nearly as strict as through the roofbox, partly because the aperture at the top of the vault is more than three times as close to the viewer's eye. The moon might have been seen every month when it crossed the summer solstition, day or night, which would have made it easier to keep track of lunar cycles from inside the chamber.

It is the position of the nodes that determines whether or not a solar or a lunar eclipse can take place. Sun and moon must be just in line, so the moon must be right on the ecliptic, thus it must be at one of its nodes. The moon courses over and under the ecliptic in a serpentine path and when it intersects the ecliptic there is always the threat of a solar or lunar eclipse. The shape and appearance of the apparition along with the wriggling shape of the lunar path with regard to the ecliptic tended to call forth the image of a dragon, a winged and fiery snake. The ability to understand the powers and stratagems of the moon requires great knowledge and wisdom.

The fact that the moon shone not only during the day, like the sun, but also at night, when its light was a real defense against danger, and the fact that its face bore many battle scars, helped give it some of the attributes of a warrior. Jacob Grimm (*Teutonic Mythology* 1892) has reported a number of greetings to the new moon which reflect a concept of it as hero, warrior, or king. These include a Lettish new-moon formula "Ah, thou, God, I see for God a new warrior!"

"Welcome new moon, noble lord; increase my gold!," and from a Hungarian healing formula "New Moon! New King!" (Roscher *Lexicon* 2754). Opie includes eight columns of New Moon customs. Many new-moon customs refer to wealth, such as turning the money in the pocket when seeing the new moon. The idea is that the number of coins will then increase. Certain plants are to be planted when the moon is waxing or when it is waning.

24. Triangular stone as Sculptured Emblem	**Possible Reference:**	**Comparable Features:**
	Same as Engraved Triangles	Carved Rungs, K1 and K52 Interpreted as Sculptured Emblems

Vallancey, an early explorer of Newgrange, saw and drew a large triangular stone set up between K1 and the entrance to the passage. If his reporting is accurate, the stone might have been a sculptural lunar emblem. The stone Molyneux described also sounds like a triangular stone: "Along the middle of the cave a slender quarry-stone, five or six feet long lies on the floor, shaped like a pyramid, that once, as I imagine, stood upright, perhaps a central stone to those placed round the outside of the mount: but now 'tis fallen down."- But this sounds very much like the same one Vallancey drew. If it was the same stone, this would seem to be evidence that at least one object from inside the chamber was moved by someone in the interval between these visits.

Another triangular form which seems sculptural rather than engraved can be seen in a photograph in the O'Riordain and Daniels *Newgrange* which shows clearly a very large, deep triangular indent on the surface of GC1. It may or may not have been a natural feature.

CHAPTER XII

COUNTING

25. Three Rosettes   **Possible Reference:**   **Related Site Features:**
Counting by Nines   Roofstone, K52, Bowl and
                        Sockets, Marbles, Nine
                        Passage Rungs

See Fig. 10 and Plate IX

Aman who could tell in advance what phase the moon would exhibit when it entered the Newgrange chamber, or when there was a chance of an eclipse, would have earned and surely been accorded great dignity and respect. This kind of skill would have been the rocket science of the time. Predicting such events required counting.

If on the night of midwinter a full moon shone through the chamber aperture, the same event would have occurred again in almost exactly nineteen years, 6939 days. This cycle is called the Metonic Cycle. It is off by only about an hour and a half.

Eclipses of both moon and sun would have been of absorbing interest to these astute watchers of the skies. Scientists still travel thousands of miles to witness an eclipse. Hartmann in his *Astronomy* suggests that one reason the Mayans developed an eclipse-based calendar was that *five solar eclipses* (only one was total) were visible there in the 14 years between AD 331 and 344. A whole generation was exposed to this cluster of ominous events.

Hartmann explains how people could have learned to predict when an eclipse might occur. The cycle that predicts these events is called the Saros: "Early astronomers discovered that if, in a given year, a particular sequence of eclipses occurred, a similar sequence would probably occur after one Saros. Because the moon's umbral shadow on the earth is so small, a fixed observer has only a small chance of seeing any given solar eclipse. But because the earth's umbra is large and because the moon can be seen from the whole night hemisphere of the earth, half the earth will see every lunar eclipse (barring cloud cover). Total lunar eclipses are therefore relatively common for any observer, and they were thus easier than solar eclipses for ancient astronomers to predict using the Saros and other cycles."

The Saros is a period of 6585 days during which a series of thirty-five solar and lunar eclipses will occur. How might the people of Newgrange have kept track of such a long period?

The system they used for counting astronomical cycles was probably developed from familiarity with the track and phases of the moon, a timekeeper from time immemorial. The root of the word "moon" is related to the word for measure. The moon's sidereal cycle is the time it takes to make its circuit of the heavens from a given star back to the same star. It is twenty-seven and a third days long, almost divisible into three nine-day periods. The synodic cycle is the time the moon takes to go from one new moon to the next. This is twenty-nine and a half days, during about three of which, called the interlunium, the moon is behind the sun and cannot be seen at all except during an eclipse, when it passes in front of the sun. There is some evidence of a nine-day week in both Celtic and Roman cultures.

In the previous chapter I suggested that the triangle was an emblem of some aspect of the moon's shapes and cycles. If it was, then it may have been the moon's relationship to *number* that particularly impressed the Newgrangemen. The number three has convenient links with the moon, beginning with its three phases. The cube of three, twenty-seven, is almost the length of the sidereal cycle and the visible part of the synodic cycle. The twenty-seven-day periods may have suggested the use of a nine-day week. The importance of the numbers three and nine may have led to an appreciation of numerical powers, including their pictorial expressions as the square and the cube. Playing with numbers and powers of three has a fascination of its own. The engineering of Newgrange gives ample proof of the intelligence and inventiveness of its builders.

Groups of nine devices occur fairly often among Newgrange devices, and so do groups of eight. The base number has a different, special value. The swastikas and shorthand reductions on R12 and R21, which are formed out of triangles combined into squares, are attached to a set of nine ascending rungs, divided into a set of three and a set of six. The meshed swastikas on R12 contain a total of eight divided squares or lozenges, counting the magical doubled square that joins them as two. The righthand recess roofstone has several striking examples of sets of three as does K52.

There is one type of device on the righthand recess roofstone that may reveal the use of a nine-based number system. In fact this is the most striking feature of the roofstone. It consists of a trio of large devices that resemble rosettes. Parts of them are concealed, some by orthostats that support the roofstone and others by supports which well-intentioned early restorers forced in under the roofstone.

PLATE XIX. Righthand Recess Roofstone

It is not possible to be sure of the original configuration of two of the rosettes but we may make some cautious guesses.

The three rosettes are located around an excellent eight-coil clockwise spiral. According to the convention adopted in this study, the clockwise spiral could refer to the planetary orbits although a reference to circumpolar rotation reflected as clockwise by the water-filled bowl below the roofstone is also possible. The eight-coil spiral would of course have been reflected in the bowl as counterclockwise.

Only the rosette nearest the northerly side of the recess is completely visible. I am going to call this one Rosette I. Age and pressure have cracked the roofstone right across this rosette, but the design is clear enough. Rosette I is formed by a ring of eight small disks of about the same size arranged around a large unpicked lozenge. This ring of disks is surrounded by several wreaths of boxing arcs. The small disk in Rosette I which is located nearest to the center of the roofstone will be called Disk 1. Just touching Disk 1 on its outside edge is a smaller circle flanked by two others. Disk 1 is further distinguished by being boxed by an extra arc.

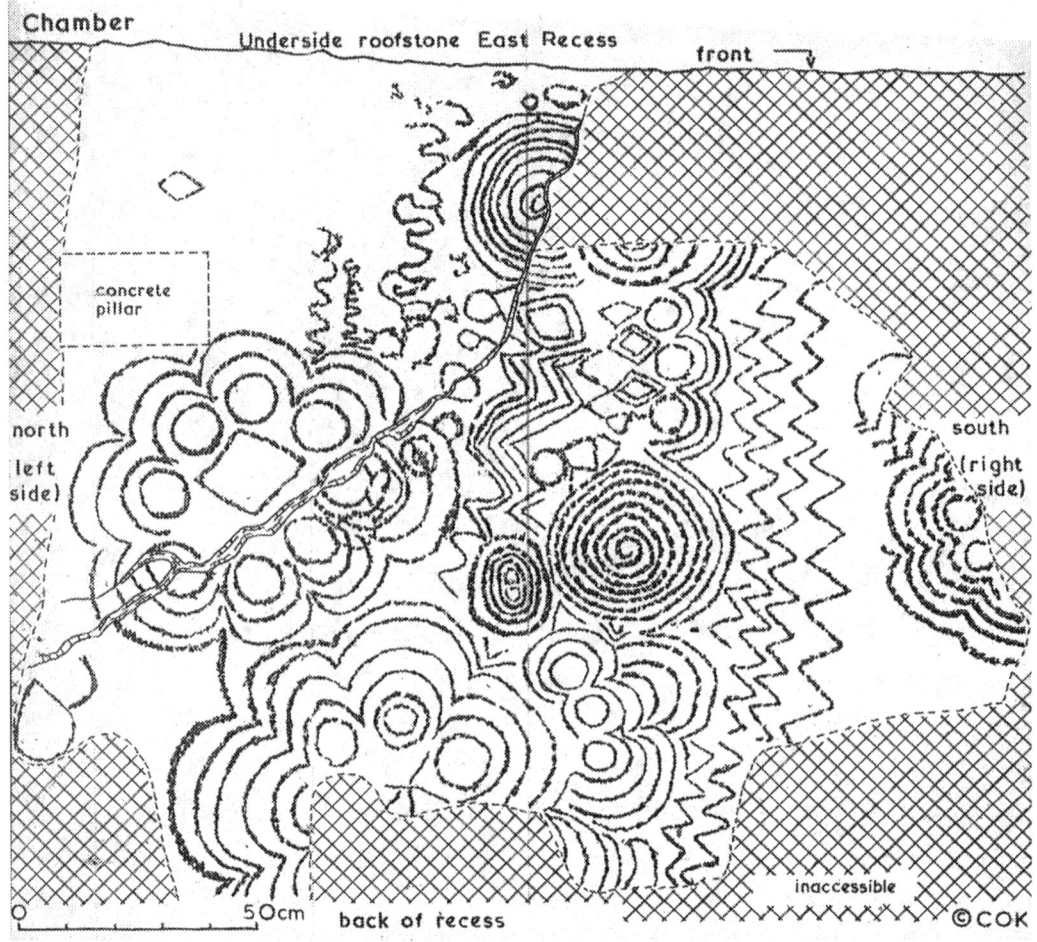

FIG. 10. Claire O'Kelly's Drawing of Righthand Recess Roofstone Devices

Rosette III at the extreme right of the design (as we look *down* on the drawing of it) is almost completely hidden by the supports of the northerly side of the recess: two disks are visible, surrounded by several wreaths of boxing arcs, not all complete. Rosette III is separated from Rosette I by a welter of different devices including a broad band of parallel chevron- rows.

The outmost boxing arc of Rosette II at the back of the recess is continuous with the outmost boxing arc of Rosette I. Only three disks and part of a fourth in its ring are visible, but the rosette looks like half of a ring which would be completed by four more disks. Close to the middle of the ring there is an irregular device of five diverging lines, the two on the right forming a V or square corner that brackets the rightmost disk. Just outside the wreath of boxing arcs that surrounds that rosette is a symmetrical row of three small disks, also arced. The middle disk of these three is in line with the bracketed disk, and boxed by six arcs.

In Rosette II, the disk which is the nearest to the middle of the roofstone has a smaller disk *within* it. I suggest that this device hints at a simple way of counting by nines. The eight disks would represent the eight digits in the system. The disk that encloses a smaller disk would have a dual value: the value of *one* at the beginning of the clockwise count around the ring, and the value of *nine*, signalized by the small enclosed disk, after one round. If the timekeeper continued to count by nines around a ring of eight disks, each time he came to the number nine he would begin the next count of nine one disk farther along the ring, advancing the small circle that signalized the place of his nine by moving it one disk clockwise. When the number nine worked its way around to where it was at the beginning of the count, completing a count of nine nines, the doubled disk would represent 9^2, eighty-one.

In the same way a person can count to eighty-one by nines using his eight fingers, by beginning one finger farther forward each cycle of nine. The change of place could be remembered by moving a ring to the beginning-finger of each cycle.(Finger rings were invented by Prometheus.) Counting nines with eight fingers could be useful. This may be a clue of sorts to explain the persistence of the fairy-tale or mythic emblem of the missing little finger, which is turned down or "cut off."

It is true of Rosette I as of Rosette II that one of its eight disks is distinguished by its relationship to a small disk. In Rosette I, an extra set of arcs embraces both Disk 1 and the small disk which touches it. The two small disks on each side of the touching disk intersect in a complicated way with surrounding arcs. The small flanking disk on the left touches Disk 2.

The disks in the three rosettes may represent either days or numbers. The choice of the disk would be fitting, as what is being numbered would probably be days, or suns, since we have reason to believe that the Newgrangemen counted the days of the year from solstice to solstice.

Two of the three rosettes on the roofstone of the righthand recess might represent a way for counting nines by moving the starting point one place as described. In the case of the almost completely obscured third rosette the possibility could not be ruled out. Since the three rosettes are similar but not identical, being surrounded by different numbers of arcs and flanked by different groups of smaller disks, it is possible that each might have been associated with a different power of nine.

The devices on the roofstone could not themselves have been used for counting. The tallies that may refer to the determination of the solstice were probably not used for tallying either. Both the rosettes and the tallies would be *emblems*, and their being placed as they are would simply be a solemn tribute to ideas developed for a religious calendar related to a funeral practice. The astronomy-based tallies and the mathematics-based rosettes would have absorbed an aura of holiness because they helped time rites that were intended to promote an afterlife in the heavens.

The row of eight devices on the roofstone lintel could have been used as part of the calendar count. This stone was public and accessible. A marker could have been moved along the row to keep track of the moving start. All eight devices on the roofstone lintel have the same outline, an X inside a rectangle, that is, a saltire, but the rectangles change size across the length of the stone, the largest being on the righthand end.

There are three nines in the sidereal cycle, about 27.3 days, just close enough to three nines to tempt a person to keep counting in the hope that it will come out even. It does come close in 81 days, three of its cycles, and this happens to be the second power of nine. Nine 81-day periods make up 729 days, that is, the third power of nine. This is only a day and a half less than two years, $730^1/_2$ days.

The Metonic Cycle, the time required for a given phase of the moon to recur on the same day of the year, is almost exactly nineteen years: 6939 days. The nineteen years are solar years, not calendar years, so that every four years the leap day is added, a little over four days for the nineteen years. In a nine-based system the period of 6939 days would be counted as 9^4 (6561) plus one year, which is half of 9^3 (364 $^1/_2$), leaving a remainder of thirteen days, that is, 9^1 plus four. Since one date that was certainly marked was the winter solstice, the extra days would probably be added at that time, which is suggestive in view of the traditional "Twelve Days of Christmas."

The Saros is the period of time after which the same sequence of thirty-five eclipses recurs. We express the cycle as 6585 days. A person using a nine-based system would express the cycle as 9^4 plus twice nine plus three days.

The use of a nine-based system would be a rather elegant way to help keep track of these long cycles, appealing to a religious sensibility that honored both sun and moon. The devices on the roofstone above the water-filled bowl may give some support to a hypothesis that both the number nine and some idea of mathematical powers had been involved in the religious system of the culture.

There is another possible piece of evidence in the righthand recess for the use of mathematical powers in counting days. This is the stone bowl and the marbles that were found in the chamber.

PLATE XX. Bowl and Sockets

The massive stone bowl was found on top of the righthand recess slab, although it has unfortunately proved to be portable enough that one cannot be sure where it originally stood. This unique bowl has two circular depressions one about seven, the other about eight inches in diameter, set into a widened and somewhat flattened part of its lip. (The value 45cm repeated in the O'Kelly works is wrong.)There is also a slight circular depression or faint marking within the main part of the bowl. It is hard to see why these depressions would have been required for laying out remains. But two, perhaps three, separate circular areas had been delineated within the bowl, and the Newgrangemen apparently did nothing without a reason.

There was another circular depression present in the chamber. This was a "ball-like object of granite, slightly flattened on two opposite sides, in one of which there is a shallow depression" which was "presumed to be a stone lamp." The depression is very shallow indeed, too shallow to hold much lamp-oil, and I believe that this flattened ball with its shallow hollow should instead be classed with the two shallow circular depressions in the lip of the stone bowl. The ball was reportedly "found in the centre of the main chamber under the basin stone which had formerly been in the east recess but had been moved to the central position some time in the 1890s." There were three depressions present, if the one in the "lamp" may be counted with the two in the bowl. If the apparent slight circular indent in the bowl may be counted with them, there were four.

The "lamp" is not unique on the Boyne. Another was found around twenty feet south of K92, not too far from Site Z, which also contained a hollowed stone slab or bowl, and another was found due south of Newgrange on the bank of the river. Another one was found in the chamber of Dowth north, which contains a large stone bowl.

I have been referring to these hollows in the bowl and lamp as "depressions," but I am now going to take advantage of a meaning of the Greek word glene as a term for them. When the Greek underworld divinity Hecate was called triglene, the word glene really referred to the eye *socket*, not the eye. The Graiae, three sisters that lived on the edge of the afterworld and could tell Perseus how to reach it, had only one eye between them, and they passed this eyeball from socket to socket.

The Newgrange sockets may also have contained balls.

Six marbles of different sizes, materials, and colors, plus two that were joined together, were found within the chamber. It would not be unreasonable to assume that there were originally more of these marbles. The three (or four) different-sized sockets, and a selection of marbles, could have been used as a kind of abacus. It might have worked like this:

Suppose that there was a full moon at midwinter, a momentous event. The Newgrangemen would want to be prepared for the time when this event would occur again. The Metonic Cycle which predicts it is 6939 days long. One nine-day week after midwinter day, the timekeeper would drop one marble, representing 9^1 days, into the center of the bowl itself, which I am going to call Socket One. Every week he would add a marble. But at the end of the ninth week, instead of putting a ninth marble into Socket One to represent 9×9^1 or 9^2, he would scoop the eight marbles out of Socket One, and put one marble into Socket Two, the smaller of the two on the rim. Each marble in Socket Two would represent 81 days as 9^2. He would have effactually moved his count one place forward, to the second power of nine.

The timekeeper would repeat this operation till, at the end of 729 days, 9×9^2, he scooped the sixteen marbles out of Sockets One and Two and dropped a marble into Socket Three, the larger of the two on the rim. Each marble in Socket Three would represent 729 days as 9^3. He would have effactually moved his count another place forward, to the third power of nine.

Seven hundred and twenty-nine days happens to be very close to two years: $730\,^1/_2$ days. This may be the point at which double marbles came into play, for every one of the 9^3 marbles would have had two significances: it represented 9^3 days, and it also represented very nearly two years. Socket Three would need to be larger than Socket One if its marbles were double, and in fact it is.

Either two-year periods or nine-year periods might have been important in whatever kind of liturgical calendar was in use. The nine-year interval is known to have been important in several traditions. The use of double marbles would provide a rough visual check for the completion of nine two-year or two nine-year periods. But the difference between 729 and $730\,^1/_2$ days would accumulate substantially over a nineteen year period. The Newgrange timekeeper already had a rough visual check for the solstice in the horizon-distance or noon-shadow-length tally, so he would be aware of the discrepancy.

Every time the timekeeper dropped a 9^3 marble in Socket Three, the solstice would occur a day and a half later. By the end of eighteen years, the solstice would occur over thirteen days later. This would probably in fact come to be recognized as another check on the date of the solstice.

The timekeeper would have continued to drop marbles into Socket Three until it was time to scoop all the marbles out of Sockets One, Two and Three and drop the 9^4 marble into Socket Four, the hollow in the stone "lamp." Sixty-five hundred and sixty-one days would have elapsed. The Metonic Cycle would be completed in 6939 days, almost exactly a year later.

Setting the portable, lamp-like Socket Four with its count of 6561 aside he would begin again and proceed to count one more year: four 9^3 marbles or 324 days, then four 9^1 marbles or 36 days, and finally five more days for a grand total of 365, completing the cycle, verified by the appearance of a full moon on the day of the winter solstice.

The Saros is 6585 days, or 18 years and 11 days. If the Newgrangeman's aim was to predict the date on which an eclipse cycle would recur, he would begin counting on the date of some eclipse, probably a lunar eclipse because many more are visible from the same location. Counting by nines as before till he dropped the 9^4 marble into Socket Four, representing 6561 days, he would need to drop two 9^1 marbles into Socket One, representing two nine-day weeks, and six days later the eclipse cycle would begin again.

The importance of number, specifically the numbers nine and eight, seems to be indicated by other striking devices engraved at Newgrange.

C16 is the righthand portal of the righthand recess, a tall, handsome stone, with a rather pointed top, set like a monitory stele beside the recess entrance. Near the top is a band of "text" handsomely framed by two fairly horizontal grooves or improved cracks. At the top are nine picked hanging triangles.

As a set of nine, this group might have been understood as an expression of homage to the moon as the "inventor" of the nine-based count. As master of the nine-day week, the two-year period of 9^3 days, and the usefulness of the long count of 9^4 days, the moon may have been considered at Newgrange to rule and guard the postmortem ascent suggested by the nine passage rungs. Both the Metonic Cycle and the Saros involve reconciling the solar and lunar cycles. Below the set of nine hanging triangles are eight picked lozenges.

R8 is located just below the beginning of the stair of ascending corbels over the passage. On the top of this stone is a pyramid of six divided lozenges. The entire surface of the stone is picked, which makes it hard to be sure of the original intention, but the lower halves of the six lozenges are picked, underneath the all-over picked dressing. There are two peculiar picked "wings" flanking the top lozenge in this pyramid. The lefthand wing is a complete lozenge like the others, its lower triangle picked, so that it could be related to the others in the pyramid in the same way that they are related to each other. The righthand wing is different. It is a picked triangle, standing on its *base* so that it cannot be assimilated normally into the pyramid. Thus the eighth lozenge in the group is differentiated as being special, which is also true of the eighth lozenge or square in the interlocked swastika device on R12, four orthostats ahead.

It is unexpected to find that stone-age people may have had the scientific and mathematical interests implied by the hypothesis that they used a nine-based number system and powers of nine, but there is no evidence that they were incapable of these interests, which have been inferred from apparatus and devices in the chamber. The engineering skills speak for the builders' intelligence. Attributing intellectual simplicity to ancient peoples can be a result of a quasi-religious faith in human progress. It is an unproven premise which encourages the student to gloss over details.

Several facts about the marbles found at Newgrange, facts which at first glance seem rather trifling, may be more important than they appear, if considered in the light of the hypothesis that they figured in a counting device.

The marbles are of different materials. Some of them are of chalk. This would seem to be a very casual, coarse material to fashion into spheres put to the solemn use suggested.

In my hypothesis about the counting process, the power of nine represented by a given marble was determined by which socket it occupied. I conjectured that each socket could hold eight marbles (or double marbles). Just before the count ticked over to 9^4, there could have been a total of 24 marbles in play, eight in each socket, the value of each determined only by the socket it occupied.

But it is possible that marbles dropped in a given socket were also differentiated by size, colour or surface material. The marbles that were found were neither all the same size nor all the same colour. If the surface appearance was another factor that helped determine the value of the marble, it might not matter what the sphere was made of, but simply that it be easy to shape and to coat with some distinguishing color or material. That might explain why chalk was a reasonable choice.

This possibility is opened by an intriguing find. One of the three marbles found beside the basin stone in Site Z *was* covered in some way. "When found it had a very dark grey, almost black, external surface and looked as if it were made of ... pottery clay....When shaken in the hand, it could be heard that there was something loose and movable inside.... [within the shell or skin was] a white powdery chalk marble closely comparable with those already described [from Z] and those from the other sites in the Newgrange area...... Looked at edge-on, the external "skin" is seen to be dark grey-black on the outer surface only, while the greater part of its thickness of 1.5 mm is of a beige-to-light-brown colour, with a very fine resin-like texture and a 3-lamina structure." (O'Kelly and Lynch "Three Passage Graves," 300-301) Whatever the nature of the external covering, it is obvious from this example that some means of differentiation had been applied to the skin of one marble.

The very fragile covering found may also have been a preparatory (adhesive?) layer between the chalk core and a more substantial outer shell.

Another intriguing find which may be relevant to this possibility was a "Gold foil 'packet' consisting of a sheet of gold foil tightly folded ["crumpled"] so that a circular shape was visible on the bottom surface as if it enclosed a discoidal object such as a coin. When unfolded in the British Museum Laboratory it was found that the impression was even sharper on the inside of the foil, but no coin or object was present. Instead there was a small folded piece of gold foil as if this had been substituted for the original object." (C. O'Kelly "A Catalogue of the Roman Coins from Newgrange, Co. Meath" p. 51)

It would be hard to say where this object originally came from. It was found about fifteen feet southwest of GC 9, the kerbstone that lies in front of K19. It was found "just beneath the surface sod....a circumstance which makes stratigraphical determination virtually impossible, particularly so as the surface in question is almost entirely a stony one, consisting of the stony slip of the mound or cairn." (Ibid. p. 46) Mrs. O'Kelly notes that in Roman times the slip had attained its angle of repose, which has some bearing on the question of when the packet was dropped.

Circumstances of the find make it impossible to tell whether the foil packet found was related to the primary use of the mound. It would be natural to assume that if a treasure-hunter of any period had been collecting gold objects in Newgrange and happened to detect a foil-wrapped object, such as one of the marbles, he could have stripped off the foil, abandoning the stone core. The pains taken to craft *spheres* out of soft chalk would be more understandable if some of the marbles found in Newrange and its satellites were originally coated or covered with something, such as gold leaf. A number of them were damaged in a way that might have occurred if they were "peeled." One would have to suppose that the discoidal object which made the impression on the foil packet was a coin which had been removed and replaced by the small piece of folded foil. This circumstance is puzzling; why was the coin replaced with foil? But the presence of the foil at the site seems significant in itself. Other mounds were ransacked by treasure seekers. It seems reasonable to believe that this was not pure speculation, and that the raiders knew that there was gold inside.

Theoretically, gold could have been beaten over a spherical core. Gold was plentiful in Ireland, is very malleable, and was beaten into plates very early in several cultures.Gold could have been panned out of the streams in the Wicklow mountains. "A considerable amount of gold has been extracted from the valley gravels north of Croghan Kinshela on the Wexford border" (*Ency. Brit.*" "Wicklow") and "In Co. Wicklow...regular workings [of gold] were established about 1796 but were destroyed during the Rebellion" (*ibid.* "Ireland" 750b). The gold would have originated in quartz "reefs," and been found in streams in the form of bean-shaped or flattened nuggets, quite malleable, which could have inspired the impulse to beat it flatter and larger, eventually leading to the production of leaf or foil.

The quartz used in the Newgrange facade may have come from Wicklow. Claire O'Kelly says "The quartz stones are mostly angular and some at least must have been quarried from a seam in the granite, possibly in the Dublin-Wicklow mountains or in Co. Tyrone." Perhaps forays to collect nuggets from the Wicklow streams drew attention to the nearby quartz, or vice versa. The bulky quartz could have been brought back along with scraps of gold.

Mrs. O'Kelly mentions apropos of a gold-plated ring, that "the practice of plating with gold leaf or foil rings of an inferior metal was common from about the fourth century BC on into Roman times." By the time of the very experienced Vikings, gold seekers would have been familiar enough with the practice to peel a gold shell off a chalk marble.

The Norse story of the "Three Princesses in the Mountain in the Blue" may shed some light on the relationship between the marble-and-socket as counting device, the foil packet found at the site, and the covered marble. We have already seen how the young soldier came to a big mound, dug loose a square of turf that covered a huge slab, and was lowered down into a deep hole into another world. He found a palace where everything was of copper, and the eldest princess was spinning copper yarn. She gave him three drinks from the horn behind the door, which made him strong enough to swing the troll's sword. Then she hid him behind the brewing vat, and after the troll came in and she had sung him to sleep, the soldier cut off his three heads with one blow. He found the second princess spinning silver yarn in a silver palace. After three swigs from the horn behind that door he could lift that sword, and after three more he could swing it. Then he was able to cut off that troll's six heads with one blow. The youngest princess was spinning gold yarn in a gold palace. After three drinks, the lad could stir the sword, after three more he could lift it, and after three more he could swing it.

But when he swung at the troll the sword was only long enough to reach eight of the heads, and he had to swing again to take off the ninth.

The troll-head sequence could be modeled on a system in which the number nine has a different value, the second stroke indicating the change of place. As all three metal sequences are similar, number and change of power are linked organically in the story. The dropping troll-heads recall the spherical, dropping marbles, while the three metal venues of increasing value recall the idea of change of place to indicate increase in power. The three spinning wheels are emblems of circumpolar rotation, elapsed time.

The module that follows the troll-head sequence in the story of the "Mountain in the Blue" is of great interest in view of the interval that had to be counted beyond the 9^4 days in order to complete either cycle. The young soldier was abandoned in the underground kingdom by his treacherous companions. He found a whistle which summoned a bird-flock and its ruler, a great eagle. The eagle carried him up when it had been provided with the carcasses of twelve bulls and a thirteenth cut into pieces. He was only able to claim the youngest princess after he had summoned the eagle again and provided two more carcasses to enable it to fly back to the underground kingdom and fetch the gold checkers which the princesses had played with there. The complicated module at least suggests the remainder of time, perhaps twelve months and a fraction? - after the last troll-head dropped in the gold kingdom. If the lad with the two treacherous, older companions is in some sense modeled on the new moon hero, the whistle, emblem of blown sound, reveals the nature of the great power behind the wheel of Time: the weather god, who lives at the apex of the celestial vault, and whose musical instrument is the wind.

The Roman Mercury, who corresponded to Hermes, ruled over commerce and was often represented with a purse full of coins. Coins are usually round metal disks, distinguished partly by size and partly by the value of their material, customarily copper, silver or gold. The antlered Gallo-Roman Cernunnos, similar to Mercury in some respects, was sometimes pictured on funeral steles pouring some kind of small objects, perhaps coins, out of a sack.

Hermes could divine from "the dance of pebbles in a bowl of water," which he had been taught to do by the Melissae or "bee nymphs." He was also the god who guided and protected the souls of the departed on their way to the realm of the dead. His wand or caduceus was wound either with two coiled serpents facing in opposite directions like the spiral and its reflection, or with two white streamers, suggesting the way the two pale streamers of the galaxy are "attached" to the pole.

Hermes had invented the lyre by stringing gut over the shell of a tortoise (he later bartered it to Apollo). The tortoise has four stout legs that hold up a vaulted shell composed of separate plates. The legs extend from under the almost circular shell at an angular distance of about 90° from each other. Newgrange has four massive groins lying almost on the cardinal points that support a vault made up of separate plates. Either of the slender, worked stones originally reported as found in the chamber would have been suitable as a gnomon, and when the sun shone in through either aperture the stone would have produced a graduated scale of shadow-strings beneath the plated vault, a sort of solar lyre in a stone tortoise-shell. Was this the Dagda's winter- and summer-summoning harp?

There is a venerable custom of putting a coin in the mouth or on the eyelids of a corpse. This came to be explained as money to pay Charon, the ferryman of the afterworld, to carry the deceased across the river Styx. The underground water-source in the Newgrange funeral chamber, to which human remains were brought in some way, was situated beside a possible system of counting cycles with round tokens. The rite that helped the deceased reach heaven was timed by at least one cycle, the beginning of the year at midwinter.

The custom of dropping coins into pools is still very much alive. The ritual action suggests a covert intention to bribe some tutelary power connected with the pool to favor the donor's wish. These customs may go very far back in time: farther than the dance of pebbles in a bowl of water by which the bee nymphs taught Hermes to foretell the future. Could they go farther yet, to the ceremonial movement of time-linked tokens in a stone-age font linked with the afterlife?

The fact that *coins* were found at Newgrange, particularly the gold solidi, is intriguing. Gold coins were reportedly found in the chamber although the reports were dismissed. Coins that were found inside could have been carried out and dropped by Norse looters. There was apparently originally a coin in the foil-wrapped packet. Although the stone door was found open, it cannot be determined when it was opened, and there is the possibility that entrance was gained through the shallowly-buried vault.

The nine-based system was probably used only for calendar purposes by the scientific community within the culture. It may always have preserved an aura of the supernatural, and for secular purposes would not have superseded the natural ten-digit-based system.

Newgrange's winter-solstice orientation automatically brings to mind the Christmas birth-date of Jesus, the Christian's guarantor of a life in heaven, a date thought to have been borrowed from early pagan tradition. Another figure whose tradition is intriguing in the light of Newgrange afterlife agencies is St. Nicholas, the quintessential saint of midwinter, and "the patron saint of practically everything." He too would have been borrowed from pagan tradition. Nicholas freed three maidens by dropping a purse of gold for each one *down the chimney* into a *stocking*. In his capacity of patron saint of judges, he leaves fitting gifts for children, good and bad, in shoes or stockings on Christmas eve. Dealers in coin, including both merchants and pawnbrokers, are under his protection - the pawnbroker's emblem is three gold balls. As Santa Claus his home is the north pole, and the reindeer, with its antlers, has attached itself to him through a vague chain of generally benevolent midwinter gift-givers. Nicholas is the patron saint of scholars, and he protects those in peril on water. As a Christian saint, he is also of course involved in Christian afterlife imagery and theology. Most of these traditions have faint echoes in Newgrange features.

CHAPTER XIII

THE HOLE AT THE TOP OF THE VAULT

26. Undivided Lozenge   **Possible Reference:**   **Related Site Feature:**

Frame, Gate   Shape of Chamber
                               Aperture

The ring of disks that forms Rosette I surrounds a large plain lozenge which takes up almost the entire space in the middle of the ring. I have suggested that the divided, half-picked lozenges (or squares) which make up the swastikas attached to the passage rungs represent some aspect of the moon, possibly as timekeeper. Divided lozenges are common devices at Newgrange.

Let us imagine how the Newgrangemen visualized the idea of ascent to the sky that is suggested by the set of horizontal rungs as a ladder. The ascent was obviously intended to take place from inside the monument. The run ended with the six rungs right next to the chamber, beside the righthand recess, and the ascent to the sky may have been conceived as taking place from this part of the chamber. The way out of the chamber *upward* would have to be through the lozenge-shaped aperture at the top of the vault. There was a low stone set into the floor of the chamber in front of C17, between R21 and the lefthand portal of the righthand recess, just under the most southeasterly point of the vault-aperture. The only feature of the chamber which it seems to have any relation to is the aperture almost directly above it. It is unornamented.

There was no structural reason why the aperture should have had just the lozenge shape that it has. When the corbels of the vault begin their ascent they start from six places: the passage, the center recess roof, and the four groins. Thus for a while the corbels surround a hexagonal shape, perhaps significant in itself, as similar to the snowflake and the beehive cell. As it ascends, the vault gradually assumes the quadrilateral shape of a rather steep chimney, culminating at the top in that irregular lozenge.

The fact that the aperture is lozenge-shaped may well be intentional. The shape may already have been associated with the moon as timekeeper, represented by the emblem of joined picked and unpicked triangles. If the roofstone was lifted, the moon itself entered the chamber every month. On the other hand, the fact that it was possible to look out of the chamber both day and night might have been reflected in the fact that both picked and unpicked lozenges appear among the devices, in addition to the lozenges divided into picked and unpicked triangles.

What I think was being measured by Rosette I and the bowl as Socket I was the nine-day week, about a third of the sidereal cycle of the moon. But it is possible that the reason this measurement was significant in this funeral setting was that some ritual was being observed which involved the entrance of the moon into the chamber and the exit of a spirit out of it. The shape of the aperture would have been an emblem of ascent and also an emblem of the cunning and crafty planetary power under whose protection the spirit ascended from the chamber. The undivided lozenge is an emblem of the narrow gate between earth and heaven.

27. Boxed Lozenge   **Possible Reference:**   **Related Site Features:**

Aperture Reflected

Shape of Chamber Aperture, Water in Chamber, Hollow Slabs and Bowl

The roofstone of the righthand recess features three excellent *boxed* undivided lozenges. This device, a lozenge within a lozenge, is also found on K67 and on C4.

PLATE XXI. Kerbstone 67

In the case of K67 I would interpret the upper, unboxed lozenge as the emblem of the vault-aperture as gate. The boxed lozenge directly below it could be interpreted as signifying its reflection. The two devices are separated by the linking line of a pair of spirals. Both spirals unwind clockwise, but in following the line back and forth from one to the other the gaze must move alternately clockwise and counterclockwise.

A physical model for reversal would be a sheet of water, reflecting the counterclockwise revolution of the sky as clockwise. We might guess that the undivided plain lozenge on K67 may be intended as an emblem of the chamber aperture, the gate of departure for the spirit, or the gate of entrance for a heavenly body, while the boxed lozenge below it is intended as an emblem of the reflected aperture created by the crucial agent, the water-filled, polarity-transforming bowl below. Reflection as an agency is thus imagined as a concentric, or boxing, frame. The lozenge-shaped outline of the reflection surrounds the lozenge-shaped outline of the vault aperture. Creating concentric outlines is a peculiar talent of a water surface.

On K67, both lozenges contain rather faint (scratched?) chevrons. Cassiopeia and the top of the Milky Way were visible from the righthand and center recesses of the chamber if the capstone was lifted away from the aperture at the top of the vault. The lower chevron device is not reversed as a reflection would be, but is identical to the upper chevron. Thus these chevrons could not be considered a proper reference to Cassiopeia and its reflection. But there is an extra stave added to each double chevron. This may signify that the reference was not to Cassiopeia, but to the Milky Way, whose emblem was the multiple-chevron row. The chevron-chain does not necessarily have the same relationship to its model as Cassiopeia, where the W is a simple copy of the asterism outline and would reverse to an M.

As in the case of K67, I am going to consider the boxed lozenges on the righthand recess roofstone as referring to the reflection of the vault aperture. This was the recess in which water that had filled the bowl or slab frequently provided a reflector. The three boxed lozenges on the roofstone appear between the large central clockwise spiral and the large counterclockwise spiral near the edge of the roofstone, not far from the long row of boxed chevron-chains. That is, the statement of this group would involve reflection as reversing counterclockwise rotation, as on K67, and also, as on K67, a reference to the Milky Way as the object within the aperture.

Two of the boxed lozenges on the roofstone are inserted into the spaces between three circles. This trio of circles is boxed, on the side away from the lozenges, by a triple row of arcs which runs alongside the long, broad band of chevrons, the Milky Way emblem that runs from back to front of the roofstone. Trios of cupmarks are a conspicuous feature of K52, discussed in Chapter XVI as referring to aspects of the interest in tracking cycles.

There is a boxed lozenge on C4, some distance below the two clockwise spirals to the right of the ship marking. The *pair* of spirals would most likely be a reference to the clockwise movement of the sun and moon. At Newgrange, pairs of spirals are usually nearly equal in size and are usually clockwise like the two on C4. It is quite possible that sun and moon were conceived as a couple, female and male or vice versa.

The boxed lozenge could refer to the entrance of both sun and moon through the open vault aperture, and their reflection from a possible film of water, in the slab of the *center* recess from which the top of the ecliptic could be seen. There is some confirmation of this in the fact that *three* boxed lozenges appear on the roofstone: the slab in the lefthand recess was slightly rimmed, and the broken slab in the center recess seems also to have had a rim.

There are also three boxed lozenges on the entrance stone. K1 displays the group in a chain on the left end of the stone. Between those lozenges and the broad groove in the middle of the stone there are three doubled counterclockwise spirals, and on the other side of the groove are two doubled clockwise spirals. The three unlucky spirals are thus bracketed by two lucky panels: the boxed lozenges which indicated reflection on their left, and the two clockwise spirals on the right of the groove. The matched pair of clockwise spirals like the matched pair on C4 probably referred to the sun and moon, which move clockwise with respect to the stars. The trio of counterclockwise spirals may have been intended to be referred to the same three stars whose counterclockwise paths could be viewed from the lefthand recess and may be the models for the devices on the backstone of C4.

K1 makes a positive statement, invoking both the transformational power of water and the transformational planetary powers involved in the cycles that governed the liturgical year. But this most important kerbstone also gives a prominent place to the lozenge-shaped aperture through which the stars and planets could visit the funeral chamber, and through which spirits could leave it for a heavenly realm.

I have suggested that the boxed lozenges refer to reflections of the chamber vault, through which certain stars may be seen. All three recess slabs may have been rimmed and if so they reflected stars framed by the lozenge of the vault aperture. When any planetary body was at the summer solstice-point, it too would have been reflected from water in the basin-stone in the center recess assuming that this broken stone too was rimmed. At certain times part of Cygnus could be seen reflected in water that stood in either the center or the righthand recess, and at certain times the sun and moon could be seen reflected in water standing in a center-recess basin-stone.

Colum's *Treasury of Irish Folklore* (p 431) cites a description of three supernatural beings descending into a well : "When heaven wills the performance of cures, the sky opens above the well, at the hour of midnight, and Christ, and the Virgin Mother, and St. John descend in the form of three snowhites, and descend with the rapidity of lightning into the depths of the fountain. No person but those destined to be cured can see this miraculous phenomenon, but everybody can hear the musical sound of their wings as they rush into the well and agitate the waters." Jewish sufferers more than two thousand years ago sought to enter the water of the pool of Bethzatha at certain times when the water was stirred up by "an angel of the Lord" (John 5).

The reference to the "snowhites" whose wings made a musical sound suggests the old account of the descent of the swans into the sanctuary of Apollo. The image of three swans also recalls the tale of the bewitched children of Lir, a sister and three brothers. Lir's best known offspring was Manannan, who has distinct lunar traits. The inclusion of St. John, presumably John the Baptist, is interesting; this saint was peculiarly the saint of water, and the Christianized trio would include him as a reference to the old weather god.

CHAPTER XIV

THE WHEELING SKY

In discussing the righthand recess roofstone, I suggested that the undivided lozenges on that surface, unboxed and boxed, represented not the moon as timekeeper but the chamber aperture and its reflected image respectively. This is a possible interpretation of the arrangement of lozenges and spirals on K67. K67 also displays most conspicuously another device that occurs a number of times at Newgrange. This is the net. Nets are called chequey or lozengey depending on whether they are made with intersecting horizontal and vertical lines like a checkerboard, or with intersecting diagonals. In chess the rooks see the net of the board as chequey, the bishops see it as lozengey. Almost all of the nets at Newgrange are lozengey.

If we may accept the interpretation of the undivided lozenge as the outline of the chamber aperture, we could see the lozengey net as a chain-like or net-like pattern imagined to be cast upon the sky by the lozenge-shaped chamber aperture as the heavens revolve behind it. Both stars and planetary bodies were caught in the net cast on the sky by the cunningly placed aperture.

28. Lozengey Net	**Possible Reference:**	**Related Site Feature:**
	The Pattern Cast by the Vault-Aperture Outline on the Sky	Lozenge-Shaped Chamber Aperture, Revolution of the Heavens above it

It would have been a combination of its marvelous net and the spring (or leak) in its righthand recess that made Newgrange unique. This would explain why examples of the lozengey net are not only numerous but also among the best-executed devices on site stones. A one-row lozengey net, or chain appears on K1, a superb net on K52, and two nets separated by a group of eight picked triangles on K67. Among other examples are a net of eleven lozenges attached to the clockwise spiral on C2, composed of four vertical rows of lozenges, alternating picked and plain. I have already discussed the net on C 16. A chain of lozenges is created in the spaces between picked saltires in a row on Corbel l of C2, above a doubled chevron row.

I conjectured that picked or dark lozenges might have been intended to represent the night outview, and plain or light lozenges the day outview, which alternated in the outview from the vault.

A few nets appear on hidden stones including K13 Back and K18 Back. K13 back includes a rather disorganized chain of unpicked lozenges. Upper spaces in the unpicked chain have been enclosed by lines to form triangles, and in one of the triangles is one of the fish-spine devices which I have interpreted as a tally. K 18 Back includes a net of thirteen lozenges The points of two of the upper lozenges are connected by a line to form a triangle, and a circle is attached to the lefthand triangle. Triangle and circle might have been intended to refer to the moon and sun in this net device.

Also hidden, within the so-called Relieving Lintel, are net-like devices on stones X, Y and Z. On Stone Y there is a seemingly unfinished design consisting of ten parallel vertical lines which divide six or seven lozenges vertically (as the stone now lies; it could hardly have been carved in this position). There is a fascinating cloverleaf mini-net of three picked lozenges, the two side leaves *boxed*, on Stone X and on the other side of this stone there is doubled chevron chain with a boxed lozenge right of it and an unboxed lozenge left of it. What looks like a partially completed boxed lozenge is above the chevron chain.

Stone Z displays a scratched pair of lozenges joined at their points. From the upper left side of the lefthand lozenge is a "ladder," and from the lower right of the righthand lozenge is a ladder with another attached to its side. This little device may have referred to the concept of ascent expressed in the passage rungs, joined with the vault's gate of passage from earth to heaven. The stone embedded in the floor of the chamber in front of C17 happens to be in a position suitable for the foot of a ladder leading up to the far side of the chamber aperture. The ladder was a very old emblem of ascent to the heavens. Hathor was supposed to hold one for departed spirits. A ladder has been imported into Christian iconography, being often included in pictures of the crucifixion. The popular belief that it is bad luck to walk under a ladder probably long antedates the Christian use of this emblem.

29. **Chequey net**	**Possible Reference:**	**Related Site Feature:**
	Astronomical Grid	Roofbox Orientation, Roofbox Rectangular Shape, Revolution of the Heavens Beyond it.

The roofbox lintel device may be the only example of a chequey net in the site.

PLATE **XXII**. Roofbox Lintel

The roofbox lintel bears a chain of eight squares or rectangles containing triangles that form saltires. The squares could be read as a one-row net or chain. The sketch indicates, by dotted lines, how the device might be completed as part of a chequey net. (The stone just under this decorated lintel is the one in which a curious sandstone concretion, described in Chapter XX was found.)

The chequey chain appears over the sun's special entrance-portal, the aperture that provides the spectacular midwinter sunrise observation. This astronomical interest, with its ancillary mathematics, was probably the latest of the three conjoined interests which are found integrated into Newgrange afterlife belief and practice. The two devices interpreted as tallies, and the rosettes interpreted as references to a counting method, seem to show that these genuinely scientific developments played a significant role in the religious system of this culture.

The only other device that seems to be interpretable as a chequey net is perhaps, in some special sense, the set of picked triangles on R12. The interpretation is possible because the mated triangles really have the form of squares rather than lozenges, and they are set on their sides not their points. I pointed out that there are resemblances between the lintel and R12, which like the lintel lies on the solstitial axis.

The roofbox is focused on the solstition, an element of the *astronomical* grid, which is formally anchored by the pole of the ecliptic and the celestial pole. The solstitial colure is an element of that grid. The lines of the lozengey net cast by the lozenge of the chamber aperture over the revolving heavens lie at an angle to the lines of the chequey astronomical grid.

The Newgrange righthand recess provided a crucial focus on the Milky Way, and this focus was partnered by the lefthand recess's focus on the circumpolar rotor. The lozengey net, which lies obliquely over the astronomical grid, predominates in Newgrange engraved design, because the afterlife interest of the faith was originally focused on the galaxy. The polar height seems to have been early, widely, and very naturally revered as a seat of supreme celestial power, manifesting itself most dramatically as weather. It was probably considerably later that the way reflection seemingly changed the direction of the circumpolar whorl was added to the interest in the weather god as a transformational feature demonstrating a control over time, seen as an aspect of the supreme power. The figure of Whirlwind the Whistler combines the aerial spiral with the voice of the wind. Lozengey and chequey nets appear together in Greek Geometric art. The two kinds of grids are related to the device which is discussed in the next section: the cartouche with enclosed half-circles.

CHAPTER XV

CELESTIAL AXES

I have discussed the nine-based counting-rosettes on the roofstone, and have explained their possible relationship to the marbles and sockets which could have functioned as a kind of abacus for keeping track of solar-lunar cycles, using powers of nine. Important as this concept is, it is not the rosettes that are honored with the central position in the roofstone. The center of the roofstone is occupied by a curious device which has some unexpected implications and some unexpected analogs in a number of cultures around the Mediterranean.

The builders of Newgrange had reason to interest themselves in the location of the north celestial pole. In the chapter on Circumpolar Shapes, I discussed the Thumb, the Drinking Vessel or Horn, and the Noose, peculiar outlines which are repeated on a number of surfaces at Newgrange and which are especially conspicuous along the solstitial axis. I pointed out asterisms with similar outlines that could have helped locate the starless celestial pole of Newgrange times. The lefthand recess is oriented in such a way that pole pointers were visible from this position, and the three counterclockwise-unwinding spirals which are engraved on the backstone of this recess may refer to three stars close to the pole.

The most conspicuous were the three in the handle of the Dipper, part of the arc, or pad of the Thumb. These three stars, η or Alkaid, Arabic for "Chief of the Mourners," ζ or Mizar, "Groin of the Bear," and ε or Alioth, "Bull," may also be represented by the three counterclockwise spirals that appear together in great splendor on the Entrance Stone. The references of the three Arabic names reveal three different conceptions of the constellation. The reference to Mourners is significant for us here; several traditions preserve the name Bier for Ursa Major, connecting the constellation with death.

Mizar is conspicuous for its small "rider" Alcor. Between the two upper counterclockwise spirals on C3 there is a curious eccentric spiral form of indeterminate polarity. The spiral form is squashed into a somewhat rectangular figure, facing toward the smaller of the upper spirals. It is conceivable that this referred to Alcor. The path of one star could reasonably be represented by a spiral, but the idea broke down when confronted by the problem of representing a group of stars.

The noon shadow that helped locate the solstice fell due north, and the groins of the chamber are roughly oriented to the cardinal points. These builders knew not only the location of the north celestial pole but also the location of the winter solstice, which was observable through the roofbox, and of the summer solstice, which was observable from the openable chamber vault. If the fan-stick and fish-spine types of devices can be understood as tallies for fixing the dates of midsummer and midwinter, these devices as well as the winter-solstice orientation show that these extreme positions of the sun were of importance.

The summer solstition is located almost a Dipper-length above the equatorial circle, and the winter solstition is located the same distance below it. Since the Newgrangemen could locate both of these positions it would have been impossible for them not to see that the point midway between them was not the north celestial pole but a point well removed from it: twenty-three and a half degrees to be exact. This point is the north pole of the ecliptic. The ecliptic and the equatorial circle intersect at the spring and fall equinoxes, whose dates fall midway between the solstices.

The north pole of the ecliptic is permanently fixed within the first coil of the constellation Draco. It is about twenty-three degrees below the celestial pole, and of course revolves around it every day with the rest of the firmament.

The solstitial colure passes through both poles. But the equinoctial colure, which is at right angles to the solstitial colure, passes through the pole of the ecliptic only. The equinoctial and solstitial colures cross at right angles on the ecliptic circle, that circle which the north pole of the ecliptic describes every twenty-four hours around the north celestial pole. The equinoctial colure is thus tangent to the ecliptic circle.

The ability to understand this complicated celestial design might well have been valued as the crown jewel of the Newgrangemen's astronomical skills.

There is one device which suggests that they did possess and prize this knowledge. The device appears as a complete figure in only one place, the center of the roofstone of the righthand recess, perhaps Newgrange's holy of holies.

Since the carving on the roofstone runs back beyond the orthostats which support it, the roofstone must have been carved before the recess was roofed.

30. Facing Circle-Segments **Possible Reference:**   **Related Site Features:**
   in Ellipse   North Celestial Pole   Openable Roofbox,
                            and North Pole of   Raisable Chamber
                            Ecliptic   Capstone, Orientations
                                                   of Lefthand and Center
See Plate XIX and Fig. 10   Recesses

The compact quadruple ellipse which appears in almost the exact center of the roofstone is a device which may be interpreted as a kind of diagram of the relationship of the two poles and the astronomical grid dependent on them.

This device consists of four small ellipses nested concentrically. Fitted within the inmost ellipse are two small facing half-circles. I will refer to them as half-circles for convenience, but they are pulled out toward each other just a little further than their half-way-marks, so that they look very slightly jar-shaped. Each half-circle fits into one curved end of the inmost ellipse. The straight lines that cut each half-circle are parallel to each other, and the half-circles face each other at a little distance, which is in fact about half the radius of each circle. The outside ellipse is about seven inches long, and each of the little half-circles is about an inch and a half long. The device is diagrammed, and its elements identified in Figure 11 (next page).

The ellipse device may be analyzed as follows. One of the little half-circles in the center of the cartouche corresponds to one half of the circle of the ecliptic. The other one corresponds to one half of the circle of the equator. The center or pole of each half-circle must lie in the middle of the straight line which has (approximately) halved it. The distance which separates the two parallel lines would represent the twenty-three-degree distance between the equinoctial and equatorial poles.

The long axis of the cartouche, which would pass through the centers of both half-circles, corresponds to the solstitial colure, which passes through both poles. At midwinter (and midsummer), the solstitial colure is on the meridian at midnight and at noon. That is, the solstitial colure then lies directly overhead, due north and south, coinciding with the north-south line through the north celestial pole. The chamber groins lie close to the cardinal points. The equinoctial colure and the east-west line at this time are parallel to each other, both perpendicular to the soltitial colure.

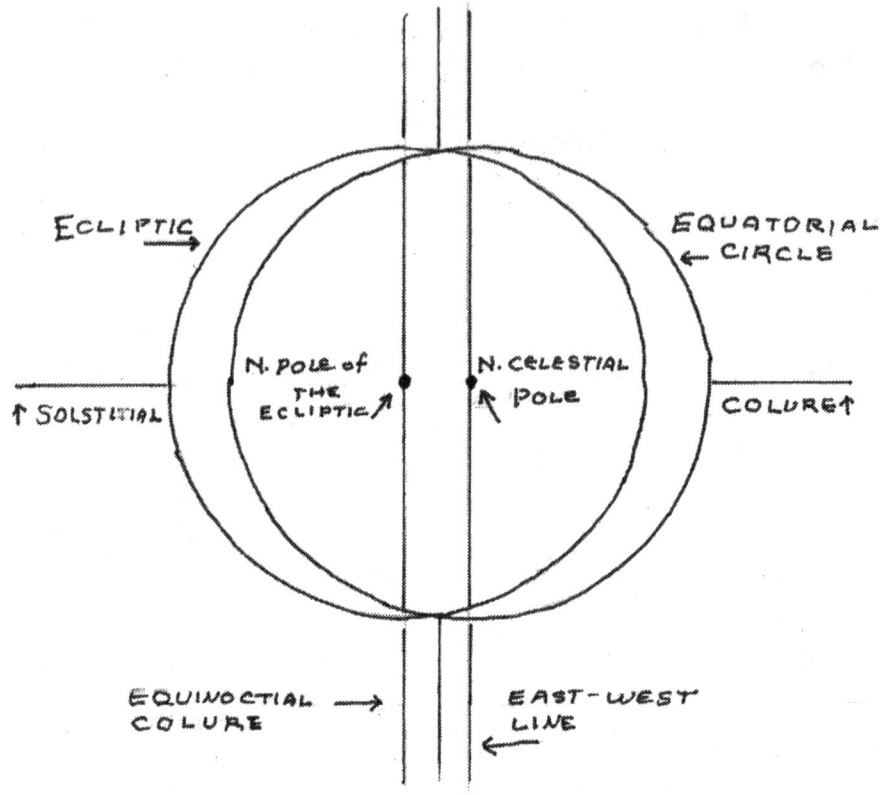

FIG. 11. Analysis of Ellipse Device

The parallel line which cuts the half-circle representing part of the ecliptic circle represents the equinoctial colure, passing through the pole of the ecliptic where it intersects the solstitial colure. The parallel line which cuts the half-circle that represents half of the equatorial circle belongs to the line that passes through the north celestial pole from due east to due west.

The reason that the roofstone diagram is an ellipse is that it is drawn around the *outside* halves of both celestial circles. Since the solstitial colure is taken to be the long axis of the ellipse, the half circles must represent the outside halves of their respective circles. The half- circle that represents half of the *ecliptic* must represent its winter half, when the sun's path lies outside, or south of, the arc of the celestial equator. The winter half of the *equatorial* circle, lying within the ecliptic, is not shown by the neolithic diagram. The opposite half circle represents the equatorial circle at midsummer, when the ecliptic arc lies *within* the equatorial arc. The summer half of the ecliptic, lying within the equatorial circle, is not shown. The diagram is a reduction, two half-circles short of the fact. We have already observed that the Newgrange engravers had developed an interest in reduction, expressed in devices on R12, R21, K4, and C8 for example.

Although both inner halves are omitted, the outline faithfully indicates the configuration which obtained overhead at midwinter. We are virtually sure that midwinter was celebrated at dawn at Newgrange. As the celebration was almost certainly preceded by a nocturnal vigil, the elegant symmetrical midnight configuration of the four celestial coordinates was familiar to the stone-age participants.

We see in this interpretation of the Newgrange ellipse a possible origin and explanation for the elliptical cartouche used in Egypt to outline or "italicize" information that has supernatural references, like the divine name of a king. When a line is drawn around both the winter loop of the ecliptic and the summer loop of the equator, the elliptical figure formed is suffused with supreme supernatural power because it binds into one emblem the dynamic hubs of two great driving powers: one governs the sun, moon, and planets, the other moves the stars. A well-known Egyptian picture interpreted as showing "upper and lower *Egypt*" being bound together may at the very least owe something to this supremely significant emblem.

Examples of other potent traditional outlines that may be related to this two-pole emblem are the Venus mirror, the Ankh, and the double axe. The loop at the top of the Ankh is pulled out along the stem, so that the center of the circular segment is higher than the juncture of the loop with the stem. However, the emblem may owe some of its power to the teardrop shape of the loop.

I noted above that the half-circles in the ends of the ellipse are slightly pursed where they face each other, that is each is a little more than half a circle. It is just possible that this may be a token reference to the midsummer configuration. The ellipse figure is generated by the fact that the poles of the two circles, and their outside arcs, are twenty-three and a half degrees apart. As seen in my analytical version of the device, another figure is generated in the middle of the design by the inside intersection of the two arcs, not indicated in the device itself. This is a kind of very fat lentoid or leaf-shaped figure, sometimes designated a "lance-head" outline.

The elliptical figure is unique among the outlines on the roofstone in being absolutely static. In contrast, the eight-petal rosettes were (as I have interpreted them) counted around, like a kind of circular abacus. Serpentine devices which may have represented the undulating lunar path represented motion. The chevrons were in long chains as if they were unrolling around the sky, which in a sense they were. Spirals compel the gaze to revolve with them. In contrast, the ellipse or cartouche is the written name, or emblem, of the linked poles of the ecliptic and the celestial pole, expressed as a supreme dyad: fixed, invulnerable, invincible.

But in fact, one element of it is in motion.

Newgrange was built with two side chambers that permitted outviews through the openable vault and only through the vault. Unlike the solstitial orientation, these views were vulnerable to precession. Precession is the slow drift caused by a wobble in the rotation of the earth which forces our north celestial pole to describe a circle with a radius of twenty-three and a half degrees around the north pole of the ecliptic every 25,000 years. Since Newgrange was built, the pole has completed a fifth of the circle it began in the time of the cave painters who shared our own pole-star Cynosura.

As the north celestial pole circles ponderously around the pole of the ecliptic over the eons it is dragging the equinoctial colure around with it, as a tangent to the ecliptic circle. As the equinoctial colure is dragged around the ecliptic it sweeps the equinoxes backward around the zodiac, at the rate of about one degree every seventy-two years. This is the precession of the equinoxes. The colures move backwards or counterclockwise along the zodiacal circle, opposite to the direction in which the sun moves through the signs of the zodiac, hence another unlucky manifestation of left-handedness. (In the northern hemisphere if we look "down" at the sun from the north, we see it travel through the zodiac in a direction opposite to the perceived counterclockwise daily rotation of the heavens, and so it is from this standpoint that planetary bodies move clockwise.)

We know that the drift of the north celestial pole was bound to pull the outviews of Newgrange's side recesses out of sight. One would have to suppose either that the builders did not know that the north celestial pole was in motion or that they did not care how long their complex of sightlines was going to remain intact. The cartouche on the roofstone reflects only the fact that the two poles are separated in the sky, that they govern two great hubs of power, and that their respective circles intersect, defining the solstices and the equinoxes. All of this must certainly have been learned before it could have been known that the celestial pole was in motion.

The unique elliptical device, centered above Newgrange's solemn font, can be recognized in other ancient pictorial contexts. At Newgrange it has been placed in what is perhaps the spiritual center of the entire site. Commenting on examples of the same or basically similar outlines Roland Hampe [op.cit. p. 50] calls this type of device "a motif which in Minoan and Mycenaean art often symbolizes the sacredness of a place." The examples to which he refers, and which he illustrates, present the device as an architectural element, in a form in which half-circles or half-ellipses define the outline, and are developed into rosettes (which may in itself be significant). The same motif may be observed in an often shown Mycenean signet ring of the 15th century BC where facing ellipses are replicated as a frieze beneath a scene with supernatural beings.

But an elliptical device that appears in certain Anatolian rock reliefs is very much like the one on the Newgrange roofstone. Larousse's *Mythology* [1968] shows three examples:

(1) From Yazilikaya, 13th century BC, Hurrian (p. 81) In the central portion of the frieze the "Sun Goddess of Arinna" followed by her son, both standing upon lions, greet the "Weather God," who stands upon two "mountain gods." The elliptical device is equipped with naturalistically depicted walking legs and feet, and is held by the son of the Sun Goddess so that the toe of its advancing foot rests on her shoulder.

(2) From Malatya, 8th (?) century BC (p.78) The elliptical device appears above the bull-drawn chariot of a "weather god" who holds a "boomerang" and a three-stick "fan."

(3) From Yazilikaya, 13th century BC, Hurrian, (p. 77). The elliptical device, equipped with walking legs and feet, is held by the god Sharrupa.

(4) Another example appears in Seton Lloyd's *Early Anatolia* (Pl. 21 and p. 176). From Ivriz in Taurus, 8th century BC, Syro-Hittite. The ellipse (footless) appears in a relief where it is the highest device in a complex of small motifs just adjacent to the head of the god Tarhundas (Pl. 21 and p.176).

As in the case of the Minoan and Mycenean examples, the Anatolian device always occupies a place of supreme honor in the groups of supernatural beings among which it occurs. But these representations differ in one significant respect from the Newgrange emblem. As noted above, some of the Anatolian examples are not static devices. The walking feet with which the device may be equipped in the open-air Anatolian examples show that here, two thousand years after

Newgrange, it was clearly understood that this feature of the heavens was not static. These walking feet are exactly like those which appear as the Egyptian determinative sign for "motion." The fate of Newgrange and other similar monuments may have helped educate the then-civilized world about precession.

We turn to another feature of the Anatolian examples that must interest us here. They occur in special physical environments. In the first place they were placed in the open air and therefore were not vulnerable to precession. Second, Lloyd [*op.cit.*202] cites Barnett as noting of Phrygian rock monuments that "the area in which they are located covers the sources of all the principal rivers of Phrygia...He shows, furthermore that almost without exception the monuments stand near to, if not actually facing, springs of fresh water..." He continues:

> "The question is of course at once raised as to whether this was a characteristic peculiar to the Phrygian monuments, and the answer, on consideration, is emphatically negative. If all the Hittite rock monuments which we have mentioned or described...be again called into account it will be recollected that almost every single one of them, from Yazilikaya beside its dried-up spring at Boghazköy to the Sirkeli relief overlooking the waters of the Jeyhan river in Cilicia, is in some way closely connected with a supply of fresh water. Finally, when one recollects that the Younger Storm God of Hittite mythology was 'a god of rocks and waters,' it becomes more and more hard to regard this as a coincidence, and one is driven to the conclusion that, both by the Hittites and later by the Phrygians, a bare vertical rock beside or near a source of water was deemed holy and a cult set up there, served by an open-air shrine."

At Newgrange a vertical rock face was present at the back of the righthand recess, and a spring (or leak) delivered fresh water from somewhere above the rock face into the slab or bowl below (possibly over a slightly in-slanted corbel), which reflected the elliptical device in the center of the roofstone.

Aegean examples of the elliptical figure had been developed into rosettes, and rosettes are also featured in many if not most Anatolian reliefs. The largest features on the Newgrange roofstone are the three great rosettes, and I have explained that these devices may be interpreted as involved in a nine-based number system used, and perhaps used only, to keep track of solar and lunar cycles.

The number of petals in the Mycenean and Minoan rosettes varies, as do most Anatolian examples. George Coffey calls attention to five Scandinavian sword-pommels in which eight elements surround the boss: in one they are spirals; in three, concentric circles; and in one, dots. Coffey was much interested in the spiral and devoted a good deal of attention to showing the similarities of Newgrange examples to Mycenean motifs, an interest which seems prescient in the present context. Included in a group of eight patterns from the Aegean, which he presents apropos of his discussion of spirals, are several examples which look as if they might be related to the Newgrange ellipse. The first of the two fragments from Mycenae which he presents (in his fig. 47) contains the main elements of the Newgrange elliptical device, decorated with ornamental framing dots.

In the Newgrange context, where the ellipse and eight-lobed rosettes appear together in the center of the most spectacular panel in the most solemn recess, it is possible to see how these emblems might have worked together. Newgrange's central recess was designed to observe the midwinter solstice (and probably the midsummer solstice as well), and its lefthand recess was designed to observe circumpolar stars. Engraved devices at the site may be interpreted as referring to both features. The righthand recess contains not only a device picturing the essential elements of the astronomical grid, but a possible counting system represented both by the rosettes on the roofstone and by the marbles and sockets, a possible counting apparatus.

One Yazilikaya relief featured a Hurrian "Sun Goddess of Arinna" and a supreme "Weather God" together with the ellipse. In these figures we may see examples of the kinds of personalities that might have been attached to the sun and the circumpolar "rotor": the marriage of two great ruling powers, one a weather-god located in the height of the heavens, perhaps represented by the celestial pole, and the other a sun goddess based on the pole of the ecliptic. The son of the sun goddess, who walks behind her on one panel, would represent a lunar power. The ellipse device appears over each of these three figures.

The Hurrian queen who, as co-regent with a Hittite king around 1250 BC may have been responsible for the Hurrian pantheon that appears at Yazilikaya, is known to have sent scribes south to Cilicia for tablets describing the proper ritual for the His'uwa festival. It has been questioned whether this festival is not similar to the vis-uwa festival, a winter solstice festival of ancient India. It is possible that the ellipse-device over the heads of the divine beings in the

(Hurrian?) pantheon has special reference to midwinter, just as may have been the case at Newgrange.

The ellipse with facing half-circles in the Yazilikaya reliefs, the versions of the ellipse device found in Minoan or Mycenean art, and the ellipse used as a cartouche in Egyptian texts are all usually placed in a way that shows that their context is sacred. The immense, often solemn significance which is attached to such two-focus figures must also have characterized the Newgrange ellipse, placed as it is.

31. Tangents.	**Possible Reference:**	**Related Site Features:**
⊙|⊙	Equinoctial Colure and Ecliptic Circle	Same as for Ellipse

There are several devices among Newgrange petroglyphs which might be interpreted as reductions or shorthand abbreviations of the elliptical device on the righthand recess roofstone. Other devices that seem to reveal an interest in reduction have already been described.

A circle to which a tangent is attached, or chains of circles linked by tangents, have been described as failed, or false, spirals. Coffey reproduces a number of them and interprets them this way. However, there is another model for them. As explained above, the pole of the ecliptic is revolving daily around the north celestial pole, describing the ecliptic circle. As the equinoctial and solstitial colures intersect on the circumference of the ecliptic circle, the equinoctial colure is tangent to the ecliptic circle. The pole of the ecliptic daily circles the celestial pole, dragging the tangent around the horizon.

Thus the circle and tangent could serve as a shorthand emblem for the system of coordinates. It would not be unreasonable to link these tangents in chains, to show that the tangent moves around the sky. It would be the same kind of thinking that would suggested replicating the lozenge into a chain to indicate the movement of the frame over the sky.

This interpretation of the circle and tangent may help explain several devices.

The back of K13 is divided roughly into quarters by cracks or planes on its surface. The horizontal division separates two surfaces meeting at an obtuse angle. In the upper righthand corner of the upper lefthand quadrant, almost in the center of the stone, there is a very bold device, about six inches long, a rough oval or ellipse whose long axis is vertical, and which contains a bold center dot. Touching the lower end of the ellipse and perpendicular to its long axis is a horizontal line, and dropping perpendicularly from the point at which the horizontal touches the oval, also on the long axis of the ellipse, is a short line. This part of the device looks a little like a crude Venus mirror, the outline long used as a symbol of the planet. At the end of the perpendicular "handle" are a circle and a cupmark, touching each other. The device might refer in some way to the configuration suggested by the ellipse on the roofstone with the addition of the circle and cupmark to suggest an eclipse, situated south of the poles on the solstitial colure.

K88 displays two rude circles of about the same size, almost touching, and just to their left there is a dot-centered circle surrounded by a cluster of fan-sticks.

On K95, three kerbstones to the right of the passage entrance, there is a pair of dot-centered circles, with a fairly straight line between them. The line is perpendicular to a line that could be drawn through the dots, thus parallel to tangents that might be drawn to the circles, so that it might refer in some way to the equinoctial colure.

Corbel 1 above C7 in the center recess includes two of the fan-stick devices that may refer to the solstice. On the lefthand edge of the stone are two multiple-boxed, tangent disks whose centers are linked by a straight line. From the center of the righthand disk there is drawn another line, almost perpendicular to the straight line, which would thus be tangent to the two circles. A large cupmark is attached to the outside of the larger circle, and as in other combinations of disk with paired circles and tangents, the cupmark might refer to a solar eclipse. Near the middle of the corbel is a very large picked disk. One model for a completely darkened disk would be a total solar eclipse.

A circle with tangent, a possible shorthand version of the ellipse with facing half-circles on the Newgrange roofstone, appears as a royal, ceremonial emblem in representations of the Assyro-Babylonian divinity Shamash, who has been associated with the sun. He grasps a rod with tangent circle in his right hand. This is the way he appears in a famous stela that shows him dictating the laws to King Hammurabi, dated around 2000 BC. Showing the king holding the tangent rod and circle, a possible emblem of supreme *celestial* law, would be a fitting way to give legitimacy to the king's great legal code.

32. Paired circle devices   **Possible Reference:**   **Related Site Features:**

Twin Celestial Poles   Same as for Ellipse

On the back corbel of the roofbox there is a pair of circles whose center dots are in line with the central dots of a fanstick device behind them. I would guess that this might be the pair of celestial poles, purposely linked here, by their position and the nearby fansticks, with the solstitial determination. Just below the dot in the middle of the fan-sticks is another dot with an emphatic arch over it. A dot with well-defined arch also appears twice on Corbel 1 C7, which is also on the solstitial axis and also bears fan-sticks. It is possible that this dot with arch was intended to refer to the pole of the ecliptic. It might also simply refer to the gnomon. The solstitial observation was linked to this configuration.

There are two definite pairs of disks on RS3. One pair is enclosed in an ellipse, and the two disks touch each other.

33. Broken egg   **Possible Reference:**   **Related Site Features:**

Ellipse as Cosmic   Same As for Ellipse

Egg?

On K18 there is a rough ellipse or oval that seems to be divided in the middle by a crooked line across the middle, so that it looks like a broken egg. Both K13 and K18, were found with their carved surfaces facing in to the mound. They must have been moved from other positions, and in style are much like stones X, Y, and Z in the "relieving lintel," stones whose designs are also now hidden.

Two facing half-ellipses resemble a halved or broken egg. Several kinds of eggs are elliptical, including those of the turtle, the ant, some birds, and certain snakes. A little forward of the elliptical figure on the roofstone are several serpentiform lines which resemble snake tracks. The serpentiform track of the moon as it loops over and under the ecliptic has often been compared with a snake or dragon. The constellation Hydra, the Water Snake, bears witness to this imagery.

The Norse fairy story of "The Giant Who Had No Heart in His Body" contains a version of a formula very common in fairytales: "Far, far away there is a lake and in that lake there is an isle, and on that isle there is a church, and in that church there is a well, and in that well there is a duck, and in that duck there is an egg and in that egg there lies my Heart." The hero kills the giant by breaking the egg.

This nest of images also occurs in stories about Koschei the Deathless, a Russian supernatural being who often tears the Russian fairytale hero away from his bride and his kingdom. Ralston [*Russian Fairy Tales* , p. 96]. says "Sometimes he is described as altogether serpent-like in form; sometimes he seems to be of a mixed nature, partly human and partly ophidian, but in some of the stories he is apparently framed after the fashion of a man." Ralston refers to Transylvanian-Saxon, Bohemian, and Gaelic versions of the "nested" supernatural egg. He states that Koschei's death is sometimes caused by being struck on the forehead by a supernatural egg. He also cites versions that place the duck inside a hare, which is an almost universal emblem of the moon. Both hare and egg are easily recognized in the forms of the lunar shadows and are the model of the egg-bearing Easter bunny.

There is a nested series of emblems at Newgrange that has similarities to this common module. Within the heart-shaped mound there is a shrine, and within the shrine there is a pool, and within the pool is the reflection of a water bird (stars of Cygnus), and also the reflection of the elliptical Egg.

Perhaps the model of this broken egg, as of other two-focus emblems, is the two celestial poles, linked together in the northern skies. One of these great hubs of power is the pole around which the heavens revolve. The other is the pole around which the sun, moon, and planets revolve. The directions of rotation traditionally affect human life quite differently. The counterclockwise rotation of the stars is associated with time and death.

Representing rotation by a spiral made it possible to distinguish polarity. Either power may be emblemized as a serpent. Asclepius had a snake-wound staff and was sometimes pictured as half serpent. Athene's son Erichthonius was also pictured as half serpent. Both of these classical figures inherited vials of Gorgon's blood: blood from one vein killed, blood from the other resurrected the dead (the veins may be specified as left and right respectively). Hermes, who guided departed spirits on their journey into the afterworld, had a snake-wound staff as emblem, the caduceus. Iris also carried the caduceus.

The constellation Cygnus ends just above Serpens Cauda the "Tail of the Snake,"and like Asclepius, Cygnus himself may have been pictured as a snake-man. One of his emblems was a serpent, the other was a lion. The lion is conspicuous for its mane, and it is thus a suitable emblem of the solar eclipse, when the sun displays its coronal mane. It would have been natural to picture the sun as the wife of a power whose home was at the height of the heavens, and Cygnus, whose name may be related to a word for "sing," blown sound, wind, may once have figured as this power.

Any power living in the height of the heavens relates itself naturally to weather: storms accompanied by lightning and thunderbolt; winds including cyclonic forms; clouds, rain and snow, and auroral fire, not to mention the whole army of the stars which wheel around the central hub. The circumpolar whorl is also master of time. At Yazilikaya this power was the Weather God.

The power of the sun which moves clockwise is linked to the source of warmth, light, germination, the renewal of life that begins at the winter solstice. At Newgrange the sun may also have been specially linked to the magic power it reveals in the flash of the dewdrop and the bridge of the rainbow. At Yazilikaya the Sun Goddess of Arinna is the consort of the Weather God.

The persona of the moon might have been pictured as the son of the sun and the weather-god. In the relief he walks behind his mother. He would have inherited some of the Weather-God's serpent tendencies, reinforced by the moon's serpentine track over and under the ecliptic. In several North European languages as in the Yazilikaya reliefs the sun is feminine and the moon masculine. The weather god is always masculine. Both mother and son stand upon lions. This is because both together are involved in the appearance of the bristling coronal mane that makes the lion an emblem of the eclipsed sun.

All three figures are distinguished by the elliptical emblem over their heads. Weather god, sun and moon were the three agents who acted out a scenario that repeats itself again and again in traditional stories: "He marries his daughter; she runs off with their son." Most versions of this scenario are violently wrenched awry in efforts to explain away the appearance of incest which develops because there are only three acting figures.

The outviews and petroglyphs of Newgrange may be interpreted as revealing an interest in the celestial triad. The three would have been conceived as superhuman personalities, the supreme father, the daughter/wife, and the son/

lover. They would have been developed around the celestial rotor, recognized by the lefthand recess orientation and spiral emblem; the sun, recognized by the solstitial orientation, disks and concentric arches; and the moon, recognized by the emphasis on the triangle and a counting system that originated with the lunar cycle.

In the Yazilikaya reliefs, two female figures follow the son of the Sun Goddess. These might have represented the inferior planets Venus and Mercury, which always remain near the sun. Two (or three?) male figures appear with the Weather God as he greets his wife. These, then, might have represented the superior planets Mars, Jupiter and Saturn. From the Newgrange chamber all of the planetary bodies were visible as they crossed the solstitial colures on their circuits of the ecliptic.

But the constellation Cygnus in itself has the three-limbed outline of the snakeman, and also runs down into the constellation Serpens Cauda "Snake Tail." It was perhaps the choice of the spiral as the emblem of rotation that suggested the image of the one-dimensional coiling snake. That choice would itself have been suggested by the perception that reflection reversed the polarity of the spiral. The reversal of polarity had been associated with regeneration. Thus the spirit, whose father was the polar whorl, might have been represented as balanced on a snake.

Reinforcing the power of the spiral emblem would be the fact that striking chains of chevrons and lozenges, like the devices common at Newgrange, appear on the backs of many snakes including the common British viper. The turtle has a reptilian aspect. The fused plates of its shell form a net pattern like the net the Newgrange vault casts on the sky, and the four stout legs at its four corners bear up its vaulted shell as the Newgrange four-groined chamber sustains its plated vault.

Both Chinese and Egyptian tradition employ the egg as emblem. C.A.S.Williams (in his *Outlines of Chinese Symbolism and Art Motives*) quotes from Davis *The Chinese* as follows:

> "Chinese philosophers speak of the origin of all created things under the name of T'ai-chi. This is represented in their books by a figure, which is thus formed: On the semi-diameter of a given circle describe a semi-circle, and on the remaining semi-diameter, but on the other side, describe another semi-circle. The whole figure represents the T'ai-chi, and the two divided portions, formed by the curved line, typify what are called the Yin and the

Yang, in respect to which this Chinese mystery bears a singular parallel to that extraordinary fiction of Egyptian mythology, the supposed intervention of a masculo-feminine principle in the development of the mundane ["world-"] egg. The T'ai-chi is said to have produced the Yang and the Yin, the active and passive, or male and female principle, and these last to have produced all things."

This figure can be seen at Newgrange in the doubled spirals, where the line reverses in the middle of the device.

The ellipse device may be interpreted as a diagram of the way the two celestial poles, as two great centers of power, are related to each other. But the two facing half-disks or circles also suggest reflection, which was used at Newgrange as an emblem of transformation in the form of reversing spirals, and the inversion of an image. The facing half-disks of the ellipse are enclosed in concentric ellipses, which shows that both parts were intended to be seen as a fused or "married" pair. We have seen this supreme dyad carved over the heads of the three main divinities in the Yazilikiya reliefs. It would have been an emblem of a supreme manifestation of natural law.

The ellipse on the righthand recess roofstone at Newgrange must have been in place before the building was completed, so that it seems doubtful whether the builders were aware of precession. But because the aperture at the top of the chamber vault was so narrow, the fact must have become obvious within a couple of generations. Many ancient traditions about supernatural beings involve a fatal conflict and transfer of hegemony from one group of divine powers to another. When it became obvious that the solstices were fixed in relation to the pole, while the constellations in which they occurred were not, power associated with the pole of the ecliptic and the planetary powers must have gained prestige at the expense of the power associated with the celestial pole, that is, the Weather God.

Some evidence in the physical fabric of Newgrange can be interpreted to suggest that its present configuration, focused on the solstice, is not original, but a re-tooling of a monument that once had two other outviews that were dependent on the celestial pole, including the Milky Way and Cassiopeia, and certain Dipper stars. If so Newgrange was a battleground of two once-married hegemonies. The planetary powers won.

CHAPTER XVI

TRACKING TIME

Kerbstone 52, like K1, is divided into two separate panels by a broad groove. The stone is almost directly opposite K1, on the other side of the mound, which led to the belief that the rumored lost passage lay behind the groove on K52, just as the sunrise passage lies behind the groove of K1. Such a groove also occurs on a stone before the west passage entrance at Knowth. O'Kelly's extensive excavation behind K52 did not reveal the passage, though it confirmed the existence beneath the Newgrange mound of a more ancient mound, this one built of turf. As on K1, the groove on K52 separates two different ideas.

PLATE XXIII. Kerbstone 52

On the left is a lozengey net, the emblem that is a tribute to the uncanny intelligence and skill of the great "smith" who designed Newgrange, its architect and engineer. Above the net are two center-reversing or doubled clockwise spirals, probably references to the chief celestial luminaries, moon and sun, whose cycles were of special interest to the builders. I have described already a fine set of concentric arcs on the right, a reference to atmospheric water, the rainbow and the waterdrop that creates it. The deep cupmarks on each end of the arch would have collected rain or dew from the grooves of the arcs, and the wet cupmarks, like concave mirrors, would concentrate sunlight within themselves, although in the present north-facing position of the stone that phenomenon is absent.

Both free ends of the righthand clockwise spiral lead into the lozengey net. Both free ends of the lefthand clockwise spiral run up and over the righthand clockwise spiral. One of these free ends goes down to connect with the net. The clockwise-moving sun is caught by that lozengey net only around midsummer when it crosses the summer solstition. The moon at this position would also be caught by the lozengey net. The other free end of the lefthand clockwise spiral continues to the right, to form a fourth arc over the three concentric rainbow arcs. The sun helps create the rainbow.

The free end of the lefthand spiral which boxes the arcs then runs down parallel to the groove in the middle of the design where it joins a crack that runs across the groove to the panel on the other side of the groove. Where the crack crosses the groove a cupmark is attached to its lower edge.

Just below the arcs and their cupmarks is a single counterclockwise spiral whose free end runs into the net. The counterclockwise-moving stars are captured by the lozengey net cast on the wheeling sky by the chamber aperture. In this panel the circumpolar whorl is definitely subordinated to the sun, moon, and rainbow emblems.

34. Trio of cartouches	Possible Reference:	Related Site Features:
	Version of Counting	Openable Roofbox,
	or Calendar Device	Raisable Chamber
		Capstone, Solstitial
See Plate XXIII		Orientations

The panel on the righthand side of the groove on K52 displays an impressive trio of boxed cartouches. These elliptical outlines are not divided like the ellipse device on the roofbox. Although they would certainly include some conscious reference to the roofbox ellipse, they are perhaps being used here like the Egyptian cartouche, chiefly as a frame with cosmic, supernatural import which hallows whatever it holds within it. Each of the three cartouches contains three cupmarks and a set of small triangular wedges, but the three cartouches are by no means identical.

I am going to call the lefthand cartouche, the one that is nearest to the groove, Cartouche I. The two spaces between its three cupmarks are filled in by two pairs of vertical wedges, point to point. Cartouche II, which is directly to the right of Cartouche I, and is linked to it by a pair of opposed wedges above and below their junction, has only two wedges, inserted above its cupmarks. Cartouche III is placed below and slightly to the right of II. It is considerably larger than the other two and not linked visually with Cartouche II as the latter is most emphatically linked with Cartouche I. Unlike the arrangement in the other two cartouches, its six elements are placed most asymmetrically within it.

Both the roofstone and K52 feature three trios of disks. Trio II is attached by boxing arcs to the outer boxing arcs of Rosette II. Trio I, a group of single disks rather difficult to make out, is enmeshed in the boxing arcs of Rosette I. Trio III is across the chevron row from Rosette III, between the clockwise spiral and the (?) concentric arcs.

I hypothesized that the rosettes were emblems of a nine-based day-counting system. The trios of cupmarks in the three cartouches may represent a slightly different but clearly related system of counting days.

The wedges in the three cartouches on K52 are a new element. I would venture the suggestion that they may represent the value of the *power* represented by the cartouche. As these wedges are triangular devices it may be that the count here is being expressed in powers of *three* rather than nine. The triangular shape would consciously refer to the triune moon.

Cartouche I, with four wedges, might represent a count of 81 as the fourth power of three, rather than as the second power of nine, each wedge representing a power. The engraver of this panel has gone to great lengths to emphasize that there is a connection between Cartouches I and II. If the wedges were accumulative, so that the two wedges in Cartouche II were to be added to the four in Cartouche I, the count would be expressed as the sixth power of three, 729 days, almost exactly two years as we saw in connection with the righthand recess.

The solar year, midwinter to midwinter, was important at Newgrange. The Saros is almost exactly eighteen years, that is, two nines; and the Metonic Cycle is nineteen and a fraction: two nines, one year, and a fraction. The joining of two cartouches may be an expression of the same type of thinking that might have suggested the use of double marbles as emblems of two-year periods. The two cartouches together might could conceivably refer to nine two-year periods or to two nine-year periods, eighteen years. This is very close to the Saros, and about a year less than the Metonic Cycle.

A nine-year period had religious significance expressed by certain myths. Minos, whom Zeus made one of the judges of the afterworld, went to a certain cave to confer with him every nine years.

Cartouche III is larger than either of the others. If Cartouche I stood for 3^4 or 81 days and Cartouche II is added to it to make up 3^6 or 729 days, not as suggested above for eighteen years, one might expect Cartouche III to make up a total of 3^8 or 6561 days. The arrangement of cupmarks and wedges in Cartouche III is significantly different from the arrangement in the other two cartouches. The three cupmarks are very unevenly spaced. The lefthand cupmark is much farther from the other two, and is separated from them by a wedge twice as large as any other in the cartouches. In fact the lefthand cupmark and wedge occupy the whole left side of Cartouche III. The other two cupmarks in the cartouche, separated by two wedges point to point, are placed well away from the large wedge, and are all crowded into the righthand half of the ellipse. The righthand cupmark very nearly touches the rim of the ellipse, and the lower wedge collides with the rim.

Could the consciously eccentric arrangement have been meant to refer to the fact that a remainder had to be added to the number 3^8 in order to complete either the Metonic Cycle or the Saros? Whatever the answer, it is probable that there is a reasonable explanation for the peculiarities of this cartouche.

The cupmarks in the three cartouches on K52 are large, deep depressions. These cupmarks look like sockets into which a ball might be fitted. If a device of this kind were lying flat on the ground, a ball or balls could be moved along the three cartouches from socket to socket to count out a cycle or cycles, in a variation of the use I suggested for the marbles and sockets in the chamber.

Both chess and checkers are played on a chequey board, and in each game the power of a game piece or "man" which reaches the eighth square, is increased: the pawn becomes a queen, the checker becomes a king. That is, the completion of an eight-step progression leads to a change in power. Perhaps both K52 and the original of this kind of game board convention were dramatic visualizations of a numerical system originally developed to track cycles by means of powers of nine with some device like an abacus.

An image of moving a ball from socket to socket occurs in the story of Perseus, Cassiopeia's son-in-law, when he traveled to Hades to fetch the Gorgon's head. Only the three Graiae or Grey Maidens, could tell him how to reach the afterworld where Medusa dwelt beside the shore. They had only one eye and one tooth between them, and they passed the eye from socket to socket. Perseus snatched that eye and held it hostage for the critical information. In one version he took the eye and threw it into Lake Tritonis; throwing a sphere into a lake to obtain supernatural wisdom has a certain resonance with the image of the spirit-guide Hermes prophesying from the dance of pebbles in water. Hermes was in fact one of Perseus's guides on his quest. The idea that a ball moving from socket to socket had something to do with the afterlife suggests the Newgrange emblem.

The ancient Irish board game called fidchell plays an important part in several Old Irish stories. The exact nature of the game is not known. Gantz glosses the word fidchell as "'wood sense' - a board game similar to chess, in which one side's king attempts to escape to the edge of the board while the other side's men attempt to prevent him." In the story called the Third Wooing of Etain, Etains's lover Mider wins the right to kiss her by winning three games of fidchell from the king.He then takes her in his arms and flies out of the skylight of the court with her. In the story of the Sickbed of Cuchulainn, Fand, the wife of the Irish supernatural figure Manannan, boasts that he could not win from her the odd game of fidchell. Both stories feature critical modules that could be interpreted as dramatizations of a solar eclipse.

The progression of a ball from socket to socket might also be pictured as a journey through three kingdoms or halls of increasing value or power. In the Russian story "Whirlwind the Whistler", the young prince sets out to free his mother, Goldentress, who has been kidnapped by Whirlwind. He meets the Copper Princess, who gives him a copper ball to follow to the Silver Princess, who gives him a silver ball to follow to the Gold Princess, who gives him a gold ball to follow to his mother. The track of the ball from realm to realm would be an emblem chosen to represent rotation and polarity.

Each princess also gives him a *ring* of the appropriate metal which contains within itself the whole of the kingdom belonging to that metal. This looks like a narrative version of the advancement of a count from one power to another, the image involving a spatial advance from one kingdom to another more precious and closer to the goal. The Russian story includes the emblem of the three balls which move of themselves from one "power" to another as well as the emblem of the rings (a reminiscence of the sockets?), which represent the total count of each power.

I have described the Norse story of "The Three Princesses in the Mountain in the Blue" as a possible dramatization of the counting system suggested at Newgrange. Heads or "balls" are removed from their sockets, the number nine is of a different order from the other eight, and the same module is repeated in venues of increasing value. In addition, both time and distance separate the three enclosures that represent the increasing powers. The device on K52 shows three enclosures each with three ball-shaped sockets, but the ninth socket, in the third enclosure, is separated from the other two and the ninth wedge is much longer than the others. This detail has a certain resonance with the detail of the Norse story that the ninth troll-head needs an extra stroke because that sword was not long enough.

When the Irish hero Cuchulainn sets out on his wooing of Emer, a young man gives him a "ball," an apple, to follow across the plain. One of the tasks Emer later sets him is to attack three groups of nine warriors, sparing her three brothers, one of whom is included in each set of nine. The two little story-modules can be recognized as fragmentary relics of modules that appear in the more symmetrical and comprehensible Norse and Russian stories. The fairy-tale count by nines and powers may represent a count toward a special conjunction of sun and moon: new moon, or an eclipse.

The hero in both the Norse and the Russian fairy stories is the youngest of three brothers. In Irish tradition great stress is laid upon the youth and diminutive stature of the hero Cuchulainn. I have explained previously that this familiar story trait could encourage us to interpret the hero, often the youngest of three, as an emblem of the new moon. Several traditional charms link the new moon with an increase in money, an emblem of counting by tokens of different values.

The interpretation of Cuchulainn, originally Setanta, as a *solar* hero would have developed many centuries later than Newgrange, probably at a time when the "Little Dog," Procyon, was a star of the summer solstice.

As the new moon is hidden within, or defended or prepared by, the sun whose radiance hides him from view, we find such examples as Parsifal, whose mother hides him in the forest from the dangers of a warrior's life, the young soldier in the Blue Mountain story, Goldentress's son Ivan whom she hide beneath her robe, and Thetis's son Achilles whose mother dipped him in the Styx in an attempt to make him immortal.

In the Russian and Norwegian fairy-tales, as at Newgrange, a transformational concept appears in which the prime agent is a special water of life or strength, to which a numerical count has been joined in some way. This appears when Ivan calms the snakes before each castle by giving them a bucket of water: that is, he reverses the polarity of these "spirals," neutralizing the threat by the power of reflection. The Norse princess gives the soldier a drink from "the horn behind the door." The Styx is a magical water. Parsifal's mysterious grail is a vessel of some sort which may be related to this concept.

In many traditional contexts the difference between right and left is developed into a distinction between waters of opposite properties. In Greek myth this distinction already appears in the difference between the effects of blood from the Gorgon's right and left vein. Goldentress has Ivan switch the places of the Water of Strength, kept on the right side, and the Water of Weakness, kept on the left, in order to trick Whirlwind. The Norse story also has two "waters": the horn behind the door which strengthens the hero, and the brewing vat which hides him and permits him to free each princess from her spinning wheel.

At Newgrange reflection neutralized the power of the fatal celestial clock. There may have been a distinction at Newgrange between water from the "winter-flowing spring" in the passage which came from the earth, if this was operative and accessible in Newgrange times, and the spring or leak in the chamber, which admitted only atmospheric water.

35. Attached lobes	**Possible References:**	**Related Site Features:**
	The Sun, Lunar Phases	Openable Roofbox,
		Raisable Chamber
See Plate XXIII		Capstone

The cartouches on K52, which I have interpreted as a possible reference to counting astronomical cycles by powers of three rather than nine, have attached to them some very striking extra "lobes," devices boxed with multiple concentric arcs.

Attached to the lower left side of Cartouche I is a large arced lobe, consisting of a circle that encloses a slender gnomon-shaped device with its point toward the cartouche. The circle is boxed with three concentric arcs. Attached to the top and left side of the outermost surrounding arc are three smaller devices, each surrounded by two arcs. The midmost of the three devices is the largest of all the cupmarks on K52. On the left of the cupmark is a triangle with its base toward the cartouche, and on its right is a triangle with its point toward the cartouche. Taking the triangles as referring to the moon, this group of three might very tentatively be interpreted as the new moon flanked by waxing and waning crescents. If one were to assume that the wedges were to be read clockwise around the "gnomon," the one with its point toward the gnomon would be the waning moon moving toward the cupmark as new moon, the other the waxing moon moving away from the cupmark toward full.

Or perhaps the much-emphasized cupmark was intended to represent a solar eclipse: the dark disk would represent the black lunar disk in front of the sun. The gnomon-shaped wedge in the circle to which the three are attached might represent the sun with gnomon. The fan-stick devices are based on the shadows cast by a gnomon, and hence are an indirect reference to the sun, whose day-count is the substance of the cycles.

Clockwise from the wedge-enclosing circle and attached directly to Cartouche I are two more arced lobes, both containing triangles with their bases toward the cartouche, presumably to be understood like the one left of the cupmark. There is only one lobe attached to Cartouche II and it contains a triangle with its point toward the cartouche. This would presumably be understood like the one right of the cupmark.

Between the two cartouches are two pairs of wedges. There is a vertical pair, arranged point to point, separated by a horizontal pair, one above the other. The upper member of the horizontal pair points to Cartouche II, the lower, to Cartouche I. These pairs of wedges, elaborately boxed by three arcs above and four below, seem intended to emphasize the importance of the connection between these two cartouches.

The lobes on the Cartouches on K52 may help explain a difference between the eight-lobed counting-rosettes on the righthand recess roofstone and the trios of disks on that roofstone. Perhaps the trios like those on K52 are intended to emphasis the role of the *moon* as timekeeper for certain dates of religious significance.

CHAPTER XVII

PLANETARY TRAVELERS

36. Returning Arcs   **Possible Reference:**   **Related Site Features:**
Orbit of Venus   Openable Roofbox,
Raisable Chamber
Capstone, Center
Recess Orientation,
Ecliptic Views, Dark
See Plate XXIII   Chamber, Long Passage,
High Vault

A curious feature of the righthand panel of K52 is a device attached to the righthand end of Cartouche II. It consists of a cupmark boxed by an arcing line that swings from side to side of the center. This returning-arc device can be tentatively recognized several times in the Newgrange repertory. It is conceivably modeled on the orbit of Venus, which is carried along the ecliptic with the clockwise-traveling sun, while swinging from side to side of the sun in its own orbit, sometimes between Earth and the sun, sometimes on the other side of the sun.

In the example attached to Cartouche II, the inmost arc moves counterclockwise, reverses to clockwise, and reverses again to counterclockwise. This is like the oscillating movement of Venus. Since the device is attached to the number-linked cartouche, one might ask whether the nine-based system was of any use in keeping track of this cycle? The synodic cycle of Venus is 584 days, which is seven times 9^2 (or seven times 3^4) plus a remainder of seventeen, not quite two nines. [An empty nest of four arcs is attached to these returning arcs, and a double arc around a wedge or gnomon is attached to that; I can make no suggestions about these interesting attached devices.]

On the back of K4, the center of the stone is occupied by a device over a foot across that consists of a clockwise spiral surrounded by what appears to be a version of the returning-arc device. In the center of K13 Back, one of the devices surrounding a cupmark may be another example. K18, far right, shows a dot surrounded by an arc that runs into a circle, also a possible version of the returning arc device. A device on K6 above a set of fansticks may be another version. There is a good, large example on K51 placed between two large W's, one boxed. Stone X may include a couple of examples.

A Lithuanian tradition pictured Venus as the handmaid of a feminine sun, sometimes her rival for the affections of the moon. At its maximum brightness Venus is the third brightest object in the sky; it casts a shadow, and makes a trail of light on a body of water like the sun and moon.

37. Seven Disks	**Possible Reference:**	**Related Site Features:**
	Seven Planetary Bodies	Same as for Returning Arcs

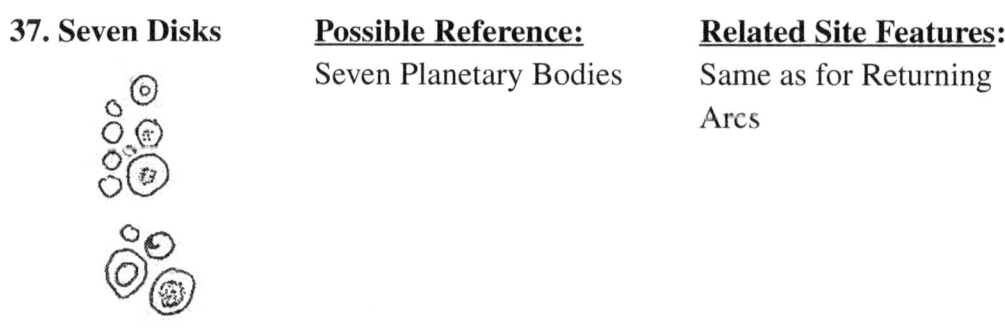

There is another device which may support a hypothesis that Newgrange stone carvers expressed an interest in planetary bodies besides sun and moon. On a rather narrow panel of R20 which was spared the pick-dressing later applied to most of the passage stones there are what Claire O'Kelly describes as "natural hollows utilized for purpose of ornament by deepening and outlining with picked circles." A very graphic photograph of this large device is included as Plate 17b in the 1971 second edition of her *Illustrated Guide,* and her drawing of the device appears in the O'Kelly *Newgrange.* Part of the device is visible at the right of R21 in my Plate XVIII.

Within the deep lower hollow is a compact group of four circles. The lowest circle is the largest. It encloses a large picked circular area. Just above and to the left is a slightly smaller circle that encloses another within it. Above the largest circle is a still smaller circle enclosing what looks like a tiny semi-circle, like a curl that touches its rim. Above the next largest circle is the fourth circle in this group, much smaller than the other three, and plain.

Within the upper hollow is a vertical row of three circles. Each encloses a different small device. The upper circle encloses a little circle; the middle one encloses what may be a circle with dot; and the lowest circle, which is the largest, encloses a small picked circular area. On their left is a vertical row of four smaller circles of approximately the same size, with a slightly smaller and fainter one at the right of the row. In short the devices are deliberately differentiated.

All seven planetary bodies could be seen through both apertures. The group of seven major circular devices on this panel might cautiously be interpreted as a reference to them. If so, I would venture the guess that the circles in the lower group would correspond to the sun, moon, and two inferior planets. These four circles are distinguished from each other by what they enclose. The lobes attached to Cartouche I on K52 seemed capable of supporting an interpretation that the large circle with cupmark on that stone represented the new or eclipsing moon. Perhaps the large circle with cupmark on R20 might also be identified with the new or eclipsing moon, and the sun by the circle that encloses another circle - or perhaps vice versa. The two smaller circles might refer to the two inferior planets. Venus by the circle with enclosed clockwise "curl", and Mercury by the small, plain circle.

The three circles that are arranged in a vertical row in the hollow above would represent the superior planets: lowest and largest Jupiter, and above it Saturn and Mars. The four small circles left of these, arranged in a vertical row beginning just below the largest circle might represent Jupiter's four Galilean moons. These moons "may roughly be classed as of the sixth magnitude; they would therefore be visible to a keen eye if the brilliancy of the planet did not obscure them. Some observers profess to have seen one or more of these bodies with the naked eye notwithstanding this drawback, but the evidence can scarcely be regarded as conclusive." (*Ency. Brit. XI* "Jupiter.")

Considering the informed attention that the Newgrangemen paid to the heavens it would not be surprising to find that some reference to the planets was included among the petroglyphs. I have mentioned that figures accompanying the sun and moon on one of the Yazilikaya reliefs may refer to planets.

The group of seven circles on R20 is intriguing, occurring as it does in a setting known to have been focused on the ecliptic, traveled by all the planets. The very restricted viewing apertures, long passage, pitch-dark chamber, and probably very clear skies would have created the best possible conditions for viewing, and the planets would have made a brilliant showing.

CHAPTER XVIII

A FOREBODING IMAGE

The set of nine rungs in the passage, which I have already discussed as probably modeled on the idea of physical ascent to the heavens, is not an engraved two-dimensional device, but a three-dimensional or sculptured emblem. The pyramidal stone which Vallancey described as standing between K1 and the standing stones would also have been a three-dimensional emblem, an emblem of "Three-ness," associated with the moon as timekeeper. K1 and K52 may also be three-dimensional emblems connected with the belief system of the people of Newgrange.

38. K1 as Emblem	**Possible Reference:**	**Related Site Feature:**
	Mutilated Form,	Central Placement in
	Premonitory Affect	Shaved Forecourt
		Liable to Ponding: Design
		Composed with Site
		Emblems

See Plates XXIV and XXVI

K1 is carved down to a fairly horizontal base-line that suggested that the stone had been set into the ground and carved above that line. That the stone was carved "in situ" as is usually said is a reasonable deduction, although it is not necessary to infer that it was never moved. The builders manipulated many much larger stones.

PLATE XXIV. Kerbstone 1

It is reasonable to believe that K1 must always have stood somewhere in the forecourt. For this reason, O'Kelly's detailed findings about the history of the turf in this area may have important implications for our understanding of it.

Turf was stripped from the surface of the ground in the forecourt of the monument at least twice. Stripping would have exposed the bare ground to the effects of rain and seepage, and the area in front of Newgrange had a great propensity for collecting water. Ireland probably always had a lot of rain, although there have been periods during which it seems to have had less than it has now. Between R7 and R8 in the passage, O'Kelly found a winter-flowing spring which has had to be controlled by drains. A spring somewhere on the ridge would have been almost a necessity, for areas of domestic habitation were found nearby, and it is unlikely that all water was brought up from the Boyne.

Seepage has often been reported around the bases of mounds, and Newgrange was no exception. Rainwater always percolated readily down through the porous cairn, and was known to continue dripping or trickling into the righthand recess bowl or slab for some time after rain had fallen. Water from this leak or spring may have overflowed to trickle down the passage or into the base of the mound from time to time. It was by conducting water into the surrounding mass that the passage water-grooves kept the passage dry. The slope was toward the forecourt, and O'Kelly describes how when the water meets the underlying clay, it tends to run down the ridge north and south. Whenever the flat clayey area in front of the passage entrance was stripped of turf, it would have been subject to intermittent ponding.

O'Kelly's guarded statement about the history of the turf is as follows: "Was it onto this second-time-stripped surface that K96 and the quartz revetment collapsed or might there have been yet other strippings? On the basis of the radiocarbon dates the Late Neolithic/Beaker-period squatting was taking place at 2000 BC and at this time the quartz revetment and some of the cairn edge behind it had collapsed. If there had been an interval of some hundreds of years between the completion of Newgrange and the collapse of the revetment, a considerable development of turf and humus would have taken place, so one must argue either that the revetment collapsed almost immediately after completion, or that there were several strippings of the turf. We can be reasonably sure of two, but perhaps there were more." (*Newgrange* p. 12)

From a practical standpoint, some kind of maintenance must always have been carried out to keep the forecourt groomed and comely, and in the absence of modern equipment, weeding the area clear of vegetation would have been about the only way to keep vegetation down. Animal grazing does it, but the by-products are a nuisance in an area with heavy foot traffic, especially ceremonial traffic. Ongoing, informal, intermittent weeding, raking, or sweeping would have left no trace, and could have been carried out whenever and as long as people had an interest in doing it.

Whenever water collected on the bare ground it would have reflected whatever was behind it. The groundline of K1 might well in that case have been a waterline. As its carving extended all the way to this line the design would frequently have been joined to its own reflection. Whether or not this had been foreseen, it would have attracted interest once it happened.

Remarkable forms and faces are often formed accidentally by features lying on the margin of a lake or pool (see Plate XXV).

The common occurrence of this striking and evocative effect might have inspired some artisan to contrive one on purpose.

During any period in which the entrance to Newgrange was configured as it is now, visitors did not enter the monument, at least not by the passage. The closing stone blocked it for some period, and K1 stood across the indent. There may also have been an infill of stones between K1 and the closing stone behind it. The collapse of the revetment may soon have hidden the entrance entirely. There may well have been a rule or taboo against approaching the entrance. As long as it was free, or was kept free, of the collapsed mound, K1 was the focus of the visitor's attention, as it is now.

PLATE XXV. Lakeside Reflection

At times when rain or seepage could produce a puddle in front of the stone, the neighbor, pilgrim or tourist would have beheld a bodiless head, with an inhumanly symmetrical face, lying on its left side, at the entrance to an underworld realm of the dead. The fame of this ominous detached head, guarding the solemn entrance to an afterworld, would surely have spread beyond Ireland. It seems significant that Homer knew there was a detached head at the entrance of Hades; there is nothing really rational about the combination of images. Travelers carry information and their hearers spread it farther. Newgrange, and something about its history, was known to the droppers of Roman coins.

Plate XXVI shows a version of K1 plus reflection, an image formed by juxtaposing a photograph of the stone and its mirrored reflection.

PLATE XXVI. K1 and its Reflection

The face so formed has big lozenge-shaped eyes, a bulbous nose, and a small, open mouth, appearing slightly pursed because of the multiple concentric lines around it. Below the eyes the face is densely surrounded by large, much-boxed spirals which might be interpreted as curls, or coiled snakes. Below the stone eye and located just on the water-line is a half-eye, its other half provided by its own reflection. The third eye is a water-eye, all reflection. Beyond the eyes and above the curls or snakes are two much-boxed arcs, features that might be interpreted as horns or very round ears.

I explained in discussing the heart-shape and cockle shell that when the inmost coil of a spiral is cut by a reflective surface, they together form the outline of a heart. The pursed, rather heart-shaped "mouth" of the face formed by K1 and its reflection is formed in this way, by an expanding curve and its mirrored image.

An astonishing feature of the K1 example is that the components of the carved face were devices that as I have explained had meaning in themselves, and were used throughout the monument. That the eyes were lozenges is fitting here inasmuch as the lozenge-shaped vault aperture was the eye of the monument.

The most famous bodiless, symmetrical head in Classical tradition is the head of the Gorgon Medusa. Homer knew it only as a terrifying apparition which Hades's wife Persephone held up to frighten those who approached the entrance to the afterworld. The Gorgoneion was customarily pictured as an absolutely symmetrical face, with wide, glaring eyes, and a broad, flat nose with flaring nostrils. Its mouth was usually fixed in a ghastly grin that exposed the gullet and showed the terrible teeth. Its face was framed by a mass of coiling snakes instead of hair. Its aspect was so terrible that it turned the beholder to stone. The landscape around Hades was littered with these petrified unfortunates.

The classical Gorgoneion is a theatrical, scary, carnivorous face. It is quite unlike the solemn, inscrutable visage produced by K1 and its reflection. K1 accords with Homer's concept only to the extent that it was displayed at an entrance to "Hades" and beyond the fact that it was frightening we do not know how he pictured it. Artistic depictions of the Gorgoneion were extremely varied, ranging from the horrific bogey to a sort of cold and menacing beauty, and the oldest versions we know are of course millennia later than Newgrange.

In fact, the hideous aspect of the conventional Gorgoneion was not the original face of Medusa. Originally a maiden of surpassing beauty, she was disfigured by Athena, who was incensed because Poseidon lay with her in Athena's own temple. There was ample time for tradition to develop and deform the image, however it originated.

The Gorgoneion appeared not only on temples but on countless homely articles of household use as well as on military paraphernalia. This is usually explained as being because it had the power to ward off evil, although the idea of warding off evil or discouraging bad luck does not seem to be a logical deduction from Homer's concept.

CHAPTER XIX

K 52: A RADICAL SUGGESTION

K52 is carved in a style very much like that of K1, a style so similar that the two stones could well have been carved by the same man. But this superb stone is placed in solitary splendor at the very back of the mound. It has been said that K52 like K1 was carved where it stands, but it is perplexing that the carver of K1 or a colleague with equal skill should have worked so far away from what must always have been the center of activity of the monument. It is also perplexing that this stone should have been set so far from that center of activity, which was probably always focused in the forecourt. Did K52 ever stand in the forecourt? This question may have a complicated answer.

Changes were often made to neolithic sites and structures. Aubrey Burl once remarked that "Changes of mind were common amongst British prehistoric societies." Of Newgrange itself O'Kelly says "The increasing thickness of the turf mound running inward under the cairn in this area suggests the presence of an already consolidated turf mound and it is possible that had it been feasible to pursue it farther, a passage- grave or other structure pre-dating the great cairn might have been encountered within it." Of a remodeling of Site K he says "In the second phase, the passage was extended to just over 3m and the mound, again circular, was extended to cover it..."

I am going to propose that the Newgrange monument we know may be the result of a re-tooling, one that took place as a result of changes in belief and practice forced when precession destroyed the outviews of the side recesses of the chamber. This hypothesis might help to explain not only the peculiar position of K52 but also of several other anomalies which were revealed by the O'Kelly work.

The celestial poles describe circles in the skies because of a wobble in the earth's axis of rotation. It takes 25,000 years for the poles to complete these circles. The interval seems very long, yet the north celestial pole has completed about a fifth of its circle since Newgrange was built. If we imagine a star located just at the pole at a given date, that star would require only about forty years, a generation, to spiral outward so far that it was describing a circle of half a degree in diameter. That is equal to the angular diameter of the moon or about one sixth the length of Orion's Belt. It seems very insignificant. But a man looking up out of a narrow stone cell whose sightlines had been critically engineered to focus on select stars would soon become aware of a change of a lunar diameter, and he would foresee the results of that trend with consternation.

In even a few decades the Milky Way could be detected edging inexorably up out of the range of Newgrange's right-hand recess. (The edge of the roofstone looks as if it might possibly have been chipped away a little, perhaps in an effort to pursue the receding targets of its sightlines.) Circumpolar stars still circled within the view of the lefthand recess, but they were not in exactly the same positions. Overhead outviews could have been pursued for a while by moving about within the chamber, and the stone bowl could have been moved. But the old fellowship of overhead stars, the familiar outlines of the powers that had been marshalled into the chamber to assist the dead to a new life in heaven, were drifting out of range. Nothing was secure but the solstitial view.

Newgrange is only one of many kinds of buildings which may have been capable of providing outviews through openable vaults or other high apertures. Such views were always available in informal domestic settings. A man under a tree, or in a cave, or in a wattled hut, or teepee, or igloo, could see stars through chinks, or the smoke-hole, and probably noted their reflections in the water-jar on the hearth. Buildings providing such outviews may have become popular over a fairly short period of time before it was understood exactly how vulnerable the rigid frames were, and to what. Small stone sites which were used and closed within a few years would have escaped the fate that closed in on Newgrange. K, L, and Z were apparently built with no intention that they would be used at all after the grave deposits were inserted.

The prestige of a building dependent on overhead star-views was eventually going to fall victim to precession, while the prestige of a building which depended on a solstitial outview alone was not. The enormous investment of wealth and power in Newgrange would have tempted its proprietors to secure its position and their own by making the most of the solstitial outview.

An important consideration is that since both the view of circumpolar stars and the view of the Milky Way were important elements in the belief that governed the funeral practice, the loss of the side-recess outviews would have forced changes in the practice if not the belief itself. The righthand recess still gives the impression of having been the ritual focus of the monument. Its sightlines through the opened vault to the Milky Way, would have been a critical element in the whole complex system of belief, as would the way reflection seemingly reversed the polarity of circumpolar rotation. Any image of power associated with the polar vortex, such as the Weather God, was compromised, as was any image of power associated with Cassiopeia and the northern loop of the galaxy.

Such ideas were compromised at Newgrange by the effects of precession. Outside of the self-filling bowl or slab, the feature which remained unchanged was the awe-inspiring solstitial observation, which had a natural transformational meaning of its own. The pole of the ecliptic had proved itself to be the most powerful member of the celestial dyad engraved on the roofstone. One would expect that the belief system would have to have been altered to reflect the new knowledge.

Let us hypothesize that in order to help make up for the shaken confidence and faith caused by precession, and at the same time to capitalize on the magnificent remaining solstitial view, the proprietors decided to enhance this asset with a towering quartz facade. First, what might have been the original form of the building? And second, how might the desired alteration have been achieved?

One of several anomalies uncovered by O'Kelly was the eccentric shape of the rim around the top of the boulder cap. The cap of selected boulders around the chamber vault rises just a little higher than its capstone. The top of this mini-cairn, like that of the large main cairn that covers it, is flat. And, like the top of the large cairn, the rim of the mini-cairn has a peculiar shape. Figure 12 is a sketch based on O'Kelly's map and plans showing how the rim lies above the plan of the chamber.

The boulder cap rim is like an unevenly-cut quarter of a pie, with the three corners of the outline rounded rather than pointed. The rounded corner in the north corresponds to the center of the quarter-pie slice. Its sides are about 90° apart. One side of the angle runs forward southeastward, parallel to the passage. The other side, which is quite a little longer, runs out southwestward. The ends of these two fairly straight but unequal sides are joined in the south by a long irregular arc, which represents the rim of the pie.

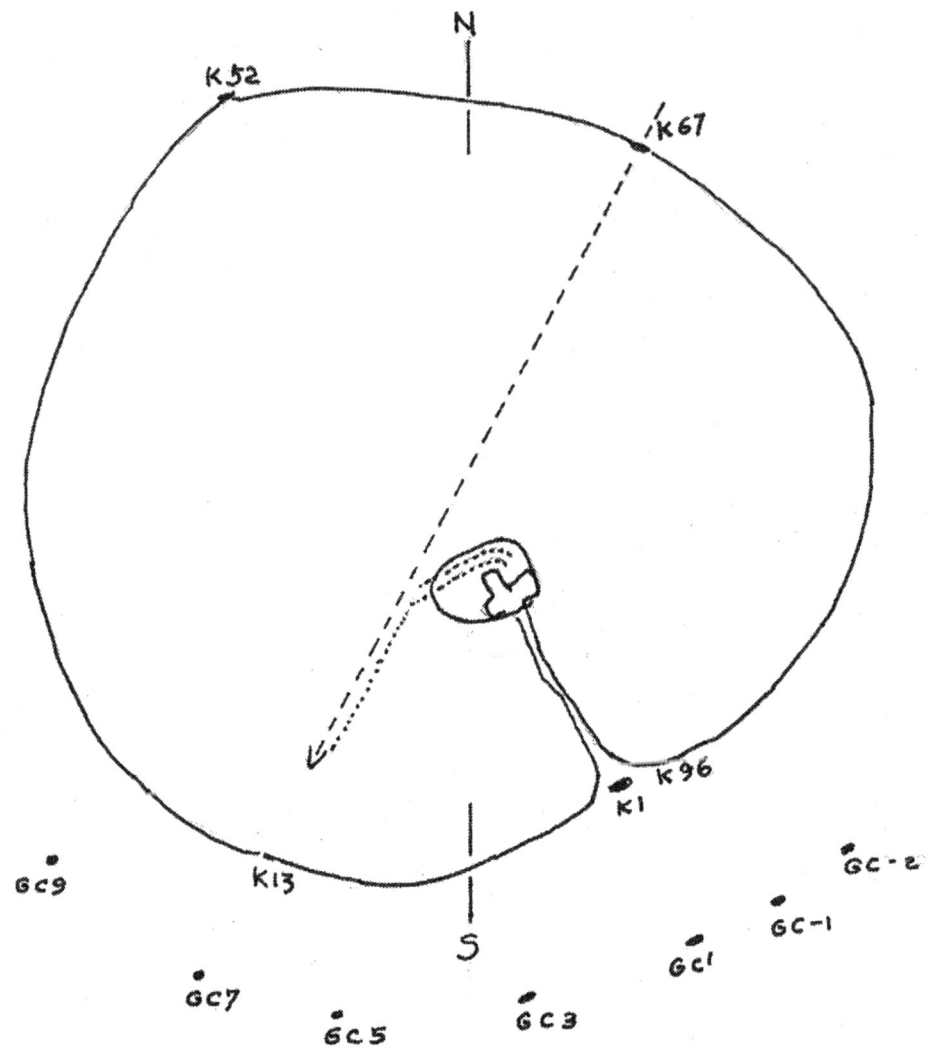

FIG. 12. Sketch of Mound with Boulder-Cap Rim
and Possible Sunset Passage

Looking down at the plan of the boulder cap and the chamber below it, the pie-wedge outline of the boulder-cap rim hugs the back of the righthand recess and the left side of the lefthand recess as tightly as possible. But the northwestern side of the cap's outline extends nine feet behind the center recess backstone, and the western side of the outline extends eighteen feet beyond the left wall of the center recess. That is, the whole chamber below is crowded under the southeast corner of the boulder-cap rim. Why does the edge of the cap extend so far beyond the chamber to the north, northwest, and southwest? If the southeast part of the rim was fitted tightly to the southeast part of the chamber on purpose, then to what, if anything, was the northwest part of the rim fitted?

The area below the rim which is not being occupied by the plan of the chamber beneath is nearly big enough to accommodate another chamber, but O'Kelly did not find another capstone within the rim, and a second vaulted chamber would seem redundant in any case. But there was ample room for a second *passage*, like the blind-ended second passage at Knowth. There was in fact room for a passage that curved all around the back of the chamber, parallel to the back of the boulder-cap rim, a U-shaped passage or cavity fitted around the center recess.

The mound of Newgrange is enormous in relation to the passage and chamber it covers. A tantalizing suggestion made by early visitors and never laid to rest was that there *was* a second passage behind the chamber. O'Kelly took the possibility seriously enough to excavate extensively behind K52, explaining that "There was also the necessity to test the oft-repeated theory that the entrance to another passage lay behind K52", adding laconically "In the event, this was not the case."(O'Kelly *op.cit*. p. 5)

It is plain that if a second passage had at some point been disused and concealed, this alone would be evidence of some change of emphasis, helping to support a hypothesis that Newgrange was substantially altered. Is there any evidence, then, of a passage behind the center recess?

Claire O'Kelly discusses one of the early antiquarian accounts: (*Newgrange*, 37) "The falling forward of [orthostat C10 on the right side of the center recess] gave rise to the notion that another chamber was present. In 1893 a Captain Keogh wrote to T. J. Westropp stating that on a visit to Newgrange he had discovered a passage between the right-hand recess and the end recess which had originally been closed by one of the orthostats of the central chamber. He apparently got his head and shoulders far enough in to see that 'the passage turned towards the middle of the mound. It is nearly filled to the top with small broken stones and the parts of the large stones forming its sides are covered with carvings and spirals'."

Mrs. O'Kelly also quotes James Fergusson as saying (1872) that by creeping behind the fallen stone (presumably C 10) "'...it is possible to see the reverse of some of the neighboring stones and it is found that several of these are elaborately carved with the same spiral ornaments as their fronts.'"(*loc. cit.*). An early visitor peering or squeezing in a little way behind C10 would have been looking into what may have been the partly-filled-in terminus of a hypothetical U-shaped passage.

There were precedents at nearby neolithic sites for a second passage, a narrow communicating gap between separated areas, and a walled-off cavity. Knowth, northwest of Newgrange, has a long second passage that enters the mound opposite the first and runs in toward the main chamber until it is about thirty feet west of it, where it makes a little bend to the right like the end of a hockey-stick and ends about nine feet from a corner of the center recess. Dowth, northeast of Newgrange, has a small rectangular room behind one recess, which is entered through a gap less than a foot wide. Site K had a miniature triangular annex attached to but completely walled off from the main chamber (although K was not entered after the grave deposit was put into it).

It was largely K52's ornamentation that suggested that it marked the entrance of a second passage. This kerbstone and K1 are in a class by themselves from the standpoint of their petroglyphs, which are similar in technique, style, and beauty of execution. Both stones have broad, smooth grooves that divide their designs into two distinct panels. As the groove on K1 lay just in front of the passage, the vertical groove on K52 reinforced the suspicion that the second passage lay behind it. Although it has been stated repeatedly of this stone as of K1 that it was carved in place because the ornamentation stops at a level ground-line this does not mean in either case that the stone must have been carved where it now stands. If K52 ever stood elsewhere a passage marked by its groove would have lain elsewhere. The presence of the similar "ground lines" and the other similarities of K1 and K52 may however reasonably suggest that the stones were once much more closely associated, perhaps once lay beside, or at least near, each other.

K1 itself was not needed to block the entrance to the passage, because this was already blocked with the closing stone. Furthermore some practical way to get up the steep, revetted mound and some practical access to the roofbox would require that K1 not completely close the ring of kerbstones.

The sunrise passage at Newgrange is marked by two kerbstones and a monolith, all lying on the line of the midwinter sunrise: K1 in the southeast, K52 in its present position on the other side of the mound, and the immense Great Circle monolith GC 1, which can be seen beyond K1 from the chamber, through the open passage.

Now, the passages at Dowth are oriented to the midwinter sunset. At Newgrange, lying approximately on the line of the midwinter sunset, there are three distinctively decorated kerbstones and a monolith. O'Kelly discovered that K13 and K18 in the southwest are elaborately carved on their backs. The style is rough and vigorous, much like that found on the now-hidden stones X, Y, and Z in the so-called relieving lintel. K67 is located on the other side of the kerb from K13. Although carved in a style very different from that of K1 and K52, K67 is also both elegant and meaningful in its composition. Outside of the kerb beyond K13 O'Kelly discovered what is left of GC7. A line drawn through K13, K67, and GC7 passes about five feet northwest of the northern corner of the boulder cap rim. If a second passage had run along that line it would seem to have missed the rounded northwest corner of the boulder cap rim by less than four feet. To put the distance in perspective, the center chamber is about seven feet long, and the sunrise passage is about three feet wide.

Let us suppose very tentatively that a midwinter-*sunset* oriented passage, which would probably have been about as wide as the present sunrise passage, did run across the back of the center recess, with a wall just under the rim of the cap. It might have made a bend (the Knowth second passage bends) in order to communicate in some way with the chamber. How far would that second passage have run out toward the edge of the cairn?

O'Kelly dug a few feet back into the cairn behind K13 and K18 in order to straighten up the sagging kerb and did not find anything unusual. But it is not likely that a second passage, if it lay here, reached to the present kerb. The most natural assumption is that if there was a sunset passage it was of the same length as the sunrise passage. If so, the sunset passage must end a good forty or fifty feet within the present mound, and the earlier mound must have been much smaller.

If in a previous phase of the monument there were both a sunrise and a sunset passage of equal length, the smaller two-entrance mound would have had a net north-south orientation. The area between the two passages, perhaps both ending in unroofed segments, would have formed a formal forecourt, facing due south, between the sunrise and sunset positions. It is possible that K52 did lie in front of a passage, a sunset passage, on the other side of a south-facing court from K1, a distance of about a hundred feet. On the other hand, the stones could have lain together adjacent to each other perhaps in the middle of the forecourt. It is significant that the orientation of the line of five mounds on the ridge is generally east and west. From this standpoint, the southeast orientation of Newgrange as it stands is in itself something of an anomaly.

In order to emphasize the importance of the sole remaining ritually important outview from the chamber, the sunrise observation, the mound needed to face southeast rather than south. The rotation of its axis would have been achieved by adding symmetrical bulges in the northeast and southwest, leaving the sunrise passage intact. The southwest bulge would have covered the disused sunset passage. The hypothetical earlier phase would have coincided with the present mound just east of the area of the present passage, near K95, and only here. The hypothesis that the present mound was enlarged implies that the immense mass of cairn material was brought and placed in two phases separated by perhaps two or three generations.

If there was originally a Great Circle of megaliths, what is left of it does not seem to have any discernible geometrical relation to the kerb of the mound. We might in fact infer from some of the above facts that the chief purpose of these standing stones was to establish certain azimuths. The term "Great Circle" applied to these stones came into use because neolithic stone circles are common, so it was believed that a complete ring may once have encircled the monument. Painstaking search has failed to determine with any certainty the sites of the rest of the stones. If only certain azimuths were important to the builders of Newgrange there would have been no need to fill in the circle. Perhaps this was one of its many distinctions: that its planners did not feel compelled to complete the customary circle when it was only a few of the points on its circumference that were important for their purposes.

It has been argued by P. David Sweetman, on the basis of evidence from circles of pits and postholes southeast of the monument, that the "Great Circle" was much later than the monument, but the evidence is complicated and leaves many questions unanswered. Where would this group of early bronze age squatters have found these stones and how would they have moved them? Since the circle would on this assumption have been erected after the mound was in a state of collapse, it is hard to imagine why these settlers would have undertaken the immense labor of partially ringing the ruinous mound with stupendous megaliths which are in any case not concentric with the outline of the mound.

O'Kelly's excavation exposed another intriguing anomaly that may be interpreted as support for a two-phase hypothesis. This is that Roofslab 3, the heaviest in the passage, was not laid directly on the supporting orthostats like Roofslab 1, but was found precariously balanced on stacked corbels. O'Kelly's elevations through the unreconstructed passage under this slab show that those corbels had splayed out so badly that the orthostats under them had leaned in until their tops nearly met, lowering the slab. Why did the builders take this risk? Did they have no taller orthostats?

But these orthostats are almost *uniformly* the wrong height - seven of the eight are about two feet too short. This naturally leads to the question, Did RS 3 perhaps originally rest two feet lower than it is now, directly on this row of shorter orthostats? The bottom of RS 3 was slightly concave. It would have fit well over the generally slightly convex profile of the row of orthostats on the right, and acceptably over the row on the left side of the passage. The inner end of the slab would have fit down between the pair of taller orthostats on the chamber side and the pair toward the entrance.

O'Kelly's drawing of the end of the passage shows that if RS 3 had rested directly on the orthostats below it, there would have been a slit between the chamber end of the now lowered RS 3 and the higher roofstone north of it. A slit between RS3 and RS4, now buried twelve feet deep in the cairn, should have admitted the beam of the rising midwinter sun much as the present slit does.

There may have been a time when the Newgrange mound sloped evenly down from the base of the boulder cap to the kerb. O'Kelly notes that the earlier mounds K and L may have been configured this way. "In L, Frances Lynch has argued that there was an unroofed outer end to the passage .... The suggestion here is that the outer part of the mound was low and probably not higher than the rather low kerb..... In K where the primary passage-grave and its kerb were low, one can envisage the turf mound curving gently down to the kerb tops, but here there may have been a turf revetment built on the kerb to hold the edge of the mound."(*Three Passage Graves* p.337)

The outer end of the Newgrange passage could also have been unroofed. The six orthostats that support Roofslab 1 are fine, well-matched, rather squarish stones whose tops form an almost level line. They would have appeared to great advantage if uncovered, as would the boulder cap. The four mounds would have presented matching facades, particularly if as suggested K, L and Z were capped with stones and the boulder cap of Newgrange itself was exposed.

Another striking discovery by O'Kelly may be physical evidence that RS 3 was indeed lifted up into its present position. In order to uncover the passage to straighten the sagging orthostats, he had to make a large cutting into the mound around it. He found that his cutting, which

"...took the form of a great embrasure...[exposed] a very similar embrasure.... It would seem that a space had been left by the builders in which the outer part of the passage could be erected.... layers of turves acting to prevent the cairn material from sliding in on them and when the passage and the roofbox above it had been completed, they filled in the embrasure just as we did when conservation work was finished"(Michael O'Kelly *Newgrange* p. 89)

But perhaps a more natural explanation of the Neolithic embrasure, which exposed Roofslab 3 along with its corbels and orthostats, is that this would have made it possible for the builders to dig back and lift the great slab. Like O'Kelly's men, the original builders of Newgrange may have dug their embrasure not to hold the mound at bay while constructing the passage, but to uncover it so that they could reconstruct it.

In the risky engineering involving RS 3 we might recognize the work of the same team that designed the unstable facade. This was a lower standard than we see in the monument as a whole, a victory of hubris over engineering. The placement of RS 3 may be another tell-tale clue that there was an earlier phase of the monument, one that was not only different in configuration, but that also held to stricter and more realistic engineering judgment.

The reason for lifting Roofslab 3 would have been that in order to add the steep revetment with its showy quartz facade the builders had to roof the first three orthostats, which were going to lie well beneath it. As the revetment would have buried the slit and its protective roofbox very deeply in the cairn, they were forced to move them forward, closer to the edge of the enlarged mound. That in turn would have forced them to lift Roofslab 3 up out of the path of the solstitial sunbeam.

It would perhaps have been during this radical retooling of the monument that the "relieving lintel" was caulked, closed, and buried along with the boulder cap. The mound which had once sloped gently from the bottom of the boulder cap to the kerb now sloped from the level of the capstone to the top of the high revetment, and the height of the mound was increased behind the boulder cap, burying the sunset passage.

All of this may have a bearing upon another unsolved problem.

If Newgrange is a "grave," what happened to the bones? O'Kelly recovered only about 2200 very small fragments of burnt bone, weighing about two pounds, under the 200,000 metric tons of the cairn. Yet "Three times fifty sons of kings" were supposed to have been laid to rest here. The site was accessible for centuries of pilgrims, squatters, raiders, neighbors, antiquarians, tourists and archaeologists. But although tidied up repeatedly in modern times, there is no evidence of a wholesale removal of enough remains to represent a burial deposit of respectable size. The two unburned skeletons reported when the site was first explored may be a later insertion.

O'Kelly states that although "...the longest dimension of a few [fragments of bone] reached thirty millimeters, in the majority of cases it was under fifteen millimeters; most pieces were considerably smaller than this." (*Newgrange*, 201). There had been so much unregulated and unreported traffic and so much undocumented prowling and meddling within the monument that it is risky to hazard a guess about what may have happened. However, the possibility that there was once another passage, along with the locations of the deposits uncovered in the excavation of three of the satellite graves, may suggest one possibility.

K, L, and Z seem to have been crammed with burial deposits, tiny bone fragments mixed up in an earthen matrix, all inserted at one time, and sealed up almost at once, and the condition of those deposits suggested that they were re-burials of remains cremated elsewhere. Although there were as described a few remains in the Newgrange chamber, no remains were found in the Newgrange passage. But at K, L, and Z, remains did lie in the passages. If there were two passages at Newgrange it is possible that the main mass of the grave deposit still lies under the mound in or alongside a midwinter-*sunset*-facing passage, whose entrance is buried some forty feet inside the kerb.

How would this hypothetical sunset passage have communicated with the chamber? The fragments O'Kelly recovered within the chamber show that remains must at least have passed through it. There may have been a time when it was possible to get behind C10 into the other cavity, although there is too much doubt about the original position of C10 to make a judgment. Perhaps access to the area behind the center recess was not a passage but a pass-*through*. In this case the gap between the two spaces could have been very narrow as at Dowth. The burned remains of the average man fill a container about the size of a small shoe-box. A hide, fiber, or basketry packet could be handed through a gap a few inches wide to someone stationed behind the chamber.

It was once suggested that the roofbox aperture might have been intended as an opening through which to communicate with the spirits of the dead, whose remains were located in the chamber. Archaeologists suggested that there may have been a slit left in the passage roof of K or L, allowing sunbeams to penetrate into a passage which had been filled with a grave deposit and permanently closed. This might imply some interchange between the sun and the spirits. The midwinter sun was certainly admitted into the Newgrange chamber, perhaps to visit spirits, but it is possible that their permanent residence was *behind* the chamber rather than in it.

Another curious possibility is that in the earlier phase the "relieving lintel," which very much resembles the roofbox, was exposed, along with the southern arc of the neatly fitted boulder cap. If this lintel had been open, like a kind of chamber roofbox, it might have admitted a midwinter sunbeam that struck the corbels at the back of the center recess. Even a small chink in the corbels would have admitted direct sunlight into a passage behind the recess that perhaps contained human remains. Or the sunbeam might have served as a signal to someone stationed in the sunset passage to perform some function connected with the remains.

The fact that the entrance to a second passage was buried deep in the mound, a passage which perhaps held a burial deposit, may have resulted in the striking tradition that Newgrange *could* not be despoiled. "I saw a house in the country out of which no hostages are given to a king, fire burns it not, harrying spoils it not; good the prosperity with which was conceived that kingly house...that is the Brugh of the Boyne that you have seen, namely the house of Oengus Og of the Brugh, and it cannot be burned or harried as long as Oengus shall live..."(quoted by Claire O'Kelly from Bruidhean Chaorthainn, *Newgrange* 46.) The tradition implies not only that the tomb could not be despoiled but also that there must have been something of value in it.

The possibility that one use of the sunset passage was to hold remains may also help to explain why the passage was buried. Because a midwinter sunset orientation was dependent only on the solstice, it was as invulnerable as the sunrise orientation, and like the sunrise passage the hypothetical sunset passage would have retained to this day some view of the midwinter sun on the horizon. However, the funerary function may have depended chiefly on the original "primary focus" of the monument, the righthand recess with its galactic outviews and water-collecting basin. When the views possible from both the right-hand and lefthand recess were lost, the funerary function may have been fatally weakened, altered, or separated from the monument whose remaining focus was now genuinely and perhaps chiefly astronomical, unless the "well" continued to play some part. The minimal remains found would have been due to accidental spill from the passage of remains *through* the chamber during the earlier phase.

The kerbstones that surround the great mound probably include all those that would originally have surrounded a smaller previous mound. In its present position K52 is meaningful only as one understands its arcane devices. They of course are of great significance in themselves. The devices on the left end of the stone may represent the way the chamber aperture captured the sun, moon, and planets, and there is a striking separate, and central, reference in this panel to the rainbow, which belongs to the very basic Swarm, or "Many-Little-" concept which links sun, stars, bees, and water-droplets, all features of an archaic funerary concept. The devices on the right end may refer to sun, moon and Venus in connection with a ritual method of counting their cycles, a method relatable to devices appearing on the righthand recess roofstone and the "marble-and-socket apparatus" below it.

So one possible reason for moving K52 to its present position is that the lefthand end of it at least was intimately related to the original transformational belief and the funeral practice developed from it, concepts, emblems, rites, and facilities (including the "well") belonging to the original configuration and ritual function of the monument. When all had been humbled or altered by precession, K52 was deliberately and spectacularly demoted.

The conceptual shock that must have resulted from the realization that the celestial pole was not fixed would have done more than provoke the great retooling of the monument. It would have shattered the unity of the original concept, which united the astronomy of the culture and its afterlife interest: a partnership of its science and religion.

Homer repeated a tradition that there was a detached head held up by the wife of Hades at the entrance of the underworld. But the Perseus tradition that describes how this head was separated from its body is also thought-provoking in view of the possibility that Newgrange underwent a radical revision due to a cosmic event. The extended Perseus tradition preserves a cluster of narrative emblems which resembles a cluster of engraved emblems recognizable at Newgrange. That is, these two contexts could have some historical relationship.

The story of Perseus can be seen as a mosaic of several doublets, narrative modules diverging radically in the course of a long history of religious politics, adhering to each other in the tradition because they were always understood to belong together.

Many of the individual modules in this story seem to echo individual Newgrange circumstances. Danae was imprisoned in a tower, or dungeon. She was impregnated by a supernatural being through a skylight. Later she was caught in a net by Dictys "Net," brother of Polydectes "Welcomer of Many," a euphemism for Death.

Medusa lived on the borders of the afterworld. Poseidon lay with her in the temple of Athena, who spitefully turned her face into the bogey-mask of the Gorgoneion. Anyone who looked at her face directly was turned to stone. Perseus found Medusa asleep on the shore, in a landscape strewn with the petrified forms of men and beasts. He beheaded her by viewing her image reflected in a pool.

Medusa bore Poseidon's twins through her cut neck: the reflection is born from within the rim of the reflector. The twins were the winged water-horse Pegasus, an emblem of the way a water surface seems to bear the observer to the sky, and the warrior Chrysaor "Gold Tensor." This name refers not to the sword but to the cord or baldrick it hung from. Chrysaor is one epithet of Demeter, whom Poseidon also impregrated with a horse and its twin. The supernatural tensor is the spiral, an emblem of circumpolar rotation. The rescue of Hesione by Telemon "Baldrick" is a doublet of the rescue of Andromeda. Big Ajax had a very famous baldrick: Little Ajax was followed everywhere by a tame serpent. Cygnus had a son named Tenes "Tensor."

A late, hostile tradition had Cassiopeia tied upside down in a market-basket a sort of net. The constellation Cassiopeia was beheaded by the stone edge of the chamber aperture.

The element "dan-" in the names Danae and Poseidon "Spouse of Dan" appears in association with the Brugh on the Boyne as the Irish Danu, a supernatural people who once frequented it. Poseidon was originally a god of fresh water, springs and wells. Dan- means flow, trickle, exudate: the same idea that appears in the image of the trickling, slow-dripping River Styx located in Hades. The blood of Medusa could kill or resurrect depending on whether it came from the right or the left vein, a reference to reversal of polarity by reflection.

The variant modules held together in the Perseus story may have diverged from a story like that of Ivan's rescue of Goldentress and the three metal princesses from the realm of Whirlwind the Whistler. He achieves his feat by following metal balls through copper, silver and gold kingdoms whose serpents he calms with buckets of water. The Newgrange chamber was spiral- or serpent-haunted. The queen-mother who was imagined to have been freed from it could have been either the constellation Cassiopeia or less probably the sun, for its visits to the chamber were brief. The model of Whirlwind's consort Goldentress however would have been the sun.

CHAPTER XX

REGENERATION AND GNOSIS

39. K1 plus K52   **Possible Reference:**   **Related Site Feature:**
    as an Emblem   Acting Genius Loci,   Stylistic Similarity of
                                   Integration of Faith   K1 and K52, Possible
See Plate XXVII   and Gnosis   Relocation of K52

Gnosis is defined as "Assured knowledge or science, especially the higher knowledge of the mysteries; knowledge of the initiated, or esoteric knowledge." At Newgrange, the science of the time, consciously integrated into the mystery of a faith in regeneration and life everlasting, was by definition gnosis - there are in fact unexpected reminiscences of Newgrange emblem-clusters in several gnostic traditions.

If K52 ever stood with K1 in the forecourt, the pair must have belonged to some earlier phase of the monument. That would have been a phase in which confidence in the scientific knowledge that supported the design of the site was still vigorously supporting an afterlife belief and practice fundamentally centered on the Milky Way and the reflections of circumpolar stars. Both were visible from the chamber side recesses. This would be a very different situation from that prevailing when both side recesses in the chamber were blinded and K1 stood alone in the forecourt, an ominous decapitated head.

If K52 was ever set beside K1, at its left end, and if ponded water reflected them together, the result would have been a solemn unearthly figure ornamented with devices celebrating a sophisticated science and mathematics.

PLATE XXVII. K1 with K52 and Their Reflections

K52 forms a short, massive, dwarvish torso for the immense head created by K1. The arms, which lie along the sides of the figure, are modeled by the rounded projection that lies along the top of the recumbent stone. The limbs are tattooed with emblematic outlines. The figure's arms reach almost to its feet, the legs being either very short or bent back at the knees as if kneeling. Below the waist, which is belted by the broad groove that bisects the stone, the body is clothed by a netted apron or plaid kilt.

This interpretation of K52 as a torso for K1 would have the merit of explaining why this stone was chosen for this carving. Claire O'Kelly has commented of K51, which is now adjacent to K52 at the back of the monument, that this stone is " ...a fine smooth rounded boulder which one would have thought would have been preferred by the master-carver of K52, since K52 has a poor surface with many protuberances, cracks and hollows and must have presented great difficulties..." According to the torso interpretation, the natural modeling of the stone fitted it well for the genuinely sculptural role I have suggested.

I have described the big-headed, stumpy-bodied figure created by the two kerbstones and their reflections as dwarvish. Several archaic supernatural figures are represented as dwarves or have dwarvish characteristics that have something in common with this peculiar apparition. Among them are the Egyptian god Bes, the Greek god Hephaestus, and the Irish Dagda. Two other supernatural beings with peculiar double names, the Phoenician Kousor- and- Hassis, and the Russian Lame- and-Crooked (or Lame-and-One-Eyed), may be related to this group.

Bes was a dwarf with outsized head, goggle eyes, large semi-circular ears, protruding tongue, curly beard of spiral locks, and very short bow legs. A bushy "tail," part of an animal hide, probably a lion's, dangles between his legs, its front paws being often draped over his shoulders and its back paws held in his hands. The figure is always presented frontally, and is absolutely symmetrical. He often appears with hands on hips, has a girdle and a sort of apron, wears a kind of amulet dangling from his neck, and has a luxuriant crown of ostrich feathers frequently represented by four or five stiff vertical tufts.

Bes was not native to Egypt. He was supposed to have come from the Land of Punt, a lost country which comparatively late tradition located on the east coast of Africa. Its location is however by no means certain. He was a popular god, principally concerned with birth and protection although there are traces of other links in archaic marginal traditions. He was a very old divinity.

FIG. 13. Sketch of Bes

The figure of Bes resembles that created by the two stones in several respects: the invariable frontal presentation, enormous head, prominent eyes, semi-circular "ears," elaborate beard of opposing spirals, girdle, very short legs and prominent arms. But most significantly, Bes like Newgrange is linked to the Milky Way. This is shown by his crown of ostrich feathers, an emblem linked to Egyptian afterlife beliefs.

The unexpected link of the ostrich with the Milky Way may be explained by a collection of mostly Arab ostrich-names situated on or near the galactic circle and the constellation River Eridanus, which also bore the Milky Way's title River of Heaven.

It should first be explained that precession has much altered what could be seen from Newgrange in its own day. If a man or woman of that time stood on the ridge around the middle of a winter night facing the Boyne, the Milky Way swept down from behind him, curling around the eastern horizon over his left shoulder, and looping down along the southern horizon, just above the southerly loop of the river, which in fact repeated the sagging loop of the River of Heaven. (Boyne means White Cow, and an Irish name for the galaxy is Way of the White Cow.)

In those days, the top of the arch, marked by Cassiopeia and Cepheus, was over 50° from the pole. From the righthand chamber recess what people could see was part of the northern loop, looking outward toward the edge of the galactic ring. This segment was very thin. But because the northern loop of the galaxy was much farther from the pole in those times, they saw more of the southern loop than is now visible in their latitude. Looking south from above the river, and through the open passage door, and of course from the top of the mound, they were looking inward across the dense center of our galaxy, a very wide, extremely ragged swathe of stars of greatly varying luminosity. Within the southern loop of the celestial stream they would have seen not only the Hydra or Water-snake with the Chalice and the Crow on its back but below them also the constellations we call Argo, Centaurus, Crux, Lupus and Ara. So practically all of the stars in the following paragraphs were visible to the people of Newgrange.

Allen's *Star Names* provides the following examples of ostrich names of stars and asterisms: Alpha Centaurus has a title Toliman, from Arabic Thalimain "Ostrich." In Sagittarius are "The Going Ostriches," and "The Returning Ostriches," "The Ostrich's Nest," and "The Keeper of the Ostriches." Corona Australis "The Southern Crown" also has a title "The Ostrich's Nest." Aquila has "The Two Ostriches." Outside the Milky Way occur several more: γ Andromedae as "The Fifth One of the Ostriches"; ζ Pegasi as "The Lucky Star of the Ostriches" (possibly occurring also for τ and υ). In Cetus appear "The Hen Ostriches," and ε and π as "a part of the Ostrich's Nest that mainly lay in Eridanus."

At the source of the Eridanus, abutting Orion, is a group called the "Ostrich's Nest,"and farther down the river are "The Ostrich" and "The Little Ostrich," followed by "The Egg." (There is a slight possibility of another group with this designation.) In addition there is a number of small stars between Eridanus and Fomalhaut called "The Little Ostriches." Fomalhaut, the Southern Fish, once adjacent to Eridanus, has a title "Ostrich." Another "Ostrich" occurs in Phoenix, once a part of Eridanus. Allen observes in connection with some of these names that "Ideler thought it inexplicable that these non-drinking creatures should be found here in connection with water..."

Allen also has a paragraph on the name Ciconia, identified with the adjutant bird, which has been attached to Ophiuchus, the Serpent-holder. Like the ostrich, the adjutant bird or jabiru is long-legged, long-necked, and heavy-bodied although unlike the ostrich it can fly. "Crane" is found for Ophiuchus and "Ibis" occurs for Sagittarius. Like the ostrich the crane has long legs, long neck, large beak and solemn gait. The stork, with a very similar configuration, is still a bird of omen, generally credited with delivering babies (the southern constellation Grus is a creation of Bayer).

Cygnus was a common classical name for the constellation we call the Swan, but it seems that its name was earlier Ornis "Bird." A Greek expression used for the ostrich was ho megas strouthos, "the big bird," or strouthos katagaios, "the bird (running) along the ground," where strouthos is a rather generic term for bird.

What accounts for all these ostriches (and other long-legged birds) concentrated around the galaxy and the other heavenly river, Eridanus? The inspiration was the form of the galaxy itself.

As the sky wheels around the north celestial pole, the summit of the galactic arch revolves along with it. The ostrich emblem is based on the fact that as the celestial vault revolves, the two stupendous "legs" of the galaxy, 180° apart, stride all the way around the horizon every twenty-four hours.

The Arabs in particular, blest with illimitable horizons and crystalline skies, saw the long legs of the galaxy race around the horizon every night. They were also very familiar with the ostrich, a long-legged runner which never leaves the ground, has a tendency to run in circles, and has been clocked at fifty miles an hour. It would be quite natural that they should make the ostrich an emblem of the galaxy.

The emblem of the striding bird is repeated by an outline formed by three bright stars in and near the northern loop of the galaxy. Deneb Cygni (the stone-age midwinter herald), Vega Lyrae and Altair Aquilonis form a triangle which has actually been figured as one asterism called "The Summer Triangle." These stars can be seen to outline a long-legged bird. Deneb marks the head, the wings are those of Cygnus, and the feet are marked by Altair and Vega. The wings are very small in relation to the size of the bird, like those of the ostrich. The foot that is represented by Vega is raised very high as the bird runs west.

Vishnu has been traditionally linked with the stars of Aquila. There are pictures of him striding that show one straight leg raised almost as high as his head. "[Vishnu's] essential feature is the three strides...with which he traverses the universe. Two of these steps are visible to men, but the third or highest is beyond mortal sight. These steps are symbolic of the rising, culminating and setting of the sun, or alternatively the course of the solar deity through the three divisions of the universe." The three brightest stars of Aquila traditionally represented these three footsteps. Deneb, Vega and Altair, which with the wings of Cygnus have an outline like that of an ostrich, can also be imagined as a stickman outline for which Cepheus provides a very outsized squarish head with a conical crown. Vishnu appears with a conical crown, and took his three steps under the form of a *dwarf*.

When we see the archaic but enduringly popular god Bes crowned with ostrich-feathers, we recognize that we are dealing with a Milky Way emblem. The ostrich feather is a critical emblem in the Egyptian picture of the afterlife. The soul of the departed had to answer for his deeds to the judge of the dead in a hall where his deeds were weighed in a great scale-balance against an ostrich feather. The emblem of the ostrich feather was contributed by the ostrich-leg outline of the Milky Way. Where did the scale emblem come from?

Again, the clue points back to a very archaic supernatural significance attached to the Milky Way. There is a cluster of Arab names located in or near the Milky Way which links emblems of weighing and the scale-balance with oath-taking. Allen cites the following.

Alpha and β Centaurus have Arabic titles "Ground" and "Weight," used interchangeably for the two stars. Gamma Ophiuchus has a title Muliphen "Of the Oath." Aquila has a title "Scale Beam" for the row δ, η and θ. Triangulum has a title Mizan "Scale Beam." Orion has "The Accurate Scale Beam" for the row δ, ε and ζ, and "The False Scale Beam" for the row θ, ι and κ. Canis Major has Al Wazn "Weight" for δ, thus probably Al Hadar "Ground" for ξ, (rather than Adhara "Virgins") since γ may be Muliphen "Of the Oath." Columba has Hadar and Wazn for α and β, the pair having the joint title Mulifain. Argo has λ Velae as Wazn, ζ Puppis as Hadar, and γ Velae as "Of the Oath." Alpha "Canopus" bore as titles both Wazn and Hadar. There is of course also the zodiacal constellation Libra "Scales," whose form does not particularly suggest the object; this scale is traditionally pictured with wildly swinging balance pans.

The shape of the Scale Balance, like the legs of the Ostrich, resembles the shape of the Milky Way as a whole. The cords of a scale balance were attached to the ends of a balance-beam, which was usually hung from its midpoint by another cord attached to a fixed upper support. In the sky, the polar point would naturally suggest itself as this fixed support, the top of the galactic arch lying below it. The long dependent "legs" would be the cords on which the scale-pans hung. All these outlines are characterized by a pair of long extensors attached to a yoke and related significantly to the *ground*. "Ground and Weight" refer to the operation of the scale.

The group of Scale-balance names, along with the Ground and Weight names, along the course of the River of Heaven are frequently found with names that refer to *Oath*. It is the nature rather than the shape of the River that has caused the link with Oath. It has been argued that oaths were originally sworn by things not gods, and rivers were apparently among the very earliest of these guarantors.

Almost invisible from modern cities because of their enormous light-spill, the Milky Way is the mightiest feature of the night sky. Its river-like shape had a tendency to associate it with precipitated water, particularly dew, which forms under skies clear enough to enhance its brilliance. Since the River of Heaven was *the* River, the widely held idea of the sacredness of earthly rivers may have arisen from the belief that they were branches of the River of Heaven. The Po, the Rhine, the Ebro, the Ganges, and the Nile were among the rivers identified with the Milky Way. Arguably, so was the Boyne. The many river-names that include the element dan- (as Danube, Don, Dnieper) may also have developed out of this association. The Christian feast of Epiphany celebrates the blessing of the rivers, linking this to the baptism of Jesus in the Jordan by John the Baptist, the event associated with the announcement of his divine identity as Savior from death. Like the water of the Ganges, Jordan water is bottled, kept, and used to bless and cure. Epiphany is celebrated on January 6th, close to the time of midwinter.

The Styx was described as a branch of Ocean Stream, and Ocean Stream, which was imagined to encircle both the earth and sea, was a name for the Milky Way. The Styx was so holy that the gods themselves swore by it, and if a god broke his word he lost his power for a year. The idea of holiness springs from the belief that the holy object must not be touched by or defiled by contact with anything less pure or perfect than itself. The old custom of swearing on the Holy Bible relied on the idea that the man putting his hand on the book was a man who was telling the truth, the whole truth, and nothing but the truth, through the assistance of his god. Lying was a defilement of the holy. Fear of punishment by the supernatural power guaranteed the oath.

The Milky Way has very often been imagined as a way of departed souls. In India it has been thought to be the source of the Ganges, with the power to cleanse, take away sin, bestow enlightenment, and ensure eternal bliss. This may be close to an original very positive conception of the Milky Way as fundamentally gracious and beneficent, a concept closely linked to the image of the goddess Ganga. Ganga might well owe something to the image developed around the stars of Cassiopeia, envisioned as a nursing mother at the source of the galactic stream. Styx was a nurturer of children. The power of the River would have guaranteed blessings to those who believed in it and paid it fitting respect and homage. The River promised supernatural protection as the rainbow bridge promised supernatural protection to Noah. The title "Of the Oath" for stars near the celestial River would have been bestowed because the River was believed to be a divine and faithful guarantor of the highest good to man, everlasting or eternal life.

Mother-goddess, ostrich and scale all have some claim to be associated with the form and aspect of the Milky Way. The scale that gave or withheld eternal life was almost certainly later than the emblem of the ostrich. The scale balance of the late, sophisticated Book of the Dead that weighs sin against an ostrich feather reveals an image of brokered salvation. Brokered salvation is the mainstay of a fossilized religion supporting a prosperous clergy. This is very different from the protection offered by the genial ostrich-crowned Bes or the cult of the freely-forgiving Ganges. The rigidity and self-interest of an entrenched religious institution relied on fear, the scales of judgment, reward and punishment. But it appealed for legitimacy to the archaic, supremely holy emblem of the ostrich feather. Similar developments can be traced in other religions.

Bes was a god of the people. He was much loved, and his image often appears on such homely articles as mirrors and toilet articles. Like the Dagda he played the harp (as well as the flute). His image was a defense against such harmful animals as lions, scorpions, and snakes. His image also appeared in bed-chambers, because he was involved with birth as well as death, and images of Bes have often been found to contain the remains of human embryos. This custom is of significance to us here because of an object which O'Kelly found carefully placed in a hollow in the back corbel of the Newgrange roofbox, a few yards from K1.

40. Sandstone Concretion	**Possible Reference:**	**Related Site Feature:**
	Regeneration	Human Remains in Chamber, Atmospheric Water Filling Hollow Slabs and Bowl, Openable Chamber
See Fig. 14.		Capstone, Midwinter Sunrise View.

"...On the upper surface of the back corbel of the roof-box [there was]...a natural shallow basin-like hollow which in wet weather, accompanied by a southeast or south wind, would fill with water and occasionally spill over and enter the passage. To prevent this, a water-groove had been cut from the west edge of the 'basin' to draw the water off...Lying in this 'basin,' in a position into which it must have been put by the builders, was a natural but very curiously-shaped calcareous sandstone concretion..." (*Newgrange* p 94; see also *Newgrange* plates 43, 52, and 64 and figures 18a, 18b, 19, and 52).

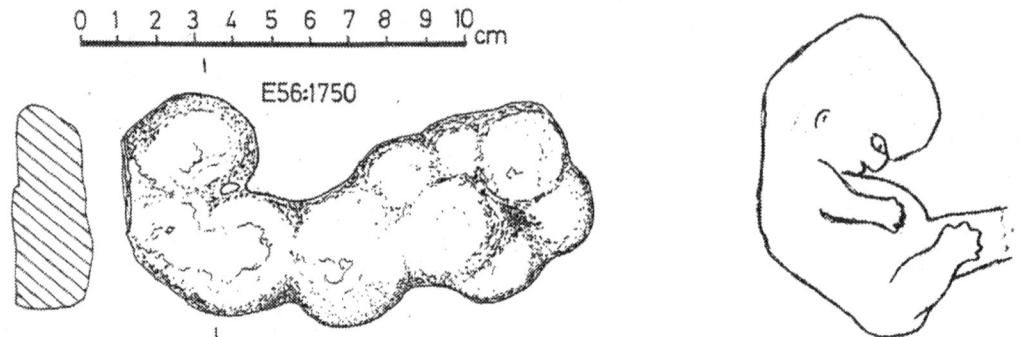

Fig 14. Comparable Forms: a. Claire O'Kelly's Drawing of Sandstone Concretion b. My Drawing of Nine-Week Embryo (actual size a little over an inch)

Mrs. O'Kelly's permission to use her drawing of this sandstone concretion does not of course imply agreement with my interpretation of it.

This little stone is about five inches long, and is thin and narrow. Judging by Claire O'Kelly's drawing, the wider end looks something like a five-lobed section of an incomplete rosette, and the narrow end resembles a human embryo in slight relief. As described in the text, the stone often lay in water, and with its own reflection the wider end would form a complete rosette, the narrow end, twin embryos.

The concept of regeneration or rebirth might well have a tendency to begin with the image of a human embryo. The intermittently watery location of this concretion recalls the embryos's amniotic pool. The cascade of stair-steps coming down from the boulder cap ensured that the water in which the image swam had the same source as that which entered the chamber bowl. The location of this evocative object, so small yet so poignant, lying right over the passage into the chamber, might easily have had graphic implications for the afterlife concept.

The dwarvish figure produced by the reflected image of K1 linked with K52 is reminiscent not only of Bes but also of the great Egyptian prototypal smith Ptah. It must have been from some archaic tradition that the mighty smith Ptah was pictured much like Bes: as a dwarf, with twisted legs, hands on hips, and huge head, shaved except for a customary talismanic slightly curling "lock." He usually appears as a solemn figure; his lower torso is wrapped up like a mummy, and he holds a stout staff which combined emblems of life, stability, and omnipotence. The lower end of the staff ends in a sort of forked split like a pair of tongs or claws. It may be significant that the zodiacal constellation Scales is also named and figured as Claws.

Like Bes, Ptah was, or became in some sense, the protector of the dead. The version with mummy-wrapped torso is, like the swaddled infant, a Snakeman outline. Ptah was the inventor of many arts and crafts including metal-working, and he was also a builder. He was being worshipped as a supreme god at Memphis at the time Newgrange was built. Memphis, just south of the Nile delta, was known as The White Walls. In its glory days Newgrange might also have been called the White Walls.

Ptah was identified by the Greeks with the divine smith Hephaestus. The figure of Hephaestus was also originally imagined as somewhat dwarvish. He was supposed to have been crippled when he was thrown out of heaven for defying Zeus and defending Hera. Homer says he had to be supported to walk. His face too was originally conceived as more or less deformed, which persisted in his late images only as squinting eyes. These traits, which might have originated as traits of a dwarf's figure, were more and more minimized in classical tradition.

Homer describes Hephaestus's dwelling as "indestructible, bright as the stars, built of bronze." He was served in his mansion by three mechanical maidens that he had made out of gold. He had also made tripods which ran by themselves on self-turning wheels to take messages between his realm and Mount Olympus. These emblems could be read as a late garbled version of a set of emblems also found in fairy tales: the wise dwarf, the magnificent mansion or palace, the mysterious master of all crafts called Lame and Crooked or Lame and One-eyed who was summoned by a whistle, the three metal maidens, the spinning wheels, the sets of three, and the self-rolling balls or wheels that guide the fairy tale hero through the otherworld kingdom. I have already called attention to similarities between these emblems and certain Newgrange features.

Hephaestus made the armor of Achilles, whose mother dipped him in the Styx to make him immortal. She failed only because the heel she held him by was vulnerable. Homer specially emphasized Achilles's magnificent *greaves,* or leg armor. In the Russian "Whirlwind" story, the name of Ivan's savior "Lame and One-Eyed" recalls Hephaestus, and it was a dwarf that provided Prince Ivan with iron talons to climb the supernatural mountain into the other world. Lame and One-eyed provided the jeweled otherworld shoes required to win the Gold Princess. The jeweled shoe is a version of the glass slipper. The glass slipper is an emblem of the reflector which plants the viewer's foot in the sky. These supernatural slippers fulfill the same function as the climbing talons. An archaic Irish version of the dwarf who provides magic shoes still lives in the person of the Leprecaun, the "one-shoe-maker" who preserves the old link with the pot of gold and the rainbow. Both Achilles's heel and his leg-armor are related to this emblem.

The Dagda, sometime owner of Newgrange, was also a kind of smith, good at every art and craft. He was also ungainly, pot-bellied, and rudely dressed. He was famed for his "wheeled fork," an enormous club, that was a burden for eight men, and left a furrow across Ireland. Its form recalls the staff of Ptah that ended in a fork-like or claw-like split. Like Bes, the Dagda played a harp. Two of his amours are reminiscent of traits of Hathor, who is sometimes identified as Bes's wife: the warlike Morigu recalls Hathor's bloodthirsty aspect; but the Dagda begot Angus on Boann, who was linked with the Boyne, Bo Finda, "White Cow," and Hathor was often pictured as a benign white cow. The old picture of the grassy mound and the milk cow again comes to mind.

Newgrange was distinguished by an openable skylight, admission of atmospheric moisture, and a visiting cow in the form of the Milky Way, features which recall still another smith. Minos had a smith named Daedalus, who built an artificial cow with an openable aperture so that the amorous queen Pasiphae could climb into it and be mated by Poseidon's bull. By one tradition she waited for the bull in a meadow *with a mirror* (*Pauly* "Pasiphae" 2077).

The openable aperture appears in what is perhaps the oldest literary tradition about a smith, an episode included in the Ras Shamra documents, which date back to the first part of the fourteenth century B.C, but are believed to contain much older mythological material. This text describes a smith or builder with a double name who is also spoken of as two brothers: Kousor-and-Hassis. Kousor-and-Hassis insisted on installing a skylight in Baal's temple. "I myself shall place them. Kusor, the mariner, Kusor, son of the law(?), he shall open the window in sanctuaries, the sky-light in the middle of temples. And Ba'al shall open a fissure in the clouds - above the face of Kusor-and-Hasisu." Kusor was adept at magic and prophecy, invented mechanical devices, and developed the fishing boat (Larousse *Mythology* p78-9). The trait of dwarfism appears marginally, in connection with Kusor's reported link with Ptah.

The double name recalls Lame-and-Crooked or Lame-and-One-Eyed, the savior of Ivan in the story of Whirlwind. In another Russian story, Katoma Wooden Hat, the figure of Lame and One-Eyed is split into two persons like Kousor and Hassis: they combine as a blind man carrying a cripple, like the blinded Orion carrying Hephaestus's servant Cedalion. Cedalion was a cyclops or "round eye," perhaps a water-jar as reflector. The pair in the Katoma story visit the Baba Yaga's hut and free her handmaiden, whose breasts she was sucking. They force her to show them two wells, one that killed and one that healed and the healing well restored the cripple's legs and the blind man's sight. One of the two kerbstones that form one figure could have been described as one-eyed, inasmuch as K1 has only one complete eye, and the other could have been described as lame, inasmuch as K52's "legs" are deficient.

There is a possible natural model for the figure of the dwarf that would have been familiar to the Egyptians as well as the Newgrangemen. The dwarf is one of several images that can be suggested by the complicated and beautiful relief modeling on the back of the common crab, whose claws might also have suggested the tongs of the smith. We know that the crab plays a critical role in Egyptian myth. It was because a crab had eaten the phallus that Isis was never able to reconstitute the dismembered body of Osiris. Greek myth tells how the crab bit Heracles when he was fighting the Lernaean Hydra. Cuchulainn's infatuated admirer Dornolla was named Big Fist, and had not only a repulsive face but limbs that all bent backwards. There are a number of other scraps of information about the crab which taken together shadow forth the outlines of some almost completely submerged concepts that may be relevant to our study.

The zodiacal constellation of the Crab, the dimmest of the zodiacal twelve, precedes the Lion and the Virgin. But small, dim, and formless as it, Cancer was supposed to be the "Gate of Men through which souls descended from Heaven into Human Bodies" (Allen). This shows that the emblem once had great importance in a post-mortem transformational setting. Two of its stars are called the Aselli, Asses, memorializing those ridden by Dionysus and Silenus during the battle of the gods and the giants; their loud braying helped win the contest. The ass has been incorporated into a story about the birth of Jesus, who called himself the door into the kingdom of the heavens. Ass is a Sorry Colt emblem, an "incomplete" horse that belongs with the reflector emblems.

In Newgrange times the sun reached the constellation around the first of May. Four fourth magnitude stars, γ, δ, η, and q form a lozenge in which glows a disk of light, the Manger or "Beehive Cluster." Seen through binoculars this cluster looks like a hole into another sky through which a blaze of far stars is seen. Its appearance strikingly recalls the incident of the Flagstone of the Little Hole, set over a hot fire, upon which the smith Domnall, Big Fist's father, trained Cuchulainn in the arts of combat (in the time of Cuchulainn the constellation was close to the summer solstice). The quadrilateral framing the bright starry blaze recalls the lozenge of the Newgrange vault aperture through which the glow of the Milky Way could be viewed.

There are several images that may be made out in the details of the crabshell modeling.

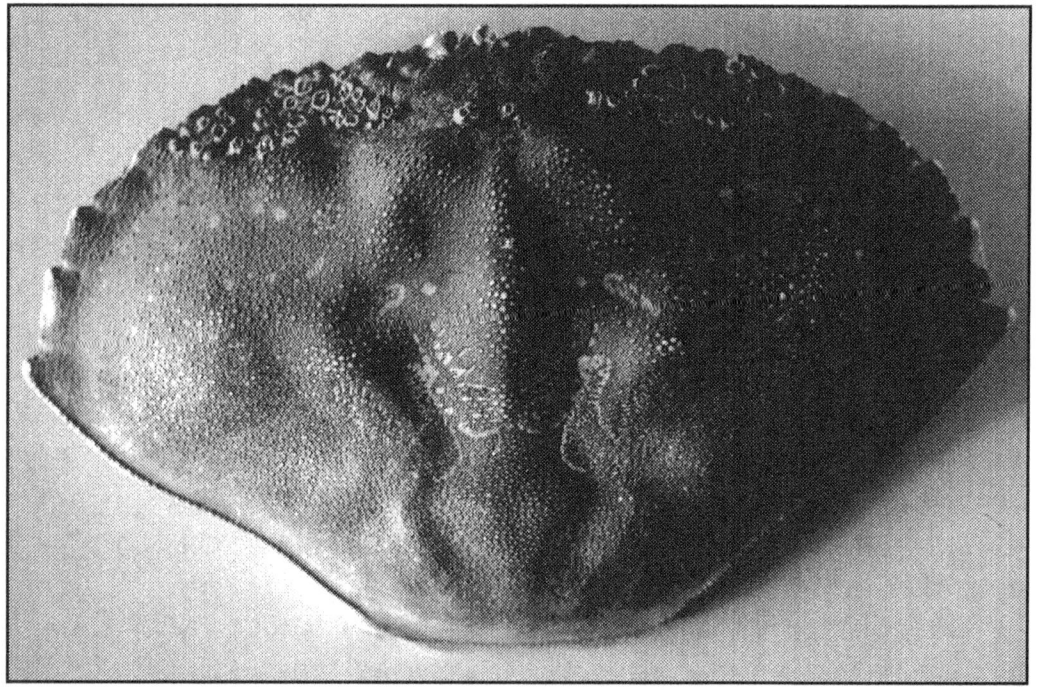

PLATE XXVIII. Crabshell Relief Images: A. Bes

The crab-back image of the dwarf is comparable in some respects to the conventional representation of Bes or the dwarvish type of Ptah. It is a symmetrical standing figure with outsized head and enormous goggle eyes. Above the head is a row of stiff little projections formed by the deeply serrated margin of shell between the crab's own tiny eyes. Below the head is a complicated raised object or process which might be thought of as a stuck-out tongue that conceals the outline of the mouth or an amulet hung around the neck. The elbows are fat and bent, the hands on the hips. The figure has spindly bandy legs. Below the torso and between the legs a sort of hexagonal shape hangs down. There is a thick band or belt around the waist. Details of the crab-back relief recall images of Bes, and the version of Ptah that resembles him. The claws of the live animal suggest tongs as does the end of Ptah's staff. Tradition said that the crab consumed the phallus of Osiris: popular tradition continued to credit Bes with control of generation, and canonical tradition retained his ostrich feather as the critical emblem in representation of afterlife destiny.

The crab is linked by several wisps of tradition with another smith: the Cabeirian Hephaestus. Pauly considers the Kabiroi to be among the oldest gods that can be recognized on Greek soil (Pauly, "Kabiroi" 1426). Hesychius pictures the crab as the child of Hephaestus, (under "Kabeiroi Karkinoi"): "The people in Lemnos hold crabs in great reverence, calling them the children of Hephaestus." (Pauly remarks that this reference explains a jest of Aristophanes in *Clouds*: "Why on earth is this chap crying as he eats? None of the crab gods has complained"). Lemnos is only about fifty miles from Samothrace, and like Samothrace was deeply involved with the Cabeiroi. Rites practised on Samothrace were anciently reported to have similarities to rites practised in Britain.

The link of Hephaestus with the crab seems inexplicable except perhaps for the similarity of claws and tongs. But it is perhaps illuminated by other modeled forms that can be recognized in the crabshell relief modeling. A figure that is rather easily made out in the pattern is the Naked Lady. This is a perfectly symmetrical female figure with well-proportioned breasts, well-marked waist, long straight legs closely pressed together, arms close to the sides, a suggestion of a small head on a sturdy neck, and two thick matching locks of hair, a figure with a marked resemblance to archaic depictions of Ashtart or the Lady of Byblos. Hephaestus's beautiful wife Aphrodite is represented as naked in several crucial modules, as when she rose from the sea, or when Hephaestus caught her naked with Ares in a net.

PLATE XXVIII B. Naked Lady

The crab's back bears another image that may be associated with Hephaestus. This one is associated with Medusa, who like Aphrodite had offspring by Hephaestus. Taken as a whole, the relief on the crab's back produces a slight suggestion of the upper half of a fright-mask, like that into which Medusa's once beautiful face was turned.

PLATE XXVIII C. Fright Mask

The raised center outline suggests the broad flat nose, and flared nostrils of a carnivorous bogey. At the sides of the face, near the edge of the shell, are two slight depressions, sometimes faintly outlined with dotted lines, which suggest enormous, down-slanted eyes (the crab's own eyes are tiny black spheres). Between these "eyes" is a complicated relief which could be interpreted as a furrowed brow. Below the nose the lower surface of the face is cut off by the lower edge of the shell. This fright-mask, surrounded in the living animal by a snaky wreath of re-curved and writhing legs, forms a bodiless head like the Gorgoneion. The traditional Gorgoneion is almost impossible to distinguish from the face of Phobos, the son of Aphrodite and Hephaestus (or Ares) so that the crab-back fright-mask might indeed represent one of the children of Hephaestus, as recorded by Hesychius.

The crab has links not only to Hephaestus but to Perseus. Aelian observes (*Lib. XIII, XXVI* p. 232): "There is a kind of marine locust, most like a little crab, on Seriphos; when they find one dead, they bury it, and when they take one alive in a net they grieve for having injured it and put it back in the sea; and they say they are *the sweethearts of Perseus* the son of Zeus..." The sweetheart of Perseus was Andromeda, who is always represented as chained naked on the shore as prey for a sea monster. Perseus rescued her by turning the monster to stone with the Gorgon's head. Seriphos is off the coast of Boeotia, a region in which the Cabeiroi flourished.

Now, the story about Perseus and Andromeda is very consciously imitated in the story of Cuchulainn's rescue of Dervorgill in the Old Irish story of the "Wooing of Emer." We easily recognize the figure of Andromeda in the person of Dervorgill, threatened by a monster on the shore (although she is clothed - she gives the hero a strip of fabric from her garment). Dervorgill's father is Ruad "Red," and Andromedas's father, Cassiopeia's husband, would be by one tradition Phoenix, also Red. But it is in this romantic story that we find included the grotesque episode of Cuchulainn's dealings with his would-be sweetheart, Dornolla "Bigfist," daughter of the *smith* Domnall. She had a crooked, crab-like form in addition to her big fist, and her head was certainly a fright-mask. In the "sweetheart" tradition reported by Aelian we may recognize not only the naked lady on the shore, Andromeda or Dervorgill, but the model of the wild Big-Fist: the fright-mask image.

The rescue of Andromeda and the rescue of Dervorgil are both discrete modules in very extended, very complex contexts. The Irish story is patently modeled on the classical story of the rescue of Andromeda, and it is extraordinary to find included with the self-conscious Irish version its jeering doublet: the episode of Cuchulainn's rejected lover Dornolla. That module is a reference to the crab tradition, seemingly much older, reportedly some of it at home in Samothrace. The grotesque Dornolla and the beautiful naked Andromeda are united in the crab as they are both in Aelian's tradition and in two of the modeled crabshell forms. The Irish word for crab is partan, "shore dweller."

Another image which is suggested by the crab-back relief pattern is the lion-scalp. This is a very realistic image, but like that of the fright-mask the face extends no farther than the nose. The most powerful affect of the lion emblem came from its relation to the apparition of the solar eclipse, with the bristling rays of the corona that form a mane for the scary black disk. I have briefly discussed this emblem (also including references to the fringe of red prominences) in connection with Fand, Etain, Dornolla, Hathor, Iris, and the Yazilikaya reliefs. The island of Cos, on whose coins the crab-back frequently appears, often modified the relief on the shell into a lion scalp. A series of coins from Lycia as well as sixth-century coins of Samos off the Turkish coast near Ephesis, shows the lion's scalp. A study of coins from the Greek islands from the standpoint of this study could clarify many questions about their subjects.

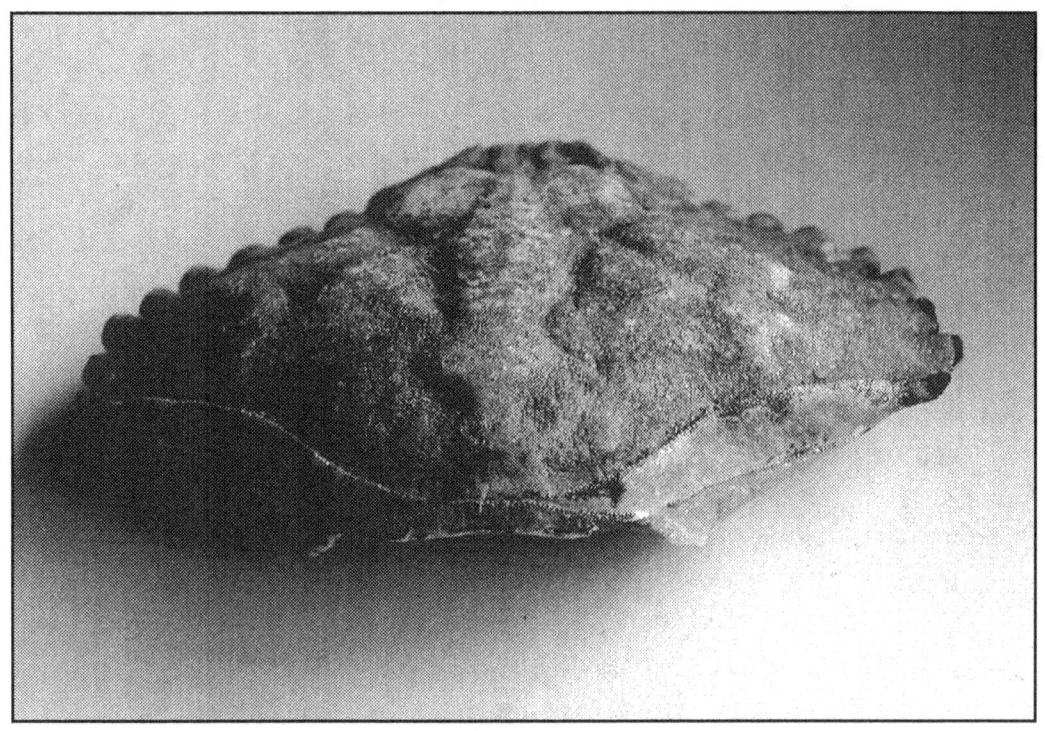

PLATE XXVIII D. Lion Scalp

The lion-scalp emblem is almost inseparable from Heracles, who wore the skin of the Nemean lion in such a way that the scalp appears over his head, the mane partially framing his face. The Nemean Lion is the one led by Iris, and by Virgo in the Zodiac. It is adjacent to the constellation of the Crab. Heracles's triumph over the lion was a symbol of the triumph of the Olympians over the power that controlled the bright-maned lion.

The association of the mane with the eclipse may have influenced the transformation of Hephaestus's wife the beautiful Medusa into the fright-mask: the transformation of the radiant feminine persona of the sun into the frightening apparition of the solar eclipse with its snaky flares and bristling coronal mane. This is the transformation seen in the double persona of the radiant Hathor who becomes a ravening man-eater.

There are similarities between the face created by K1 with its reflection and the Gorgoneion: the enormous eyes, broad nose, furrowed brow and framing spirals. There are also many important differences between them, especially the depiction of the mouth. The K1 mouth is small and pursed, the Gorgon's face has an enormous mouth, usually set in a grin that exposes the huge protruding tongue.

But Medusa has been represented in many ways. In J. K. Anderson's *Gorgons* there is reproduced "from an Attic amphora, c 670 B.C. Eleusis Museum" a pair of rather harmless looking gorgons whose heads are jars. Four parallel lines form a broad band around each jar. Two rows of teeth, like blunt vertical pegs, are drawn inside these bands, but there is a vacant space in the middle of each row of teeth and in the space there is a small upturned line like a little smile. The down-slanting eyes are much like the ones outlined by dots on the crab-back, but they have big black pupils. Snakes are attached to the jars and the creatures' shoulders. The bodies of these Gorgons are covered with fish-scales, and they have horses' or asses' legs. A triangular panel of wavy lines representing water is placed between the eyes of each of these faces which could imply that a separating, "reflecting" panel of water is involved in the existence of the face. This very different version of the gorgon gives the impression of being extremely archaic. A famous Boeotian amphora shows the body of the "Mistress of Animals" as a jar, and indicates by a fish drawn on the jar that it contains water. Her up-bent arms are formed by an enormous, clumsy W.

If it could be established that the Newgrange monument represented a very positive afterlife faith, and if it were accepted that the K1 "face" was a unique emblem associated with it, one would wonder how there could be any relationship between the uncanny inscrutable K1 visage and the carnivorous bogey of the traditional Gorgoneion which Homer depicted at the mouth of the afterworld.

When the pole of the ecliptic was recognized as more powerful than the celestial pole, Helius inherited the divine honors of the sun, and these were finally appropriated by Apollo. The defeated feminine persona, once imagined as a peerless beauty, was purposefully disfigured with the dreadful fright-mask suggested by the eclipse she had once controlled as solar power. If the K1 image ever served as a model for the image Homer thought that Hades's wife held up at the gate of the afterworld, that face disappeared when the forecourt was no longer groomed to provide ponded water, and the stone itself disappeared under the cairn collapse. As the stone-age faith withered away, the hostility of subsequent religious faiths would have gradually disfigured the memory of the enigmatic image guarding the collapsed mound and its defeated hope into a bogey. But the power of the emblem persisted.

CHAPTER XXI

RAM, GOLD, AND SET-OF-POWERS

One figure that can be imagined from the outline created by the joined kerbstones K1 and K52 with their reflections is, surprisingly, that of a fancily decorated ram. The composite image is not unlike the body of this animal seen head-on, a view that emphasizes the big head, heavy body and short, stumpy legs. The stocky K52 "torso" is fairly well proportioned for the body of a ram, and K1 could be seen as the large head with great spiral horns. The spiral nearest to K1's lozenge-shaped eye lies below it and a little toward the upper edge of the stone: a ram's horn frequently curls down and out in a rather similar fashion, below the eye. There is a smaller spiral below this one, and though certain sheep have extra horns, this spiral is extended into the dividing groove and could have been meant simply to link the design on the stone to the passage entrance or to the mound itself. The nose of the K1 face is a little elongated like a sheep's, and the corner of the eye is drawn outward horizontally like a sheep's, although it is opened wider. Like the sheep's, the eyes are slightly slanted, and like that of the sheep, the mouth is very small and prim or pursed.

The ram might have been thought of as having two different kinds of supernatural significance. Its spiral horns are its weapons in the great battles waged to win the ewes. The accompanying banging and crashing could serve as an imitation of the ponderous rumble and crash of thunder, so that the ram would easily be assimilated into an astronomical interest centered around the spiral-figured circumpolar rotor. A personification of this power was the Weather God. The ram was often employed as an emblem of supreme godhead, as in the case of Ammon. Hermes was intimately associated with the ram.

The top of an upright valentine is formed by juxtaposed spirals of opposite polarity. When you face a ram you see this valentine figure; the horn on your left curls out and down counterclockwise, the horn on your right, clockwise; the narrow chin is the point. The valentine is an emblem of reflection, the agency that reverses the polarity of rotation and creates a time-free plane of stasis, the infinitely thin reflective surface. That is why it is an emblem of romance or marriage, the union of opposites.

There are I believe only two examples at Newgrange of the heart-shape displayed by the ram's horns. One is the present plan of the mound, which is slightly cardial, and other is the central device of the carving on K1 when it is completed by reflection. This device forms the mouth of the "face." The valentine shape is the same as that of the joined valves of the cockle shell, a staple feature of cardial ware. A few cockle-shell fragments were found around Newgrange.

The horns of the bull or cow are often compared with those of the moon, but the horns of the ram too may have been an emblem of the lunar crescents. The bull's horns rest on top of its head, but the horns of the ram enclose its face as do the horns of the moon. The sheep is usually white like the moon. Lunar phases helped time Jewish festivals and determine the date of Christian Easter.

The ram or lamb emblem recurs again and again in tradition. Adam's favored son Abel kept sheep; a ram saved Isaac's life; Jacob married Rachel "Ewe"; the Israelites ransomed their first-born sons from the angel of death by smearing the blood of lambs on their doorposts; ram's-horn trumpets caused the fall of the walls of Jericho, and are still blown in sacred ceremonies. Some representations of the Romano-Celtic Cernunnos depict him as a ram-headed serpent with fish tail. It is the sheep that stand on god's right, the goats on his left. Christians rely on the blood of the lamb.

Goats' horns are usually not as spectacularly spiral as sheep's. Forms more like goats' horns are the chevrons of Cassiopeia, or the V of Taurus. The beautiful golden lumina of Auriga "The Charioteer" is called Capella, the "Little She Goat," and the charioteer has two little kids on his shoulder. The zodiacal Capricorn "Water Goat," has the tail of a fish, which could be a reflection emblem.

The genius loci of Newgrange that was created by K1 and K52 with their reflections could be seen as rather ram-like. On the "skin" of this ram-like form were carved emblems that may be related to a system of counting long solar-lunar cycles using four powers of nine, a system in which it is possible that gold was linked with the fourth power. The site was built around an idea of transformation or escape from death.

Traces of the peculiar cluster ram, gold, and set- of- powers can be recognized in a number of widely separated and much later traditions that deal with escape from death, sometimes with some reference to a prior custom of human sacrifice.

When Athamas was about to sacrifice his son Phrixus to Zeus, the boy and his sister Helle were spirited away by a flying Ram with Golden Fleece. The Ram was later sacrificed and its fleece was hung in the temple of Ares. Jason, son of Arne "Ewe," was sent to bring the fleece back to Greece and placate the ghost of Phrixus, whose four sons he brought back with the fleece.

When Abraham was about to sacrifice his son Isaac to Jehovah, the boy was saved by a ram which miraculously offered itself in his place. He later married Rachel "Ewe" who stole a set of images or teraphim belonging to her father as she and Isaac fled. Their number is not specified. The images were divine or cult images, or "powers," apparently used for divination. The images were rather small: Rachel hid them by sitting on them.

A lamb with Golden Fleece begins the story of Atreus and Thyestes. Both brothers were famous astronomers, and at least one of them could predict eclipses mathematically. A lamb with Golden Fleece appeared in their flocks and both claimed it. A horrific fratricidal war ensued, including a cannibalistic banquet.

Dardanus founded Troy. The element dan- in his name is the same as that in the name of the Irish goddess Danu. Dardanus's by-name was Corythus "Helmet" and the related word korupto means "butt with the head." The ram's helmet is its horns. Dardanus arrived from Samothrace with his wife Chryse "Gold" in an air-filled animal-skin coracle ballasted with four stone weights. The coracle that bore the pair over the sea is the equivalent of the winged ram with golden fleece that saved Phrixus and Helle. Like Rachel, Chryse brought along her sacred "images," a set of tokens or "powers" on whose possession the safety of Troy would depend.

Dardanus's mother was the Pleiad Electra "Amber" who changed places with the star Alcor, also called Alope "Vixen." Amber's use as a good luck charm or talisman can be traced from the present day all the way back to palaeolithic times. Its Greek name electron meant to ward off, and the way amber holds static electricity shows that it was the electrical storm, the deafening, fiery, sometimes fatal assault of thunder and lightning which was to be warded off. Modern Greek "worry beads," which were originally made of amber, are called kechrimpiari, "touched." It is when amber is touched or rubbed that it acquires its electrical charge. These beads are functioning as amulets. Rosaries made of amber are advertised as having a dual power. The relationship between amber and electricity sheds light on the story that the Pleiad Electra incurred the wrath of Zeus when she *touched* the Palladium. The circumpolar whorl is the home of the lightning. The son of Io and Zeus son was named Epaphus "Touch." Iris's mother was also named Electra. Her father was Thaumas, possibly also from a word meaning "Bushy," referring to the supernatural Fox. The rainbow, produced by sun and rain together, follows the electrical storm.

Before their flight from "Egypt," the Israelites smeared the blood of lambs on their door posts to save their sons, and before they left, the Jewish women stole the Egyptians' gold jewelry, which is to say, gold in discrete units, and took it with them.

The four children of Pallas and Styx were a "Set of Powers." Pallas was the son of Crius "Ram." Pallas's name (like that of the Trojan Palladium and Pallas Athene) may come from pello, "swing, whirl, brandish," possibly linked with circumpolar rotation, and Styx is linked to the Milky Way. Zeus took sole custody of the four children of this couple. Their names show that they were pure abstractions: Bia "Force," Kratos "Strength," Zelus "Emulation," and Nike, "Victory." Only Nike, who looked very much like Iris and was often confused with her, had any form or history. She was often portrayed as a miniature winged form carried by Pallas Athena. Iris is firmly linked to gold through the rainbow.

The rather ram-like image produced by K1 and K52 joined with their reflections might have been said to have golden fleece because of the devices carved on the surface of K52. These devices on the surface of K52, imagined as the hide of a ram, might be considered to give it the value of gold, the highest power in the cycle-counting system. According to the hypothesis I have been advancing, the removal of K52 was connected with the disappearance of the original views from the side recesses and the discrediting of the holy dyad associated with the cycle-counting ritual. This model scenario might have been involved in the development of stories about a fleeing couple and a golden fleece.

Several traditions associate Set-of-Four, Gold and Ram. However it is possible as hinted above that the ram in the emblem-cluster took the place of an original fox. Fox is of interest because of the great age of the sun/rain sayings tradition, where the fox marriage may be the oldest strain. I noted above a possible connection between fox and amber. Was the idea of counting by powers of nine that is seen in the Three Kingdoms stories once the property of the Fox, at a time before the Ram entered the tradition?

Stone-age men produced fire for themselves by rotating a stick or bow drill. This suggests a link between lightning and the celestial "rotor." The two Dipper asterisms circling close to this polar rotor have outlines comparable to those of the long-tailed, short-legged fox. The fox, a flesh-eater, displays the red-white-black tricolor which is the fieldmark of fire. The vixen's many little kits fed by many little teats relate her as well as the sow to the important category "Many little-" which includes the ancient "Succulent Cluster" and "Swarm" emblems.

It seems possible that it was a stone-age culture that developed the module of the Fox Marriage and even perhaps the nine-based tally convenient for keeping track of solar-lunar cycles. The fox might have been associated with the Big Dipper. He would be linked with weather, especially electrical fire. His mate the vixen, however, might have been associated not with the fox-like outline of the Little Dipper but with the solar disk which displays the red-white-black color marker during the eclipse. This suggests a model for the fox marriage.

Kuusi's selection of sun-rain sayings suggests that the fox was a prime emblem in a very ancient tradition that linked it with storm, sun, and the otherworld. The geographical dispersion of fox traditions might shed light on the origin of the people who originally developed the nine-based counting technique implied by certain Newgrange features.

This possibility may bear upon the question asked by Claire O'Kelly (*Newgrange p 48)* about the provenance of the ideas expressed in the Newgrange monument:

> "Is it fanciful to suggest that the people who built the Boyne tombs had a mythology of their own and a repertoire of poems and stories? To what extent was the design and structure of their monument governed by their myths and beliefs, perhaps inherited from far-off ancestors in far-off places? The Boyne passage graves are only one component of a widespread cult of megalith-building and it could be argued that the gods or spirits to whom the people of Newgrange gave allegiance were part of a wide-ranging pantheon or mythology, one which is no longer regarded as being wholly confined to the Celtic realm."

The interpretation of Newgrange engraved devices put forth in this study opens up some possible avenues for solving the problem of where Newgrange afterlife concepts came from by studying the distribution of similar clusters of emblems in other contexts.

For example, traces of Fox and Vixen can be detected in many of the traditions cited in this study. The name Athamas may come from thama "close, thick" or thamnos "bush," recalling the fox's descriptive appellation "Bushy." The name Phrixus comes from a word that means "bristling," also suggesting "Bushy." Athamas's second wife was Ino, a Bassarid, or Fox Maiden in the train of Dionysos. The name Io is a variant of Ino and her story is a variant of the story of Europa, which may be from eu- plus a form of rhops- " Very Bushy," possibly Vixen (her father was Phoenix "Red," perhaps Fox). Europa was the mother of Minos and Rhadamanthys, two of the three judges of the afterworld.

Jason's mother was Arne "Ewe," but his helper in his quest was Medea "Cunning," a common appellation of the Vixen. Dardanus had a wife Bateia "Bushy Shrub, Bramble, Blackberry" suggesting both the bushiness and the red-white-black color fieldmark of the Vixen.

Isaac had twin sons. The elder was Esau, described as red and hairy, suggesting "Fox." The younger son, Jacob married Rachel "Ewe" and acquired her with her father's set of teraphim, that is "images" or "powers." The story emphasizes the fact that Jacob "Supplanter" tricked the rightful heir Esau out of his birthright, feared vengeance, and went to great lengths to propitiate him.

Fox plays the cat's role in a Russian version of Puss and Boots. This story is about a poor and ragged lad re-clothed in princely garments beside a bridge or (otherworld) river, through the advice of an animal helper. The model of this narrative is the transformation of the ruined fleshly garment into the royal robes of eternal life, so the appearance of the fox in this context is important. (The cat, who usually has this role, has been dubbed a "domestic fox." Cats like foxes are very cunning, have long expressive tails, are carnivores with a taste for mice, are excellent mothers, and are archetypally chased by dogs.) Oedipus freed Thebes not only from the Sphinx but from the Teumessian Vixen, which was eating an infant a day. She was pursued in a circle by Laelaps "Left-lapsing," the counterclockwise- coursing hound. The vixen was destined never to be caught and the hound was destined never to miss its quarry. An exasperated Zeus finally turned both of them to stone.

The story of Medusa is a doublet of the story of the Vixen Alope. Like Medusa and Demeter Alope bore Poseidon a foal-*twin* (her story contains twin versions of finding Hippothous). Medusa could be viewed only in a reflector, and Alope was turned into a spring. The name Medusa as "Cunning" might refer to the vixen.

Such fragmentary almost obliterated allusions (there are many more) establish some presence of a fox and vixen pair in connection with the cluster of emblems that includes Set of Powers and Gold. Fox seems to carry this tradition back far behind myth and fairy tale into a culture of totems and what is usually called shamanism.

In China a significant part of that cluster of emblems which we have seen passing over from Fox to Ram in some European and Near Eastern contexts appears in Chinese folk tradition with Fox, but not with Ram.

Of Fox it is said "At the age of 50 the fox can take the form of a woman, and at 100 can assume the appearance of a young and beautiful girl, or otherwise, if so minded, of a wizard, possessing all the power of magic. When 1,000 years old, he is admitted to the Heavens and becomes the 'Celestial Fox.' The celestial Fox is of a golden colour and possesses nine tails; he serves in the halls of the Sun and Moon, and is versed in all the secrets of nature. The *Shuo Wen dictionary* states that the fox is the courser upon which ghostly beings ride.. the fox was originally a lewd woman in times of old.....for her vices she was transformed into a fox."

In Japan it is the Celestial Fox, not a ram, who owns the emblems Gold and Nine. The Sun remained a goddess of great importance there. Her principal legend features a mirror with which the desperate gods once lured her out of a cave. The Japanese vixen is very much a figure of the other world. The Japanese rice-god Inari has two foxes as his messengers; the fox itself is worshipped as god of rice. I would interpret an involvement with seed as originally referring to the generation of supernatural seed rather than to agricultural plenty, although the emblem would never exclude the latter. Death is a more universal preoccupation than plenty, although they are of course intimately related in times of dearth. The fox had the power to cure diseases, another transformational feature. In Japan as well as in China the fox is associated with wealth. An association with wealth involves money, that is, counting with tokens of different values, usually including gold.

The Ram/gold/set-of-four cluster of emblems seems not to penetrate all the way to the Orient. One might infer that the original cluster was Gold, Nine, and Fox. Ram might have been a dramatic intrusion into a very archaic, much more widely spread Fox context which had originally included roles for lightning and amber for example and which already responded to the rainbow as an emblem of the Fox marriage, a marriage understood as a postmortem emblem. The emblem ram would have developed in response to a conception that the reflection of circumpolar rotation had a role as post-mortem transformational agent. The spiral that makes it possible to differentiate spiral polarity is an important device at Newgrange.

If the K1-K52 image was ever imagined as a Ram with decorated hide, the prestige of Newgrange, propelled by political forces, might have fueled the diffusion of the emblem Ram to both northern Europe and the Aegean. The image would need to have taken form at a time when the engravings on K52 were understood as I have understood them. When this emblem met a powerful solar rainbow emblem such as the classical Iris it might have tended to detach her from the fox and vixen figures and associate her with a Ewe, and there is some evidence that this did affect the tradition of Iris. Jason's mother has been made a Ewe because Jason appropriated the Ram's golden Fleece - however he did so with the aid of Medea "Cunning," perhaps "Vixen."

(The interpretation of the double images as the dwarvish image described previously would of course raise a completely different set of questions.)

K1 and K52 as joined and reflected would be a feature in a set that served a funerary site, and I have hypothesized that each feature in that set was intended to raise a new spirit in place of the dead body, and set it on the path to everlasting life in the heavens. The Ram with Golden Fleece bore Phrixus through the skies to a new life. The ram like apparition at Newgrange with its Fleece of transcendent emblems was once connected in some way with an astronomical and mathematical wisdom that had developed in association with an afterlife faith which was probably much older. That faith included an image of flight, or ascent to the skies. It is notable that although there are engraved devices at Newgrange which could have been used to locate the then celestial pole, there is none that resembles the bright circumpolar Dipper asterisms whose outlines resemble stick-drawings of the long-tailed, short-legged fox.

CHAPTER XXII

ANCIENT FAR-WESTERN LANDMARKS

O'Kelly remarked that it can be argued that "...the megalithic religion was disseminated, not by invasions or immigration or any other kind of mass-movement of peoples, but by a spread of ideas..." (O'Kelly *Newgrange* 122). I believe that it is very helpful to put into some sort of perspective the distance that separated Newgrange from developed cultures to the east of it. As it happens, the Lewis and Clark expedition across the American continent was made under conditions that could be said to have something in common with those in which both Neolithic ideas and traditions about Neolithic sites may have been spread. The well-documented journey covered several thousand miles of wild territory among populations just emerging from the stone age.

The expedition set out from St. Louis, Missouri, in May of 1804. It was composed of about thirty people, including a Frenchman, his infant son, and his Indian wife who knew the Shoshone language. They traveled chiefly on waterways, by canoe and pirogue, using oars, poles, tow-ropes, and sails, building the boats as needed en rout. They completed four pirogues in ten days, five canoes in another ten-day period, and (taught by the Mandans) made a bowl-shaped coracle out of one buffalo hide in a few hours.

They lived on game where it was plentiful, as it often was, and when it was not, they ate dog, horse, fruit, roots, fish, and (once) mushrooms. They used interpreters when available, but often communicated by signs, which they unexpectedly found both accurate and efficacious. They once had to put together some important pieces of information by translating through English, French, Minnetaree, Shoshone, and Chopunnish and back again; it took them half a day.

They traded beads, tools, kettles and clothing for what they needed. They traded horses. They profitably exchanged not only information but entertainment, including fiddle music and dancing. They obtained a great deal of respect and assistance by practicing medical arts which Lewis learned from his mother, "an active amateur physician", and from a crash course he took from a "celebrated American physician."

Using great tact and discipline they managed to get along with Indians both friendly and hostile. They crossed snow-capped ranges and rivers broad and wild. They battled bears, mosquitoes, and doggedly defended their stores from thieving Indians and marauding animals. Having lost only one man (to illness), they got back to St. Louis in September, 1806.

As the crow flies, the distance they covered, between St. Louis and Astoria on the Pacific, was about the same as the distance (as the crow flies) that separates Newgrange and the city of Odessa on the Black Sea. Or, one and a half times the distance they covered was (as the crow flies) about the same as that which separates Newgrange from Baghdad, or the mouth of the Nile. Or, *two* and a half times the distance between St. Louis and Astoria, somewhat longer than the round trip the expedition made, is about the same as the distance between Newgrange and the Indus valley. Comparing the geography of the regions on relief maps, their mighty rivers and formidable mountains, helps to evaluate the obstacles which separated cultures from each other in very early times.

Newgrange in its prime was one of four or five monuments occupying its ridge, and the Boyne cemetery contained many other monuments of many different kinds. Ireland as a whole was densely populated by Stone-age sites. The word "infested" has been used. Thousands of people must have been familiar with the locality. Newgrange was conspicuous because of its commanding position and the symmetrical flanking mounds K, L, Z, and probably Z_1, which would once have contributed greatly to the total effect.

In profile, the monument was built like a squat, truncated pyramid, girdled around the base by a low wall of slabs, many engraved with geometrical devices. The mound may at one time have presented somewhat the same appearance it does now: faithfully restored by O'Kelly, the four-foot kerb supports a facade of sparkling crystalline quartz about nine feet high.

The arrangement of darker boulders now inserted at random throughout the quartz facing may before the collapse of the facade have traced some signature design, distinguishable at some distance. The facade of a Sumerian temple at Uruk (c 2900 BC) is finished in "a mosaic of greenish-yellow and blue-black clay cones" arranged in a pattern of multiple linked chevrons and nets of boxed lozenges, (Wolff *Origins of Western Art*, Pl. 95) devices which as it happens are among the commonest petroglyphic outlines at Newgrange.

Lhwyd reported seeing a standing stone on top of the mound. The flat top (and perhaps part of a lower bench over the boulder cap) permitted the staging of public ceremonies. The top was well-adapted for use as a lookout, or as a station in a signal grid, visible by day or night from other sites. For the general populace, the nocturnal vigil that would have preceded the dawn observation must have been staged in the open. The rising sun could be seen from the top of the mound several minutes before it struck the roofbox slit and penetrated into the chamber, and the view of the Milky Way was stunning.

Insofar as a memory of Newgrange could be expected to endure, it would have been colored by the fact that the building occupies a position easy to characterize geographically, lying as it does on the extreme Western margin of Eurasia. A memory or report of the building would naturally include an impression of the walls. Since the steep revetment may have collapsed quite soon after its completion, (the reconstructed revetment is cemented in place) a memory of Newgrange as a walled monument would date back to a period long before 2000 BC, when the revetment began to collapse, leaving a darkened "grotto" under an overgrown tumulus.

The truncated cone may have been remembered. A Phoenician emblem-cluster called the Sign of Tanit usually includes a truncated cone; a hand, whose palm would display the "reflection" of the W of Cassiopeia at the source of the Milky Way; and a shallow rimmed shape like a reflector. The W and reflector were crucial elements of Newgrange faith, and if the Phoenician emblem did by any chance refer to some recollection of Newgrange, the truncated cone would go back to the remembered shape of the walled monument.

It did seem to be known that sunlight had entered or could enter into the mound. The O'Riordain and Daniels *Newgrange* refers to a calendar that included a note about this, and the O'Kellys were familiar with the tradition. The connection with the winter solstice was apparently not known.

This site must have retained some numinous power known to visitors in touch with centers of Classical culture, because of the coins dating from the first to the fourth century found just beneath the sod at Newgrange along with a few other Roman effects. As a matter of fact both Beaufort and Fergusson stated that gold coins were found in the chamber, although these statements have been perhaps too readily dismissed. People who casually picked up valuables or curiosities in and around Newgrange did not always turn them over to the authorities, such as they were.

It has not been possible to determine whether Norsemen did or did not enter this mound, but it is certain that if they came they came to loot, and they would certainly have removed anything of value they may have found. It is striking that Roman finds dating centuries before the advent of the Norse were found so near the surface of the ground. Coins of about the same dates are found in abundance in Norse hoards. Is it possible that some were lifted from Irish sites including Newgrange? None were found near Dowth or Knowth.

Many classical references make it clear that the legendary landscape of the far West or Northwest, a region lying "on the shores of Ocean" or of "Ocean Stream," was understood to be full of buildings. There were walls, towers, palaces, and even cities. Hesiod's *Theogony* includes descriptions of a number of structures which were located in the West and associated more or less intimately with the afterworld or otherworld. Some details about these buildings are striking when considered in the context of the Boyne cemetery. The amount of dilapidation that has taken place there during only the last few centuries is an indication of how much more of the site may have been in existence in classical times, and how much better their state of preservation must have been.

Hesiod described Tartarus, an underground place where the gods imprisoned their defeated foes the Titans. It lay near Ocean and Mount Atlas. "....Round it is planted an unyielding palisade which the nether world has thrown up in three ranks around the top of the ridge...(726)...Poseidon fixed stout gates upon it, and a wall runs around it on every side, and there are sparkling gates and an adamantine threshold with foundations stretching evenly along, fitting well together, of native construction." (*op. cit.* 810). The word usually translated bronze or adamantine seems to be used chiefly to convey the idea "everlasting." Tartarus also had keys and a gaoler named Campe, "Crooked." The crooked constellation Cassiopeia had an old title "Laconian Key." The Laconian key was shaped like a W. Poseidon was originally a fresh-water god.

Near the wall of Tartarus, was Night's palace. Night was a primeval being sprung from Chaos and Erebus "Covered." She was the mother of Nemesis "Apportionment" (which was a legal concept), of the Fates, and of the Hesperides "Children of the West." As Hesiod describes it, "There stands the awe-inspiring palace of dark Night...in front of it...[Atlas] stands staunchly upholding wide Heaven on his head and tireless hands, where Night and Day draw near and greet one another as they pass the great brazen threshold; the one comes down into the interior, but the other comes to the door..."(*op. cit.* 744). Atlas was a Titan who was turned to a mountain of stone when Perseus showed him the Gorgon's head. Newgrange could be said to uphold heaven on its head. The hint of two entrances, one of them accessed by Night from above, the other accessed by Day at the door, is provocative.

"Lying beneath cold Atlas," says Ovid (quoting Agenorides), "is a place secured by a rampart of massive structure, in whose entranceway two sisters lived." These were the Graiae, who were daughters of Phorcys, as were the Gorgons. The Graiae had one eye (and one tooth) between them and passed the eye from socket to socket. There was a tradition that Phorkys and his daughters were neighbors, and he is shown with them meeting Perseus on a 4th century Attic pyxis. According to Palaiphatos (cited by Graves), "Phorkys was a Cernaian man. Racially, the Cernaians were Aithiopians, but they lived on the island of Cerne outside the pillars of Hercules: they cultivated Libya however." The word Libya may be related to the word libas, anything that drops or trickles.

The Pillars of Hercules are the rocky promontories flanking the Straits of Gibraltar that separate the Atlantic from the Mediterranean. Graves refers to an account by Diodorus Siculus about Cerne: Myrine, an Amazon queen from Libya, invaded Cerne, captured the capital city of the Atlantians, and then defended them from their foes the Gorgons. However, the Gorgons counter-attacked and drove Myrine out. "...Her dead lie buried under three huge mounds..." The three great mounds Newgrange, Knowth and Dowth come to mind. Protected by the Mother of the Gods, Myrine eventually reached Samothrace, "which Myrine consecrated to her, founding altars and offering splendid sacrifices."

It was in Samothrace, according to Artemidorus (in Strabo IV 198) that rites were celebrated similar to those practised on an "island near Britain." These rites involved Demeter and Kore, but the Samothracian Kore was the Kabirian maiden born by Demeter to Iasion. Iasion was by some traditions the brother of Harmonia. Harmonia's name suggests the idea of the graduated scale of musical pitches that is analogous to the idea behind the fanstick and fish-spine devices as tallies. Harmonia became established in tradition as the bride of Cadmus, founder of walled Thebes and engraver of its "Cadmeian Letters."

The house of Styx was located in the afterworld, usually associated with the far West. "Terrible Styx, eldest daughter of Ocean, who flows back into himself...lives apart from the gods in her glorious house vaulted over with great rocks and propped up to heaven all around with silvery slabs [a word often used for an inscribed slab or gravestone]. Rarely does...[Iris]... come to her with a message over the sea's wide back. But when strife and quarrel arise among the deathless gods, and when any one of them...lies, then Zeus sends Iris to bring in a golden jug the great solemn witness to truth of the gods, from far away, the famous cold water which trickles down from a high and beetling rock. Far under the wide-pathed earth a branch of Oceanus flows through the dark night out of the holy stream, and a tenth part of his water is allotted to her. With nine silver-swirling streams he winds about the earth and the sea's wide back and then falls into the main; but the tenth flows out from a rock...Such a solemn witness to truth then did the gods appoint the eternal and Ogygian water of Styx to be; and it spouts through a confined place." (Hesiod *op. cit*. 775).

Oceanus is explicitly distinguished from the terrestrial sea. He is called "Ocean, who flows back into himself," a rational way to describe the Milky Way, as the River of Heaven that encircles both earth and sea. As the right-hand recess of Newgrange was oriented toward at the top of the Milky Way in such a way that a reflection of it was visible in a vessel of water, it could be said that in one sense some of the galactic stream entered into the receptacle over the rock behind it. Dew forms on clear nights when the Milky Way is brilliant. To the extent that dew as well as rain dripped into the recess one might have said poetically that a branch of the Milky Way flowed out from a rock and spouted through a confined place into the recess. The consistent description of the flow of Styx as trickling or dripping is striking. Hesiod uses the word kataleibetai "trickles" for Styx. He also uses hiesi "flows as tears." Homer uses kateibomenon "dripping." Water dripped into the Newgrange recess.

Styx was a daughter of Oceanus, and by one tradition she became by Zeus the mother of Hades's wife Persephone. She also had a title kourotrophos, "nurturer of children," which was born by all the Oceanids including Electra. This probably supports an association with supernatural regeneration. Achilles's mother Thetis dipped him in the Styx in an attempt to make him immortal. Thetis was on excellent terms with the smith Hephaestus, and got him to make Achilles's armor.

Another building located in the far west was the Tower of Cronos standing beside the highway of Zeus "where the breezes of Ocean blow around the Islands of the Blessed" (Pindar *Olympic Odes* 2 69-71) The Milky Way was thought of as a pathway of the gods and of the departed spirits who inhabited the Isles of the Blest in the West. Pindar relates that the Fates led Themis "beside the heavenly spring of Ocean towards the august ladder [or staircase?] bright of Olympus, to be the first wife of the savior God." The ladder or staircase is interesting in view of the nine rungs in the Newgrange passage and perhaps, if it was in an earlier phase uncovered, the stone "staircase" formed by the passage roofstones. People still hesitate to go under ladders, and the ladder was introduced as an emblem in depictions of the crucifixion of Christ.

Thebes was not traditionally located in the West. The name was borne by several cities, and I discuss it here because it was famous above all for its gates and walls and because it had an afterlife dimension. The old acropolis or walled stronghold of Thebes was itself called "Isle of the Blest" (Artemides quoted by Roscher).

Thebes was built by Cadmus. He was sent by his father to find his sister Europa "Vixen?" (daughter of Phoenix "Red," Fox?) who had been kidnapped by Zeus. His search was in vain, and the oracle at Delos told him to follow a certain cow and found a city where she lay down. He needed lustral water to sacrifice the cow, and went to the spring of Ares, which was guarded by a dragon who may in fact have been Ares's son. By one tradition Ares was also Cygnus's father. Newgrange was engraved with many counterclockwise spirals whose model may be the spiral by which circumpolar rotation was represented. The spiral tends to spin off the snake emblem to which wind and lightning add wings and fire.

I have described how Cadmus killed the dragon and sowed its teeth, and how an army of lancers sprang up from them. Cadmus threw one stone into the midst of them, and they set about mechanically killing each other until only five were left. I explained that a model for this famous and peculiar module is the way one stone, a gnomon, produces a set of self-cancelling pairs, an acceptable emblem of two graduated sets of noon shadows, opposite each other on either side of the solstice, which match or cancel each other out except for the few in the middle of the series which cannot be distinguished from one another. Within this little group of survivors the solstice is located, being (in theory) the middle number.

If the walls of Thebes, like the walls of Newgrange, had been laid out in dependence on the midwinter sunrise, one phrase which has taxed the ingenuity of mythographers would be clearer: "...Cadmeia [the citadel of Thebes], put completely under the control of winter..." (see Roscher, "Kadmos," 940.) Another perplexing quotation may hint at the presence of cosmic "music" in a post-mortem context: "...They who had been put under the control of the Muses' (or musical?) instruments were awakened from any grief..."(Roscher, "Kadmos," 115)

Cadmus's bride was Harmonia, whose name represents concord in music, but has a prior significance of fitting together, joining, setting in order, governing. There is also a tradition that Harmonia was his second wife, his first being Europa. This is intriguing in view of the possibility that the fox and vixen represent a layer of tradition older than that represented by Newgrange and its emblems.

Another feature of the tradition supports the hypothesis that Thebes was built in conformance with an understanding of the location of true north and the nature of the solstice. The walls of Thebes were raised by Amphion and his brother Zethus. The music of Amphion's lyre impelled the stones to move into place by themselves. Amphion's brother and co-builder was Zethus, a name probably related to zeteo, "search out, inquire into, investigate," like the name Zetes, closely linked with the Strophades or "Turning Isles." The names Zethus and Zetes suggest the hound as tracker and pointer.

When Newgrange was built there was no pole star. But locating true north was important to help establish which shadow was the noon shadow, that is, the one that fell due north. A hunting dog which tracked an unseen quarry was a good emblem for circumpolar stars which could point out the location of the hidden pole. So if Thebes was laid out on the principles of Newgrange, then Zethus as the hound, the "hunting dog" that sought out and identified the north celestial polar point, as well as the lyre of Amphion that identified the winter solstice, helped build the walls of Thebes, exactly as it might have been said that both helped build the walls of Newgrange. Dog or hound names have historically been found attached to circumpolar constellations.

There were traditions about the dragon-haunted spring of Ares that resonate with the "spring" in the Newgrange chamber.

"...Hidden water was also brought [to the rest of the city] from the Cadmeia [or citadel] through conduits made by Cadmus, provided, they say, in ancient times." (Roscher, "Kadmos," *op. cit.* a31) These arrangements for bringing water from the citadel were hidden from view. Conduits into the Newgrange chamber must remain a hypothesis, since the vault could not be dismantled, but there was water there.

Of special interest in view of the burned bone fragments found near the "spring" in the Newgrange chamber is another Theban tradition, described in a papyrus fragment from the Antiope of Euripedes (*Flinders Petrie Pap* t 2 p. 7): "...But when you perform the funeral rites for your wife you lay on the pyre the remains of the miserable wretch which you have gathered up, in order to throw the bones you have burned into the spring of Ares..."

By one tradition Cadmus and Harmonia ended their earthly lives in Illyria, a name commonly derived from "lyre." The musical names accord with the idea of a building laid out in accordance with the operation of a shadow-lyre tuned to celestial order. By another tradition, they were ultimately transformed into serpents and carried to the Isles of the Blest in an ox-cart. The transformation was punishment meted out for Cadmus's killing of the dragon that guarded the Ares spring which by one tradition was the son of Ares. The serpent pair is a version of opposite-polarity spirals, like the East Indian Naga couple, an entwined serpent-pair. One name of the Dipper was "Ox Cart." The Blessed Isles were traditionally located in the Far West.

In several traditions the lyre continues to have a positive if not a triumphal affect in tradition while the dog develops an affect tinged with evil, misfortune, death and ruin. This could have arisen from the fact that precession altered the role of individual circumpolar shapes such as the Dog or Hound in locating the drifting celestial pole, whereas the solstice, determined by tallies, "graduated scales" like lyre-strings, remained constant.

Cadmus was credited with many cultural accomplishments or inventions. As a stone mason he built a hundred stone cities. He also invented Cadmeian letters. The special term stoichea is used for these letters invented by Cadmus instead of the word grammata customary for written characters or letters. Stoichea connotes elements or rudiments, "a first beginning, first principle or element." A stoichos is a small upright post or gnomon or its shadow. Cadmus taught the lyrist Linos the rites of Dionysos as practiced by the Egyptians, and Linus wrote these down in "Cadmeian-Pelasgian letters." (Roscher, "Kadmos," 104) The Pelasgi were a "prehistoric race of unknown ethnological affinities," living around the Mediterranean basin. Traditions about Cadmus' invention of writing depend mostly on Milesian sources. The Milesians played an important part in the traditional history of Ireland.

Thebes "...was curiously emblazoned with Phoenician artistry...with a seven-track gateway...Cadmus imitated seven-zoned heaven by his art" (see Roscher, "Kadmos," 101). That the walls of the city were not simply beautified is implied by other statements. After providing a named gate in the wall for each of the seven planetary bodies, Cadmus gave the "holy city" "...a name the same as that of the Egyptian city of Thebes...curiously adorned [or wrought?] [it was] an earthly type equal to Olympus." The phrase "Phoenician artistry" brings to mind the Phoenician sign of Tanit, the set of emblems consisting of truncated cone, shallow dish, circle or sphere, and associated upraised palm, suggesting the walls, reflector, polar rotor, and Cassiopeian W which I have discussed in connection with Newgrange. A unique feature of Newgrange which would have impressed itself on tourists and pilgrims prior to the total collapse of the revetment is of course the striking devices engraved on its "walls."

The palace of Aiolos was another place that was called Isle of the Blest. Aiolos' palace had a wall, described like the walls of several otherworld structures as "brazen." It was given a geographical location in the Tyrrhenian Sea but was described like Delos as "floating" (Cadmus was sent to Delos to get instructions for founding Thebes). "Floating" is a riddling way to describe a location which revolves or moves in relation to its environs as the earth moves in space. By one tradition the name of Aiolus' island was "Lipara", a name which means Fatland, as does the name Pieria which has developed from Pi-wer-iu, an old name for Ireland. Aiolos was the ruler of the winds. That is, he was a figure of the Weather-god who ruled in the height of the heavens.

Phorkys, father of the Gorgons and the Graiae, was usually described as living in the far West. In this case the Cave of Phorkys or Cave of the Nymphs would presumably have been located in the West, not (as in the Ithacan tradition) off the coast of Greece. The Cave of Phorkys is described as the site of rites of death and transfiguration. It had two portals: the northern portal was for men, the southern, for gods. It contained stone amphorae in which bees stored honey, and there was a plentiful supply of spring water within, as well as stone basins to hold it. Inside the cave were stone looms on which Naiads wove purple garments.

Rites of death and transfiguration or rebirth probably also characterized Newgrange. As in the Cave of the Nymphs, there are two openable ports at Newgrange, the two apertures that as the sky revolved past them projected "woven nets" upon the sky. The frame in which the vault culminated had a northern outview from the standpoint of the left-hand recess, and the roofbox frame looked out to the south-east.

I have suggested how at Newgrange there may once have been two "portals" of another kind, that is, two entrances, one to a southwest passage and the other to the present southeast passage. The two would naturally have been associated with some contrast in their use, possibly by mortals on the one hand and supernatural powers on the other.

The Cave of the Nymphs was frequented by bees who stored honey in stone jars. This would suit the "Many-Little" concept that included bees, water-drops, Melissae, Danaids, and stars conceived as celestial bees, swarming in the column of the Galaxy, beings who produced or were associated with dew. Like the Cave of the Nymphs, Newgrange had a plentiful supply of water from the "spring" above the deeply hollowed slab, or the stone bowl if the latter stood in the right-hand recess. This was precipitated water with a possible complement of dew contributed by the boulder cap, which if and when uncovered would have tended to function as an aerial well. Water may also have been available from the winter-flowing spring found in the passage.

The nymphs of Phorcys's cave wove purple garments on stone looms. The weaving that was done at Newgrange was also on stone looms, if the apertures may be considered the "looms" that wove the chequey and lozengey nets. And the colour purple suggests the murex shell that was the source of purple dye: this shell is a clockwise spiral whorl, hence an emblem of the *reflected* circumpolar whorl which was the focus of the right-hand recess and the diurnal unroller of the chains and nets. The nymphs wove *garments*. One fairy tale type of which Puss in Boots is a well known example describes how the ragged hero is outfitted with royal garments. Saint Paul uses the image: The reborn christian is to "...fling off the dirty clothes of the old life, rotted through with lust's illusions and to put on the clean fresh clothes of a new life." (Eph 4:22 Phillips translation)

The well of Nechtan is described in Old Irish sources. It seems to have been located in or near Newgrange and was linked with it at least indirectly. By one tradition Boann, with whom the Dagda had an affair, was Nechtan's wife and Elcmar was her brother; by another tradition Elcmar "Envious, Spiteful" was her husband. The Dagda's son by Boann was Angus. The names Nechtan mac Labrada suggest "washed, clean," and "speaking." Clean speaking, as true speaking, would suit the owner of this well, since it punished liars. The Dagda owned the Brugh, that is, Newgrange. The names Nechtan and Elcmar would stress positive and negative aspects of the same figure.

Nobody but Nechtan's three cupbearers could look at his secret well without losing his eyes. Their names are similar to those of the three Classical judges of Hades, the realm of the Styx: Rhadamanthys, Aeacus, and Minos. Like Nechtan's Well, the Styx punished liars or oath-breakers.

One of Nechtan's cupbearers was Flesc "Wand, Rod." The Greek Rhadamanthys is probably from rhabdo "wand" and manthys "divining."

Another cupbearer was Lesc, "slow, loath, unwilling, unwelcome, undesired." The Greek Aeacus was punished by having his springs and rivers infested with snakes so that they dwindled to fouled trickles, and killed his people. Styx is usually described as ateibomenon "down-dripping, slowly trickling." The name Styx may be derived from stugeo "loathe," but this may be a secondary development inspired by the association with Hades. The name may have come originally from stadzo "drip, let fall drop by drop." The same idea of an exudate, a liquid dripping, trickling or flowing very meagerly, is expressed in the element dan- which lies at the root of such river names as Eridanus, a name which has been applied to the Milky Way, Danube, and Don. The root also appears in the names of Perseus's mother Danae, the Danaids, who were condemned to carry water in sieves, Don, a Welsh supernatural being linked to the Milky Way, and the Tuatha De Danann, who were believed to have frequented Newgrange. The fatal "spring" that dripped or trickled into the righthand recess basin at Newgrange was a possible model for this widely-dispersed idea. Another model would be dewfall.

Nechtan's third cup-bearer was named Luam "Pilot, Navigator." The third judge in Hades was Minos, a famous navigator. Every nine years, he conferred with Zeus in a cave. By one tradition Minos was the son of the smith Hephaestus, who was also associated with a nine-year period. Nine-year intervals are relevant to a solar-lunar cycle or half-cycle.

The traditions suggest that each of the three cupbearers was associated with a separate concept. Each of the three Newgrange recesses was also associated with a separate concept. The left recess was pole-centered. The names Rhadamanthys and Flesc both suggest a pole, as rod or "wand." The right recess was focused on a fatal water- source. The story of Aeacus and the name Lesc suggest similar association: a slowly dripping source, with an ominous aura of reluctance or dread. The center recess was centered on solar-lunar cycles. The navigators Minos and Luam may have been associated with a rapid, traveling round-hulled moon.

The three interests may have developed separately. They seem to reflect different transformational models. Each may have had a separate history long before and long after they were combined in sites like Newgrange.

Nechtan's well has a crucial role in a story linked with Newgrange which may have a bearing on the positions of K1 and K52. The Dagda slept with Nechtan's (or Elmar's) wife Boann. Afterwards, she visited Nechtan's spring to wash out traces of her guilt, but the spring raised itself up and drowned her. By another account she denied to her husband that she had slept with the Dagda, then went to the well to purify herself, and strode around it three times *counterclockwise*. She was accompanied by her lapdog Dabilla, who thus acts out the name of the famous Classical hound Laelaps, whose name means "Left-Lapsing, or Counterclockwise." Boann's dog would be a representative of the circumpolar dog suggested by several old star and constellation names. The name Conchobar taken as cabor or pole of the dog could go back to the same traditions.

The water broke out of the spring and overtook Boann and Dabilla as they fled to the sea. Dabilla was *split into two pieces on the rocks*, memorialized in the names *Lake of Two Stones*, Hill of Dabilla, and Mount of the Covenant. The name Dabilla itself may be from dabach "tub, pool, hollow, a water container." It is the name of a lake, or of the River Blackwater, which joins the Boyne. One "tub" of "black" water whose overflow could be said to make its way to the Boyne was the hollow slab in Newgrange's dark righthand recess. The word Covenant suggests the concept of judgment implied in the traditions that Nechtan's well, like Styx, punished oathbreakers or liars.

By still another account, Boann arrogantly circled the spring three times to test her powers, and *three waves broke out of it and annihilated one of her eyes, one of her legs, and one of her arms*. To hide this humiliation she fled to the sea but the water followed her, creating the Boyne. This mutilated half-figure, split in two lengthwise from crown to foot, could have as its model a figure which was once completed by K1 and K52 with their reflections, and was destroyed when turf overgrew the neglected forecourt that had provided the reflector needed to complete the figure.

I hypothesized that an earlier phase of Newgrange may have had a sunset as well as a sunrise passage, a net north-south orientation and a southern forecourt. Both passages would have been used within the short period which separates sunrise from sunset at midwinter in northern latitudes, in a ceremony that dramatized the transition from death to life. Something of this sort might lie behind the saying that Angus, son of Boann and the Dagda, was conceived and born on the same day.

Another woman who was described as divided into two halves was Hel, mistress of the Scandinavian afterworld: *her body was half flesh-color and half blue-black*. K1 and K52 are warm-colored stones which might be called flesh-colored. If reflected in water, the complete figure was half flesh-colored and half blue-black. If Hel was modeled on this object it would have to go back to a phase of the monument when both stones stood together in the forecourt, as would have been true of the tradition of Boann and the tradition of Medusa before Perseus beheaded her.

Could the old belief in a *Golden Age* have originated in some memory of the Boyne culture, its faith and the emblem Gold? Hesiod writes:

"First of all the deathless gods who dwell on Olympus made a golden race of mortal men who lived in the time of Cronos when he was reigning in heaven. And they lived like gods without sorrow of heart, remote and free from toil and grief; miserable age rested not on them; but with legs and arms never failing they made merry with feasting beyond the reach of all evils. When they died, it was as though they were overcome with sleep, and they had all good things; for the fruitful earth unforced bare them fruit abundantly and without stint. They dwelt in ease and peace upon their lands with many good things, rich in flocks and loved by the blessed gods. "

Hesiod says that this race survives still, and that "...they are called pure spirits dwelling on the earth, and are kindly, delivering from harm, and guardians of mortal men; for they roam everywhere over the earth, clothed in mist [and keep watch on judgments and cruel deeds], givers of wealth; for this royal right also they received..." (*Works and Days* 110-26) The mention of judgment, longevity and wealth recalls the wondrous far-western island culture which Silenus described to Midas.

CHAPTER XXIII

FAITH, AFFECT, AND PRACTICE

Interpreting Newgrange devices as emblems related to its features has produced many unexpected insights. Because the set of models the emblems refer to is present and recognizable in the site, and because these emblems have distinctive outlines verified by site engravings, it has been possible to point out sets of different emblems with similar outlines in other contexts. As would be expected after such an enormous lapse of time and over such wide expanses of territory, we find these emblems detached from the original afterlife framework.

In considering how these emblems appear in other much later contexts it is useful to remember that the word emblem had the original sense of an *insertion*, a *detachable relief ornament* used as a decoration. This is a determinative characteristic here. Most of the emblems which I accept as modeled on Newgrange transformational agencies that have survived in other contexts do indeed stand out from those contexts, whether verbal or pictorial, as seeming to be of a different style or order: arbitrary, irrational often grotesque. Examples are Dornolla "Big Fist," Cadmus's self-cancelling dragon's teeth lancers, or the three Grey Sisters' shared eye.

Emblems involved in the kinds of contexts I have discussed are often marked by an appearance of great age. They jut out from their narrative contexts like fossils, casual, discrete, not integrated into the rest of their contexts in a normal way. They may appear as conscious archaisms, or freaks: rustic, or comic or undignified, treated with condescension, cynicism, hostility, amusement, or a kind of knowing mystification. Sometimes they are glossed by pedantic etymologies or genealogies, or bizarre rationalizations. They are however quite consistently, if indirectly, associated with death, or with the supernatural. All of their characteristics tend to support a hypothesis that these sets of emblems are older than their contexts, in which they have been preserved like groups of insects in amber.

They may owe their survival partly to an enduring taste for the sensational and the funny. But there is probably another element in their survival, an involuntary reverence for traditions handed down by our ancestors, particularly traditions that seem to bear on the supernatural. The very incomprehensibility of the emblems seems to guarantee some kind of archaic credentials.

Similarly, so-called superstitions such as throwing salt over one's shoulder, throwing coins into pools, observation of lucky and unlucky directions and so on are performed within a peculiar mental pocket or recess. Such usages are behavioral fossils, jutting out from the normal pattern of contemporary habits. The mind of a person saying self-consciously "touch wood" is as it were momentarily insulated from his normal mental contents and behavior; the phrase is enclosed in psychological brackets. The insulation or bracketing is just exactly the vacuum caused by the missing supernatural context. Many superstitions seem to be at home in the set of agencies that may have operated in the neolithic postmortem transaction practiced at Newgrange. The phenomenon is analogous to the insulated pocket in which an archaic transformational emblem often seems to be traveling through the changing landscapes of narrative traditions.

Emblems often do appear as insertions embedded in the contexts that have been improvised for them, except for a few traditional tales in which very conservative storytelling techniques protected sets of emblems in rational narrative contexts from the pressures of other religious orthodoxies.

Most of the contexts are verbal, such as stories and superstitions which may reveal glimpses about the natures of their emblems, as well as hints of how they fit together. Greek myth reduced Iris to a rainbow goddess, but preserves various scattered traditions about her, one that she visited Styx to obtain the holy, dripping water that guaranteed the gods' oaths, one that she carried the caduceus, one that she led the Nemean Lion on a leash, and one that her daughter was Persephone, Hades's wife, who held up the Gorgoneion at the gates of the afterworld. At Newgrange sun and rainbow emblems, the rising midwinter sun, pairs of opposite spirals like those of the caduceus, and a bowl into which water dripped, are guarded by the mask-like form of K1. All were here at Newgrange integrated in the service of a single afterworld transaction. The Norse and Russian fairytales cited above preserve recognizable sets of emblems in integrated modules, that shed some light on the way their emblems were believed to cooperate in a supernatural transaction.

Even though such narrative contexts are so much later than Newgrange, these persistently adhering sets of emblems may suggest possibilities about how the set assembled at Newgrange may have fit together in its funeral practice, and help to form some idea of the kind of ritual activity that may have taken place at this site.

It was a stubbornly conservative piety that preserved the water-bowl as the ritual focus of Newgrange's late and very sophisticated synthesis. The same devout conservatism tends to preserve archaic emblems in much later religious contexts. Archaic emblems believed to have power to assure an afterlife are probably among the most conservative elements in human history. Wells, springs and pools are invested with supernatural power to this day, and baptism in water hallowed by the sign of the cross remains the central Christian rite.

The people of Newgrange had gone to great lengths to draw the powers of the heavens into their postmortem precinct and had also managed somehow to include within the most elaborate recess of the chamber a pure source of precipitated and atmospheric water. In fact, features capable of holding water were found not only in the Newgrange chamber, but in all three of its satellites.

Site K was surrounded by a penannular ditch which had contained water, and the ditch had been re-dug in an enlargement of the monument. K had a small triangular annex, attached to the right side of the chamber and equipped with a double wall on the chamber side. The *double* wall suggests that this could have been a little cistern, once caulked to hold water. The triangular shape itself would be significant: an emblem. I have suggested that both the engraved triangles and the triangular stone reported at Newgrange had a lunar model. The chamber was too small to stand in, but before it was roofed and closed, water in the triangular cist would have reflected the sky, including at times the trinitary moon.

Site L contained some fragments of pottery which apparently were "originally in the end chamber of the tomb." The curvature of one shard "suggests that it came from a round-bottomed pot of large size." Site Z contained a sizable basin stone within whose shallow depression was a circular hollow, recalling the depressions in the lip of the Newgrange stone bowl.

The much later concentric arcs of circular pits east of the Newgrange entrance were lined with clay, and whatever else may be said of them they were in an area into which water from within the porous mound drained, and they were capable of holding water in addition to whatever else may have lain in them. The water reflected the sky.

Water can purify, refresh, give life. In addition its powers of reflection have transformational significance in a post-mortem situation: water hides whatever is put under it, re-clothes it in a starry mantle, generates a mysterious twin of whatever lies beside it, creates a new image by doubling the outline of what lies beside it, stops time by reversing the direction of circumpolar rotation, and puts heaven beneath the feet of a person who looks down into it. Each one of the rounded river-rolled stones used in the construction of the mound, and each one of the rounded river-rolled boulders that decorated the facade, acted when wet as a convex mirror reflecting the world around it in miniature like an eyeball. This was also true of the concoid stone found standing in front of the passage entrance of Site K.

These magical properties may have been imagined as powers of a supernatural agent. Poseidon for example was originally a god of fresh water; the zodiacal constellation Aquarius "Waterman" suggests some early, undifferentiated personification of a celestial water-giver, and John the Baptist retains a definite importance in Christian iconography and story. Jesus used the imagery of life-giving water in regard to his mission. The properties of water may have been ascribed originally to the Weather God, at home in the heights where both the terror of storms and the blessings of water originate.

All water-filled hollows that are exposed to the clear night sky reflect the stars, the polar whorl, and the Milky Way. The Milky Way under which dew forms in many little drops is a dense glittering column like that formed by swarming bees. The many little stars may have associated themselves with many little bees and their many little nectar droplets and cells of honey. Perhaps one reason flowers have figured in funerals from time immemorial, is to attract and please the celestial "bees," which Greek ceramic pictures as melissae, small winged female forms hovering over sepulchral urns in the company of Hermes, the spirit guide. It was melissae that taught him divination from the dance of pebbles in a bowl of water. In Ireland, the fairy host were thought of as "*Little People*." As a stream the galaxy has a milky look. Perhaps it was these kinds of images that led to the idea that the afterworld, the ultimate land of promise, is a land of milk and honey. The virtues of both would have been associated with the water surface that reflected the stars and the Milky Way.

Celestial powers must have been drawn into the chamber because they were believed to have transformational powers that could help the spirits of the departed attain a new life and prosper in it. The engraved motifs are emblems of these powers. The W and chevron chains imitate the outlines of Cassiopeia and the Milky Way, the disk is the outline of the sun, the triangle pictures the mystic three-ness of lunar phases and cycles, concentric arcs depict the rainbow, the fish-spine and fan-stick devices diagram the midpoints of noon and solstitial shadow sequences, the rosettes are emblems of the nine-based time-counting system, Thumb, Beaker and Noose are possible locators of the celestial pole, seat of the weather god, spirals refer to circumpolar rotation and its reflection, the ellipse with enclosed half-circles diagrams the linked celestial poles. Personae of one form or another may have been developed around any or all of them and received ritual honors in season.

How were the various powers involved in religious observances and funeral transactions imagined? There is evidence in some northern pantheons for a feminine sun, a natural personification of beauty, warmth, faithfulness and nurture, perhaps with the personified planet Venus as her attendant. These pantheons include a masculine moon, a natural personification of adventurousness, activity, changefulness, trickiness, measurement and wisdom.

Weather gods are almost always present, and invariably masculine in gender, responding to the tremendous power of the celestial rotor, lightning, thunder, storm winds and precipitation. The devices which I suggest were used to locate the celestial pole deliberately avoid the old animal imagery suggested by the dippers. The inference is that there was a conscious rejection here of totemistic powers among circumpolar constellations, such as the fox, jackal or hyena, the Dog, and the Bear. When polarity became a critical element of rotation, and had to be represented by the spiral (or swastika), the serpent and serpent-wound pole would have contributed to, and probably come to dominate the imagery of the Weather God at the polar height. Because of his serpent-wound staff or serpent torso, the healer Asclepius may have originated as a weather-god.

Various emblems might have developed around the double chevron of Cassiopeia. The Cernaian hind was always represented with antlers: her name was Taygete "Dew Fetcher." The chevron-elbowed Ishtar-type, buxom and amorous, is another possible emblem. Cernunnos with his antlers and money-sack (?) is prominent in Gallo-Roman times.

Stories developed around supernatural agents would have included examples of what we recognize as "magic": instantaneous reversals and transformations. This would be a development of the important concept of the transformational instant or plane. This critical instant or plane is the crux of both the Midwinter event and the reflective surface. In fairy stories otherworldly characters such as clever dwarves and wise old women with supernatural knowledge and devices often bring about such transformations.

The celebration of cycles and a respect for number as sacred or holy was probably the last element of the eclectic Newgrange faith. It would have been the basin filled with water dropping from the sky which preserved the soul of the faith and practice. The ancient reverence for the waterdrop, dew in particular, hallowed the whole religious synthesis.

Several Newgrange devices can be interpreted as the result of an unexpected proficiency in abstract analysis, and of equal interest is the fact that some of them can be seen as abbreviations or shorthand versions of more explicit devices. Both characteristics encourage the development of other forms of writing. I say *other* forms because I am convinced that the engravings at Newgrange qualify as genuine written text, which should yield more insights as it continues to be studied.

There is evidence that Newgrange timekeepers kept track of several solar-lunar cycles, and it would have been natural to visit the site at frequent and regular intervals to celebrate events in these cycles. Both solstices were observable from the chamber. The equinoxes must have been important too not only as the midpoints between the solstices but also in connection with the Milky Way. The round of religious celebrations would have been anchored by these four dates.

In Newgrange times, at the spring equinox, the sun approached and began to cross the Orion arm of the Milky Way. At the fall equinox, it prepared to cross the Cygnus arm. As both sun and galaxy were important, these two dates would quite possibly have been marked in some way. The equinoctial colures were not visible from inside the building (unless, perhaps, if it were exposed, through the chamber roofbox). As the moon seems to have been of great importance at Newgrange, and the sun was the star of the solstitial observance, it is possible that the moon was the focus of observation at the equinoxes. The moon still helps time the Christian resurrection- observance of Easter in the spring.

The fate of the regenerated spirit may have been modeled on the progress of the new-moon hero. By partaking of a supernatural drink, by fulfilling a set cycle of time counted by a nine-based sequence, and frequently by being clothed in new, royal garments, the young fairy-tale hero wins the gold princess, inherits half the kingdom, and lives happily ever after. Addresses to the new moon cited by Roscher and Grimm salute the new moon as hero: "New Moon, New King! I see for God a new warrior!"

The new-moon imagery may have owed something to the way the lunar chalice gradually fills with light and empties as the moon rejoins the sun. In India for example the moon was imagined as the cup of soma, a divine elixir of immortality that was drunk by the gods themselves. In the far north, the goddess Idun gave the gods magic apples which ensured their immortality, a story which may be related to accounts of how the new-moon hero follows an apple or golden ball from one metal kingdom to another in his quest. Cuchulainn followed a self-rolling apple in his quest to win Emer. Juno also had golden apples, guarded for her by the serpent Ladon in the Islands of the West; and the serpent himself is an emblem of the circumpolar spiral. The drinking horn offered to the horseman on the Norse stella is crescent-shaped. The crescent shape also suggests a boat- or coracle.

The regular celebration of supernatural events governed by a seasonal calendar was probably felt by neolithic believers as by believers in our time to be good in itself. Regular offerings of respect to supernatural beings with power over human destiny are natural and prudent. They also multiply opportunities to celebrate with other believers, help sustain the ecclesiastical fabric, and support the clergy, all of which nourish religion, if not the life of the spirit.

One of the most important characteristics of a religion is its emotional tone, its assurance or lack of it. Gregory Dix says of the Dark Ages that "...the struggle with evil and calamity [was] so close and so terrible that there [was] never time or breath to stand for a moment and look at the holiness and beauty and redeeming wisdom of God, which is - after all - the end of religion."

There is an opulence about the Boyne cemetery that suggests that the folk of Newgrange were generally comfortable in their world. It has been said that in Europe in very early days the abundance of game was almost unimaginable. On the Atlantic coast it must have been true, as on the Pacific, "When the tide is out, the table's set." A comfortable standard of living would probably have been reflected in a comfortable view of the hereafter. One could expect that the tone of worship at Newgrange was generally reasonable and optimistic.

Something of the note of positive assurance that I conjecture may have characterized the faith of Newgrange, can be observed in the words of a Pygmy quoted by Colin Turnbull. " 'The forest is a father and mother to us, and like a father or mother it gives us everything we need – food, clothing, shelter, warmth...and affection. Normally everything goes well because the forest is good to its children." Of disaster which befalls them, "they sing in this one great song, 'There is darkness all around us; but if darkness *is*, and the darkness is of the forest, then the darkness must be good.'" (*The Forest People* pp 92-3) Christians said "Our God is light and in him is no darkness at all."(I John 1 5).

It is certain that early surmises about blood sacrifice within the chamber were wrong. It has in fact been argued that the motives for blood sacrifices may arise later rather than earlier in a culture, and there is no evidence at Newgrange for the ignorance, alienation and dread that prompt them. "For the pagans the meatless dishes were a form of bloodless sacrifice to the gods." In the Old Testament bloodless sacrifice occurs prior to animal sacrifice. Adam's eldest, Cain, offered Jehovah grain and though he later killed his brother, the usually vengeful god treated him on the whole very leniently. (One of Cain's descendants was famed for music and his brother was famed for technology.) The foxy Esau, Jacob's elder brother, was disinherited because he exchanged his birthright for a *vegetarian* meal.

As here interpreted, the religion of Newgrange like its building would reflect a curious, confident intelligence. The details of the monument and its engraved text suggest that its funeral faith and practice were thoroughly imbued with the science and mathematics of its time. The builders met engineering challenges with energy and skill. Like ourselves they lavished resources on pursuing a rational interest in the heavens, and the devices engraved in the site's holy of holies seem to display a reverence for the importance of number that is a feature of modern science. Facilities exist throughout the site which made available the sensible perception of space-travel obtained by looking down into a star-reflecting water-surface. This has a certain resonance with the modern passion for traveling through space to find planets with water on them. The nocturnal water-gazer at Newgrange already stood in deep space on a watery planet.

Newgrange was built to operate within a supernatural continuum, a framework that was much more durable than either the monument or the particular ethnic identity of the peoples that transmitted it. The spiritual heritage these people shared was one branch of a widespread and long-lived tradition which probably once qualified as a world religion and many traces of it live on in existing traditions, stretching throughout and far beyond the boundaries it once occupied. I have called attention to scraps of "superstition," fairy stories, myths and mythological fragments, and religious traditions, as well as such graphic remains as reliefs and painted ceramics in which sets of similar emblems may be recognized.

There is in fact a great deal of material which might be reviewed profitably in the light of the Newgrange monument and its engraved devices. The key to restoring the lost link between the monument and its supernatural framework is the careful study of details of its structure, and the identification of the engraved devices as emblems of the agents that forwarded its afterlife intention. The main problem in developing an accurate picture of the belief and practice of the people of Newgrange is to clarify the relationships, temporal and geographical, between the various insights that were combined in that unique synthesis of faith and science. A study of emblem clusters in other contexts should help to determine where these ideas originated, in what directions they spread, and the geographical influences and religious and political influences that caused the differences in the ways they developed. The O'Kelly work has laid the groundwork for this effort.

The capstone of Newgrange and its immemorial well are sealed up with concrete now. Its fragile scraps of bone have been duly counted and filed away. It is a tribute to the stubborn vitality of the faith of this staunch old sentry on the borders of the afterworld that so many of its emblems and tales still live among us.

We are surrounded by fragments of the old supernatural continuum. Ladybirds are warned of fire-threats, pins are picked up, the stars and new moons are noted, city fountains are littered with coins and wishes. At Midwinter, families pass the festal dishes around the table clockwise and save the V-shaped breast-bone of the bird to wish on. The birth of the swaddled infant who will save from death is celebrated with gifts and songs, while three holy visitors guided by a star bring a gift of gold. Meanwhile Nicholas, Midwinter's special saint, is drawn by antlered reindeer from the pole, descends through apertures in roofs, and rewards good behavior.

In our own times a scrupulously secular science pursues the origin of the universe, galaxy after galaxy. Newgrange focused its hopes for escape from death with grave intensity on the galaxy in which we stand. The old photograph of a milk-cow grazing a few feet above the chamber, taken in what Michael O'Kelly (who also reproduced it) called "the romantic days of candlelight and cows," has an ironic poignance in the light of the possibility that the light of the Milky Way could once shine through the chamber vault, while rain and dew dripped down to fill the hollow slab and prophetic bowl.

PLATE XXIX. Newgrange with Cow

PARTIAL LIST OF SOURCES CONSULTED

Newgrange and Its Neighbors

Brennan, Martin. *The Stars and the Stones: Ancient Art and Astronomy in Ireland.* Thames and Hudson, Ltd., London. 1983.

Burl, Aubrey. *Prehistoric Avebury.* Yale University Press. Newhaven and London, 1979.

Clark, R. M. "A Callibration Curve for Radiocarbon Dates." *Antiquity* XLIX, 1975.

Coffey, George. *New Grange and other incised tumuli in Ireland.* 1912. Blandford Press reprint. 1977.

Cooney, Gabriel. *Landscapes of Neolithic Ireland.* Routledge, London, 2000.

Hawkes, Jacquetta and Christopher. *Prehistoric Britain.* Penguin, London, 1943.

Hawkins, Gerald S. *Beyond Stonehenge.* Harper and Row, New York, 1973.

MacKie, Euan. *The Megalith Builders.* Phaidon, Oxford, 1977.

Mac Uistin, Liam. *Exploring Newgrange.* The O'Brien Press, Dublin, 1999.

O'Kelly, Claire. *"Passage-grave art in the Boyne Valley, Ireland."* Printed by John English & Co. Ltd. Wexford. 1975. [reproduced from *Proceedings of the Prehistoric Society,* London. Vol. 39, 1973.]

O'Kelly, Claire. *Guide to Newgrange,* Second edition. Printed by John English & Co. Ltd., Wexford, 1971.

O'Kelly, Claire. *Illustrated Guide to Newgrange and the other Boyne Monuments,* Third edition. Printed by John English and Co., Ltd., Wexford, 1978.

O'Kelly, Michael J. *Newgrange: Archaeology, art and legend.* Thames and Hudson. Ltd., London, 1982.

O'Kelly, Michael J. "Some Soil Problems in Archaeological Excavation." *Journal of the Cork Historical and Archaeological Society.* 56, 1951.

O'Kelly, M. J.; Lynch, Frances; and O'Kelly, Claire. "Three Passage-Graves at Newgrange, Co. Meath." *Proceedings of the Royal Irish Academy*, Volume 78, C, Number 10. Dublin, 1978.

O'Kelly, M. J. and O'Kelly, Claire. "The Tumulus of Dowth, County Meath." *Proceedings of the Royal Irish Academy,* Volume 83c. 1983.

O'Riordain, Sean P. *Antiquities of the Irish Countryside*, Fourth edition. Methuen & Co. Ltd., London, 1965.

O'Riordain, Sean P. and Daniel, Glyn. *New Grange and the Bend of the Boyne.* Frederick A. Praeger, New York, Washington, 1964.

Stout, Geraldine. *Newgrange and the Bend of the Boyne.* Cork University Press, Cork, Ireland, 2002.

Sweetman, P. David. "A Late Neolithic/Early Bronze Age Pit Circle at Newgrange, Co. Meath." *Proceedings of the Royal Irish Academy,* Vol 85c. 1985.

Thomas, N. L.. *Irish Symbols of 3500 BC.* Mercier Press, Dublin, 1988.

Stars

Allen, Richard Hinckley. *Star Names: Their Lore and Meaning.* Reprint: Dover, New York, 1963. First published as *Star Names and Their Meanings.* G. E. Stechert, 1899.

Astronomy of the Ancients. Edited by Kenneth Brecher and Michael Feirtag. MIT Press, Cambridge and London, 1979.

Detailed Star Map: "Die Sterne: Stand der Sterne im Jahre 2000 nach dem sternkatalog des Yale University Observatory 1964." 29th Edition. Hallwag Publishers, Berne Switzerland, 1997.

Hartmann, William K. *Astronomy: The Cosmic Journey.* Wadsworth Publishing Co., Belmont, California, 1985.

Inglis, R. M. G. *A New Popular Star Atlas (Epoch 1950).* Gall and Inglis, Edinburgh and London, 1959.

Lum, Peter. *The Stars in our Heaven: Myths and Fables.* Pantheon, New York, 1948.

Mitchell, John. *A Little History of Astro-Archaeology.* Thames and Hudson, London, 1977, 1989.

National Audubon Society. *Field Guide to the Night Sky.* Alfred A. Knopf, New York, 1991.

Philips' Planisphere for Latitude 42° North. George Philip and Son, Ltd. London, 1982.

Pickering, James Sayer. *The Stars are Yours.* Revised edition Macmillan, New York, 1953.

Rand McNally Celestial Globe. Ed. Oliver J. Lee. Rand McNally, Chicago, Early 1960's.

Young, C. A. *Uranography: A Brief Description of the Constellations Visible in the United States with Star Maps, and Lists of Objects Observable with a Small Telescope.* Ginn and Company, Boston, New York etc., 1889.

Zim, Herbert S. and Baker, Robert H. *Stars: A Guide to the Constellations, Sun, Moon, Planets, and Other Features of the Heavens.* Golden Press, New York, 1951.

Natural History

Abbott, R. Tucker. *Sea Shells of the World: A Guide to the Better-Known Species.* Golden Press, New York,1962.

Armstrong, Margaret. *Field Book of Western Wild Flowers.* G. P. Putnam's Sons, New York and London, 1915.

Cook, Theodore Andrea. *The Curves of Life: Being an account of spiral formations and their application to growth in nature, to science and to art; with special reference to the manuscripts of Leonardo da Vinci.* Reprint Dover Publications, New York, 1979.Originally published by Constable and Company, London, 1914.

Culbreth, David M. R. *A Manual of Materia Medica and Pharmacology:* Sixth Edition Revised. Lea & Febiger, Philadelphia and New York, 1917.

Day, John A. and Schaefer, Vincent J. *Peterson First Guides: Clouds and Weather: A Simplified Field Guide to the Atmosphere.* Houghton Mifflin Company, Boston, 1991.

Fraquet, Helen. *Amber.* Butterworths, London and Boston, 1987.

Guiguet, C. J. *The Birds of British Columbia (6) Waterfowl.* British Columbia Provincial Museum; Department of Recreation and Conservation Handbook No. 15. A. Sutton printer, 1967.

Halfpenny, James and Biesiot, Elizabeth A. *A Field Guide to Mammal Tracking in North America.* Johnson Books, Boulder, Colorado, 1986.

Jago, Lucy. *The Northern Lights.* Alfred Knopf, New York, 2001.

Kelman, Janet Harvey and Smith C. E. *Flowers.* Thomas Nelson and Sons, New York, 1952.

Lecht, Jane. *Honeybees.* National Geographic Society "Books for Young Explorers," 1973.

Lewis, Meriwether, and Clark, William. *The Journals of Lewis and Clark : A New Selection with an Introduction by John Bakeless.* The New American Library, Inc., New York, 1964.

Pandell,Karen and Stall, Chris. A*nimal Tracks of the Pacific Northwest.* The Mountaineers, Seattle, 1981.

Peattie, Donald Culross. *Trees You Want to Know.* Whitman Publishing Company, Racine Wisconsin, 1934.

Peterson, Roger Tory. *A Field Guide to Western Birds.* Houghton Mifflin Company, Boston, 1941.

Rice, Patty C. *Amber, The Golden Gem of the Ages.* Van Nostrand Reinhold, NewYork, 1980.

Steel, Duncan. *Eclipse: The Celestial Phenomenon Which Has Changed the Course of History.* Headline Book Publishing, London, 1999.

von Frisch, Karl. *The Dancing Bees.* Harcourt Brace Jovanovich, New York and London, 1953.

History and Pre-history

Brailsford, John. *Early Celtic Masterpieces from Britain in the British Museum.* British Museum Publications Limited, London, 1975.

De Santillana, Giorgio, and Von Dechend, Hertha. *Hamlet's Mill.* David R.Godine, Boston, 1969.

Dix, Dom Gregory. *The Shape of the Liturgy.* Dacre Press, Westminster, 1945.

Hampe, Roland, and Simon, Erika.*The Birth of Greek Art from the Mycenaean to the Archaic Period.* First Published in German. Oxford University Press, New York, 1981.

Hawkes, Christopher and Jacquetta. *Prehistoric Britain.* Penguin Books Ltd., Harmondsworth, Middlesex, 1943.

Higgins, Reynold. *Minoan and Mycenaean Art.* Revised Edition. Thames and Hudson, New York, 1981.

Hoyningen-Huene, George, with text by George Steindorff. *Egypt.* Revised edition. J. J. Augustin, New York, 1945.

Lewis-Williams, David. *The Mind in the Cave.* Thames and Hudson, London, 2002.

Lloyd, Seton. *Early Anatolia.* Penguin Books Ltd., Harmondsworth, Middlesex, 1956.

Mallory, J. P. *In Search of the Indo-Europeans: Language, Archaeology and Myth.* Thames and Hudson, London, 1991.

Piggott, Stuart. *Prehistoric India.* Penguin Books Ltd., Harmondsworth, Middlesex, 1950.

Prevost, Bernard, et al. Societe du Palais de la Civilisation Catalogue. *L'Or des Cavaliers Thraces*: *Tresors de Bulgarie.* Montreal, 1987.

Schweitzer, Bernhard. *Greek Geometric Art.* Edited by Ulrich Hausmann / Jochen Briegleb. Translated by Peter and Cornelia Usborne from German *Die Geometrische Kunst Griechenlands.* Phaidon Press Ltd., London, 1960.

Turnbull, Colin M. *The Forest People: A Study of the Pygmies of the Congo.* Simon and Schuster, New York, 1962.

Wilson, Penelope. *Sacred Signs: Hieroglyphics in Ancient Egypt.* Oxford University Press, New York, 2003.

Wolff, Walther. *The Origins of Western Art: Egypt, Mesopotamia, the Aegean.* Universe Books, New York, 1972.

Myth, Fairy-story, and Superstition.

Asbjornsen, Peter, and Moe, Jorgen. *Norwegian Folk Tales.* (Various editions and translations). Originally published in 1845, 1852.

Afanasiev, Aleksandr. *Russian Fairy Tales.*Translated by Norbert Guterman.Pantheon Books, New York, 1945.

Colum, Padraig. *A Treasury of Irish Folklore: The Stories, Traditions, Legends, Humor, Wisdom, Ballads and Songs of the Irish People.* Crown, New York, 1962.

Tom Peete Cross and Clark Harris Slover, Editors. *Ancient Irish Tales.* Henry Holt, New York, 1936.

Ganz, Jeffrey, Translator. *Early Irish Myths and Sagas.* Penguin Books, Harmondsworth, Middlesex, 1981.

Hesiod, The Homeric Hymns and Homerica. Translated by Hugh G. Evelyn-White. William Heinemann Ltd, London; Harvard University Press, Cambridge, Massachusetts,1967.

Homer. *The Iliad* and *The Odyssey.* (Various editions and translations.)

Jacobs, Joseph. *Celtic Fairy Tales..* D. Nutt, London; G. P. Putnam's Sons. New York and London, 1892.

Jacobs, Joseph. *Indian Fairy Tales.* D. Nutt London; G. P. Putnam's Sons, New York, 1912. (A. L. Burt Co., New York. [n.d.])

Mary McGarry. *Great Fairy Tales of Ireland.* Wolfe Publishing Limited, Avenel Books, New York, 1973.

Lang, Andrew editor. Collections: *The Red, Blue, Green, Yellow, Violet,Pink, Olive, and Brown Fairy Books.*Various Publishers and dates.

Larousse *Encyclopedia of Mythology.* Translated from the French by Aldington and Ames. Prometheus Press, New York, 1950.

Larousse *New Enclyclopedia of Mythology.* Translated by Aldington and Ames. The Hamlyn Publishing Group Limited, NewYork, 1968.

Mabinogion: A New Translation by Ellis, T. P. and Lloyd, John. Oxford,1929.

Malory, Thomas. *Le Morte d'Arthur.* Dent, London, 1906.

The Nibelungenlied. Translated by Shumway, D. B. Houghton Mifflin, Boston, 1909.

Opie, Iona and Tatem, Moira, Editors. *A Dictionary of Superstitions.* Oxford University Press. Oxford, New York, 1992.

Ovid. *The Metamorphoses.* Translated by Mary M. Innes. Penguin Books, Ltd.. Harmondsworth, Middlesex. 1955.

Wolfram von Eschenbach. *Parzival: A Romance of the Middle Ages.* Translation by Mustard, Helen M. & Passage, Charles E.. Random House, New York and Toronto. and Alfred A. Knopf Inc. 1961.

Porphyry. On the Cave of the Nymphs. Translated by R. Lamberton. Station Hill Press, Barrytown, New York, 1983.

Ralston, W. R. S. *Russian Fairy Tales.* Hurst & Co., New York, 1873.

Rees, Alwyn and Rees, Brinley. *Celtic Heritage.* Thames and Hudson, London,1961.

Rhys, Ernest and Grace. *English Fairy Tales*. J.M. Dent & Sons, London, E. P. Dutton, New York, [1916].

Steel, F. A. *English Fairy Tales*. Macmillan, New York, 1979.

Stephens, James. *Irish Fairy Tales*. Collier Books [Macmillan], New York, 1962.

Stevenson, John. *Yoshitoshi's Thirty-Six Ghosts*. Blue Tiger Books, Hong Kong, with University of Washington Press, Seattle, 1983.

Swanton, John R. *Haida Texts and Myths*. Smithsonian Institution Bureau of American Ethnology, Bulletin 29, 1905.

Thurneysen, Rudolf. *Sagen aus dem alten Irland*. Übersetzt von Rudolf Thurneysen. Wiegandt & Grieben, Berlin, 1901.

The Thousand and One Nights; or the Arabian Nights Entertainments. Porter and Coates, Philadelphia, [n.d.]

Williston, Teresa Peirce. *Japanese Fairy Tales*. Rand McNally & Co. Chicago, New York, London. 1904.

Wilson, Richard. *The Russian Story Book: containing tales from the song-cycles of Kiev and Novgorod and other early sources*. Macmillan and Col., Ltd., London, 1916.

Yeats, W. B. *Irish Fairy and Folk Tales*. A. L. Burt, New York. [Orig. *Fairy and folk tales of the Irish peasantry*. W. Scott, London, 189-].

Irish Heroic Sagas.

Aided Con Culainn ("The Death of Cuculainn"); Aided Oenfir Aiffe ("The Death of Aife's Only Son"); Compert Con Culainn ("The Conception of Cuchulainn"); Fled Bricrend ("The Feast of Bricriu"); Mesca Ulaid ("The Intoxication of the Ulstermen"); Scela Mucce Meic Datho ("The Story of Mac Datho's Pig");Serglige Con Culaind ("The Sickbed of Cuculainn"); Tain Bo Cualnge ("The Cattle Raid of Cooley") from the Book of Leinster; Tochmarc Emire ("The Wooing of Emer").

General Reference

The Encyclopaedia Britannica. Eleventh Edition. Cambridge University Press, London, 1910.

Encyclopaedia Judaica. Keter, Jerusalem, 1972.

Funk and Wagnalls. *New Standard Dictionary of the English Language.*Funk and Wagnall Co, New York and London, 1924.

Graves, Robert. *The Greek Myths*. Penguin Books, Harmondsworth, Middlesex, c1960.

Pauly/Wissowa *Real-Encyclopädie der klassischen Altertumswissenschaft*. Neue Bearbeitung. J. B. Metzler, Stuttgart, 1920.

Röhrig, Lutz. *Das Grosse Lexikon der sprichtwörtlichen Redensarten*. Herder, Freiburg, 1991-1992.

Roscher, W. H. *Ausfürliches Lexikon der griechischen und romanischen Mythologie*. Teubner, Leipsig, 1884-1937.

World Book Encyclopedia. Field Enterprises Educational Corporation. Chicago. 1966.

www.ingramcontent.com/pod-product-compliance
Lightning Source LLC
Chambersburg PA
CBHW080408290526
45791CB00008BA/2189